SACRED JOURNEYS

The Conversion of Young Americans to Divine Light Mission

SACRED JOURNEYS

The Conversion of Young Americans to Divine Light Mission

James V. Downton, Jr.

Columbia University Press   New York   1979

Library of Congress Cataloging in Publication Data

Downton, James V
  Sacred journeys.

  Bibliography: p.
  Includes index.
  1. Divine Light Mission.   2. Conversion—
Case studies.   3. Guru Maharaj Ji, 1957–
I. Title.
BP605.D58D69   299   79-546
ISBN 0-231-04198-5

Photographs: Number 2 is reproduced with the permission
of the *Daily Camera* (Boulder, Colorado). All others are
courtesy of Divine Light Mission.

Columbia University Press
New York   Guildford, Surrey

For my father and mother, James and Vera Downton

Acknowledgments

I would like to express my appreciation to a number of people who contributed to the development of this book. I am especially grateful for the cooperation of the followers of Guru Maharaj Ji whose stories make up the core of the work. With very few exceptions, their trusting attitude, generosity, and honesty never wavered, which made our association warm and valuable beyond the pragmatic goal of finishing the manuscript.

To my wife, Mary, and my children, Katherine and Diana, I owe a special note of thanks for giving me the time and support for my writing. Mary read and criticized various portions of the book, which definitely improved it.

I am also very grateful to Lucy DuPertuis, a follower, for reading and criticizing earlier drafts of the book. Her help was invaluable to me. Others working at the Divine Light Mission headquarters in Denver were also helpful. Cliff Bowden and Joe Anctil read the manuscript and proposed revisions, most having to do with factual material. While not always agreeing with me, both respected my point of view and made no effort to change it, which I appreciated. I was especially happy for the opportunity to work with Cliff, who had been working on a Ph.D. in sociology before joining the Mission and therefore could understand the theoretical side of the study.

ACKNOWLEDGMENTS

I would also like to thank Suzy Pensinger for transcribing the interviews; Ron Rinkle for organizing the questionnaire data and doing a statistical summary for me; Joan Biagi and Dick Skeen for their assistance in tracking down the literature dealing with conversion and commitment, and Judy Warren Little for helping me to organize the interview data.

Let me thank the members of the Council on Research and Creative Work at the University of Colorado for funding the transcription phase of the study.

Finally, I am grateful to Robert Hunter who, as director of the Bureau of Sociological Research, in 1972 provided me with a typist to help with the transcription process and also provided me with a quiet office where I began organizing the materials.

Contents

Illustrations follow page 150
ix

chapter
ONE

Introduction

When I was a little boy, I was just like every other little boy going here and there, playing. When I was six, my father gave me Knowledge. I was given Knowledge and I didn't realize it right away. But I understood it was my duty and I began to meditate and in about a month I realized it. When I was eight, late Maharaj Ji left his body. He was very sick in Delhi. There were all these telephone calls. I was at home and it was time to go to school, so I went to school and I was sitting in the classroom and the driver from Delhi came and called the teacher out to tell her about Shri Maharaj Ji. The madame came back into the class and said to me, "Go."

I went home and everyone was weeping. I was just sitting there not weeping and something began to happen to me. I began to feel that I am not this body; that I could not move these lips. I always thought that the soul would leave by the mouth, but my mouth was shut. Still I felt like I was leaving my body and my soul was everywhere going out. And this voice came to me saying: "You are He, you are the one to continue."

Then I puzzled over the voice. Thirteen days later, I was doing pranam to my father's ashes and bones. You know, in India, they

1

INTRODUCTION

burn the bodies and thirteen days later you collect the ashes. I bent down to touch the ashes, and the voice came, "You are He, you are the one to go and give this to the world."

I didn't want to be Satguru. I would have been satisfied to be a mischievous little boy. I didn't understand why it is me. I would have been satisfied to be the humblest servant of the Satguru and not to be one myself. It was not my desire. But the late Maharaj Ji had left one letter when he was away. He sent his love to his oldest three sons and complete prostrations to his youngest. So they crowned me with the crown of Rama and Krishna and put the tilak on my forehead, and again the voice came: "This is the last I will tell you. You are He, you must take this Knowledge out to the world."

Then for the first time I did not give satsang. The satsang just came and I began to speak (Guru Maharaj Ji, 1974).[1]

Guru Maharaj Ji was born Prem Pal Singh Rawat on December 10, 1957. His father, Shri Hans Ji Maharaj Ji, was already recognized as a Perfect Master* and lived with his wife, Mata Ji, and his four sons in the Prem Nagar ashram† in India. Guru Maharaj Ji, like his brothers, was treated like a divine being by the many Mahatmas‡ and premies§ who served his father in the ashram. Thus, he received the attention and affection of his father's devotees,‖ who happily responded to his every wish. Luxury and service were his birthright and later became his personal life-style when he was elevated to his father's position as Perfect Master at the age of eight.

It was a surprise to many people that the youngest of the children would assume the father's spiritual role, for the expectation was

---

* A "Perfect Master" is one who is regarded as a teacher of spiritual perfection.

† An "ashram" is a monastic living arrangement for those who want to seriously dedicate themselves to spiritual devotion and practice.

‡ "Mahatma" means "great soul" in Hindi. In the Mission, Mahatmas were empowered by Guru Maharaj Ji to reveal the source of life which is called the "Knowledge." After the movement became westernized and Indian Mahatmas either were leaving or being demoted, the designation "Mahatma" was replaced by "Initiator."

§ "Premie" literally means "lover of God" and is a term applied to members of Divine Light Mission.

‖ A "devotee" is one who has surrendered to a guru and to the inner spiritual experience he or she is thought to represent.

2

that his eldest son would succeed him. In another sense, the elevation of the youngest to spiritual prominence was no surprise at all, for stories are told about his extraordinary dedication to the Knowledge,* which he demonstrated almost from the moment when his father, and guru, had revealed the life force to him. From the age of six, he is said to have voluntarily immersed himself in spiritual practices, sometimes meditating for hours at a time. His exuberance for the Knowledge made him a sensation at satsang,† where premies say he spoke spontaneously to mass audiences with the assurance of someone many years older. After succession to his father's position, the young guru continued attending school and officiating at the spiritual activities of the movement, which had attracted a sizable following in India by then.

By the end of the 1960s a few dropouts from the American counterculture had made their way to India in search of a guru. A handful heard about Guru Maharaj Ji, received the Knowledge from one of his Mahatmas, and returned to the United States as his followers. The guru was just emerging into adolescence when, in 1971, a few of those American premies invited him to the United States for the first time. His decision to accept the invitation against the wishes of his mother, Mata Ji, was the first sign of his developing independence, which eventually culminated in the widely publicized feud between them several years later. In India, his mother and eldest brother, Bal Bhagwan Ji, had dominated the Mission with the "boy guru" assuming a more symbolic, but still potent, form of spiritual authority. In theory, he was at the top of an organizational pyramid which bestowed on him the privileges of legislator, executive, and judge—rights generally taken for granted by gurus. But, due to his age, authority was more broadly shared throughout his family. His mother was recognized as the "Holy Mother" and his three older brothers were widely regarded as Divine, each representing a spiritual virtue. Premies prostrated to them as they did to Guru Maharaj Ji,

---

* The "Knowledge" is the primordial energy, or source of life. This life force is revealed to people during the Knowledge session and is the inner experience premies mediate upon.

† "Satsang" literally means "the company of Truth." Satsang is spiritual discourse about the Knowledge.

3

even though in India and the United States he was the only one spoken of as "satguru," the Indian term for Perfect Master.

The guru's first visit to Colorado in 1971 created great excitement, similar to that of a Christian revival meeting, as a sizable crowd of young people from the counterculture gathered in the mountains to see the 13-year-old guru whom people were calling the "Lord." Some were just curiosity seekers wanting to see the show; others were seriously looking for a guru to follow. Many stayed to receive the Knowledge from one of the guru's Mahatmas, Indians clad in orange saffron robes and lending mystery to the initiation ceremony by the sheer contrast of their speech and demeanor to American customs. Soon after the first visit, a wave of premies were covering the area like zealous missionaries, spreading the word that there was a 13-year-old saint in the mountains who could reveal God. The boldness of this claim and the thought of a teen-aged Perfect Master was enough to capture the attention of countless numbers of hippies who had already begun a spiritual search. Before long, the young guru was joined by members of his family and other Mahatmas to set into motion an important phase of what they hoped would become a world-wide peace effort. Divine Light Mission had come to America.

Attracting young, white, middle-class youth, the movement expanded rapidly from 1971 to the close of 1973, at which time the Mission's leadership estimated American membership to be about 50,000. That was the number of people who had received the Knowledge; the deeply dedicated followers were a considerably smaller group. In the beginning, the organization was fairly loose-knit, and premies did what they could on their own to interest people in receiving the Knowledge. By 1972, ashrams were beginning to open up across the country and premies were flying to India to acquaint themselves with the movement there. The mood was optimistic. Premies were encouraged by the sight of hundreds of people crowding into the ashrams asking to receive the Knowledge, many staying several days until a Mahatma arrived to initiate them. With enthusiasm on the rise, the coffers of the movement filled, making expansion possible.

A medical clinic was opened in New York City to administer to

4

INTRODUCTION

the health needs of the poor, with plans for similar facilities in other large cities. Secondhand stores were started to recycle goods at prices within range of low-income families. Small business organizations were developed spontaneously by premies which contracted for jobs in the community to do painting, carpentry, landscaping, and similar services.

The national and international headquarters of the Mission in Denver naturally swelled in size to meet the demands of the movement's growth, activities, and goals. By 1973, it was staffed by 125 full-time coordinators, who were responsible for operations in the 55 countries on six continents where the Mission was active. The latest technical know-how was used. A computer was even purchased for keeping tabs on the large membership and for filing and documenting financial records. By the summer of 1973, there were an estimated 1.2 million members worldwide, with India accounting for the bulk. Of the estimated 50,000 who had received the Knowledge in the United States, about 500 were living in 24 ashrams in 24 cities, while information centers were being started in smaller cities and towns.

Within the Mission a belief was developing among premies that the day was approaching when the masses would recognize the virtues of their guru, receive the Knowledge, and join them in their mission of peace. Outside the movement, its future seemed uncertain, for public attitudes were far from sympathetic. People were hostile toward the guru. Reports in the media were unfavorable, repeating often that he seemed to live more like a king than a Messiah.

When word first began to circulate within the Mission about a massive festival to be held in the Houston Astrodome premies were ecstatic. Like a symphony building to a crescendo, their hopes for a dramatic change in the world were rising. Millennium 1973, the name given to the festival, promised them what they longed for most—a sign that a new age of peace was coming. For the Mission's leadership there was an accompanying wish that the members of the news media would at last see Guru Maharaj Ji as positively as they did, and hundreds of reporters were invited from across the country. By the time of the festival the runaway expectations of some premies

5

INTRODUCTION

had led them to believe that masses of ordinary people would descend on the Astrodome, a few thought Guru Maharaj Ji would transform the world singlehandedly, while wild rumors spread in half-jest about the possible appearance of extraterrestrial beings.

But the Astrodome did not fill to capacity, the world remained as it was, and representatives of the media were angered, not impressed, by what they saw and heard. Many premies were disappointed. Reassessment began to take place within the movement, as the organization faced the task of paying off a $600,000 debt from the festival and the necessity of cutting back on its programs. (These events and other changes will be described in more detail in a later chapter.)

The millennial appeal of the Mission prior to Millennium 1973 revolved around two beliefs: that Guru Maharaj Ji was the Lord, and that a new age of peace was about to begin under his leadership. Actually, millennial beliefs had been germinating in the counterculture long before the arrival of the guru on the American scene, for many hippies were anticipating the "second coming" and the dawning of the Age of Aquarius. The Mission's millenarian overtones seemed to offer hope to thousands of young people in the counterculture who had become disillusioned with earlier attempts to change the world and were turning to a spiritual solution in the hope that it might accomplish what a political and cultural revolution had failed to achieve.

The belief that Guru Maharaj Ji was the Lord conformed to the eastern spiritual tradition, where surrender to the inner spirit and obedience to a spiritual teacher had been regarded for generations as customary steps in the attainment of spiritual enlightenment. Trying to follow Guru Maharaj Ji's teaching created uniformity of conduct and fashions among premies while it ensured their practice of meditation, satsang, and service. These practices were considered essential for staying in harmony with the inner spirit.

Disillusioned with conventional American religious groups in their youth, premies emphasized the importance of the Knowledge experience as the source of their spiritual awakening and as the basis

6

INTRODUCTION

for seeking more love, peace, and happiness in their lives. Upon entry into the movement, there was no vast literature for them to study, such as we find in the Hare Krishna movement, nor was there an elaborate theology. Instead, they regarded their relationship to the universal spirit and to Guru Maharaj Ji as sufficient for undoing what they saw as the undesirable features of their social conditioning, which they believed would give them a fuller and more joyful experience of life.

Many people who watched the 13-year-old guru attract a mass following in 1971–73 were amazed. They wondered how a mere boy could be regarded as Perfect Master and why so many young people, dressed in counterculture style, were anxious to follow him and to lay prostrate at his feet. Some parents were appalled and disappointed when their children became involved and scholars were wondering whether Guru Maharaj Ji's followers were not just another wave of desperate people in this country trying to "escape from freedom."

I have talked to many people in the last five years who were skeptical and sometimes antagonistic toward Guru Maharaj Ji and Divine Light Mission. Yet, most were not very well informed about either the guru or the movement, nor were they interested in learning how premies might be benefiting from their involvement. For example, one woman whom I had met at a party in 1973 nearly shouted, "Oh, I am quite willing to accept all the different spiritual movements in the country, but not the one with the boy guru. That one I can't stand." As we talked, it became apparent she knew little more than what she had read in the newspapers about the Mission. In fact, she had never even met, let along talked at length with, a premie. Because she felt Divine Light Mission was contrary to her values, she was more than ready to condemn and reject it.

When I first started this study, I too was made skeptical by some of what I saw in the Mission. Even now, I am aware of certain pitfalls to individualism in such movements. Yet I knew in the beginning that to perceive it as a threatening and bizarre phenomenon could only be an excuse for not examining it carefully and objectively. Instead, I wanted to set my personal biases aside as much as

7

INTRODUCTION

possible in order to understand it as a part of human experience, as ordinary people trying to find spiritual answers to the ultimate questions of purpose and meaning.

Religious movements were a new area of research for me when I began this undertaking in the summer of 1972. Having just completed a book about commitment and charisma in political revolutions, I was disappointed that I had been unable to fully grasp the personal drama which leads ordinary people to experience a change of values and to choose revolution as a way of life. Much has been written about the leaders and the organization of social movements, but little is known about the conversion and transformation of followers who put their security in jeopardy for the sake of change. Therefore, when I turned to study Divine Light Mission, I was certain that I wanted to focus on the lives of premies, looking especially at how they had become followers and how they had changed as a result of their involvement in the Mission.

There were two ways I could have carried on the investigation. One was to join the movement and study it as an insider. That choice was not a viable one for me, however, because I had no intention of becoming a devotee. To join without a genuine interest seemed a sham, not to mention the fact that masquerading as a premie would probably have given me a distorted picture of the movement. So I took a second approach, which was to remain on the outside and to explore the Mission as a visitor.

For about a month, I spent time at the ashram in Boulder, Colorado, watching, talking to premies, and participating in some of their rituals. I certainly did not agree with everything I saw or heard; in fact, there were some premies whose beliefs seemed quite unrealistic, for example, some believed that the guru could transform the world singlehandedly if he chose to. However, I respected many of the Mission's goals and the motives of those involved. They seemed sincere about what they were doing and were committed to many positive values, such as love, peace, and cooperation. Feeling I could treat the Mission fairly, I decided to begin interviewing premies. By that time, most of the local followers knew who I was, so I was in a good position to make further contact with them.

INTRODUCTION

The selection of premies for interviewing took a fairly natural course, through random contact, asking if they would participate, then scheduling a time for the first interview. Given the casual nature of the setting then, this approach worked quite well, although I did end up interviewing more premies who lived in the ashram (13) than on the outside (5). The stories of the two groups, however, were quite similar.

My only concern in selecting people was to equalize the representation of the sexes. I thought it would be interesting to discover if the accounts of males and females would differ, but, except for minor details, this was not the case. Other than the sex of the premie, I had no knowledge of the person's background before the first interview— for example, whether he or she had a history of psychological disturbance, had attended college, used drugs, etc.

Initially, my intention was to interview twenty premies in depth. Only nineteen cases were completed, however, because the twentieth person was transferred to a distant city while our discussions were underway. By that time, I had become aware of a pattern in the accounts of premies and additional stories were not adding many new elements or insights. One case was eliminated from those completed because I suspected that the individual's motives for participating had not been completely honest; he spent most of the time trying to convert me and almost no time talking about his personal life. In all the remaining cases, premies spoke with frankness and honesty, revealing intimate details of their lives which many of their friends, and certainly their parents, were unaware of.

The interviews were each tape-recorded in three segments, and taping was done wherever it was possible to find a quiet and secluded spot, which proved to be a challenge at times. Many meetings were in the basement of the ashram, where the incessant sound of clanging water pipes from the kitchen made conditions less than optimum. On one particularly busy day, when the ashram was filled to capacity with visitors, a premie and I squeezed into a storage room, where we spent a cramped three hours in the midst of old clothes, suitcases, discarded living implements, and whatnot.

The first interview covered the early lives of premies up to their

9

contact with the movement. The second probed the period from contact to the "present." The final interview focused on their life within the Mission and the difficulties of propagating the Knowledge in the surrounding community.

My main purpose was to get as complete a story as possible without leading premies on with prearranged questions. I wanted to encourage them to tell their stories in their own way. My role was merely to see that they told detailed stories. Therefore, the one question I asked over and over again was simply, "Could you tell me more about that?" I raised this question whenever I wanted them to fill in the substance of something they had touched upon only briefly or had skipped over entirely, thinking it was not worth talking about. Questions arose from the first interviews which I felt moved to ask in later ones, pertaining, for example, to the premie's relationship to his or her parents, attitudes about conventional American religion, success in making friends, drug use, and the like.

Follow-up interviews were conducted over the next several years with seven premies who seemed representative of the larger group. I maintained contact with all eighteen, however, in order to keep track of their activities within the Mission, to observe any changes, and to initiate follow-up interviews with any who chose to leave, as three eventually did. In the summer of 1976, an extensive questionnaire was mailed to the remaining fifteen, exploring changes which had taken place in their lives and in the movement since they had joined. In 1972, a questionnaire covering basic background information was completed by the eighteen, by other premies from the Midwest and South, as well as by forty college students who were not followers of Guru Maharaj Ji and twenty-nine members of the Hare Krishna movement. The information from these various sources provided a comparative perspective which was indispensable for understanding what, if anything, was unique about the background of premies to make their lives take a spiritual direction. (For a brief discussion of the methods and results of that questionnaire, please see "A Statement on the Method" at the end of the book.)

I was aware of the subjective quality of retrospective accounts, since the past obviously takes on a somewhat different character after

INTRODUCTION

conversion. But "reality" is always subject to individual interpretation: perceptions of reality differ in the stories of premies, in my interpretation of each of their accounts, and, finally, in my analysis of all their stories combined, which we could call "theory." I do not pretend that my rendering of reality in this case is the "true story," but only one of many that could be written.

I have been trained to look for and understand the social and psychological processes that appear in all social movements and during different periods of history. To see such processes operating in the Mission is not a condemnation of it, for they can be found in all similar movements. In fact, while cautioning against the dangers of prolonged dependence on the guru, I conclude in a later chapter that premies seem to have grown personally in many positive ways from their involvement in the Mission.

The book is organized in two parts. Part I includes four individual case histories. Part II, the bulk of the work, traces the stages in the conversion and commitment of premies and an analysis of some of the social and psychological dynamics of change. I conclude the book with a short discussion of the future prospects of the "spiritual revolution." Throughout, the names of premies have been changed to preserve and protect their identities.

11

Part
ONE

Four Stories

Perhaps the closest we can get to the full human drama of Divine Light Mission is in the personal accounts of premies. There we see how social forces, psychological conflicts, decisions, and chance influenced them to take a spiritual direction.

Four accounts make up this part of the book, each adding a different dimension to the larger scenario. These stories reflect the views and language of premies during 1972, as they reconstructed the past and spoke with conviction about the future. Changes which premies and the movement have undergone since then are taken up in the chapters titled "Changes" and "Defection."

Even though these four personal histories are important as examples of how the dynamics of change work at the individual level, one could read only one or two cases without missing the essence of the process, since that is covered in depth in Part II.

chapter
TWO

Alan

When I was young, my father was sort of a drunk and my mother and father fought a lot. I can't remember a lot about that period, since I was only about nine years old, but I do remember when my mother decided to leave my father. I didn't know anything about it until one day a couple of my uncles came to our house, packed up a bunch of stuff, and we drove off. I didn't see my father for a long time after that. But my mother talked about him a lot, telling us how bad he was. I guess that made a big impression on me.

After my father and mother split up we moved to Kentucky, where my mother got a job in a factory. Usually, me, my brother, and sister were the only ones at home. My mother didn't want us to have any of our friends over after school, 'cause she didn't want to be bothered. So, us kids would fight and yell at each other a lot. Sometimes it was okay, but usually it was pretty sad.

After we left my father, my mother had to be both a father and mother to us, so she yelled a lot at me. She was pretty strict, like we always had to come right home after school. I guess she loved me, because mothers are supposed to love their kids, but she wasn't too good at expressing it.

15

ALAN

She used to get uptight 'cause she didn't like her job and she thought that people were against her. She talked about the people she worked with and especially her boss, who she said yelled at her all the time to work faster. She was just not very happy.

By the time I reached junior high school I was a loud mouth, always cracking jokes and getting kicked out of class. I guess that was because I was insecure and I felt I had to act up to draw attention to myself. You know how kids belong to certain groups and if you're not accepted into their group they won't talk to you. Well, I had a hard time relating to that. I thought it would make me happy to be involved in social things, but I couldn't get into it.

When I was in high school a lot of guys I knew had girl friends, but I didn't because I was really shy. I could chat with people to pass the time, but I couldn't say anything really important 'cause I just didn't feel I could share my feelings with anyone. I thought that was something you were supposed to keep inside.

I could be with other people and still be alone, feeling I wasn't really with them, wanted by them, or involved with them and what they were doing. I really noticed that happening in high school at times, which made me feel depressed. It seemed like my life was just going to school, coming home, and doing homework.

In high school, I did get into some fights, yet I really wasn't that aggressive. I used to talk a tough game, but I never really did much. Sometimes people would push me around, which bothered me because I thought I was supposed to push back, but I just didn't feel like it. Sometimes there were angry words, like I'd try to get involved with people and they would tell me to leave them alone.

During that time, I didn't have anyone I could really call a friend. Sure, I had people I hung out with, but we didn't really know each other that well. We'd hang out together at school, but after school I wouldn't see them.

In high school I started to rebel on the inside, although not on the outside. I was thinking a lot because I knew I wasn't happy and I was trying to figure out some way to be happy. I got pretty good grades, but after a while I didn't even study that much. I got into daydreaming a lot and would let my mind wander all over the place.

16

ALAN

I knew I wasn't good at relating to people, that's why I talked a lot and why, on the surface, it looked like I could relate, when I really couldn't. I didn't have any girl friends, so I thought maybe that was my problem. I tried to figure out how not to be shy. But I never saw anyone after school and it was really hard to get to know anyone in between classes.

My mind became more and more involved in thinking about me. I wanted to get socially involved, but I had no confidence in myself. Even when I tried my mind would be thinking, "You're going to blow this." If I did relate to someone I'd start to wonder why. I had all these different impressions of how people were. Some people were stronger or tougher than me, so I stayed away from them. Others were better than me or weren't as good as me, so I didn't get involved with them either. I couldn't see any unity, just all separate people. It was a really paranoid trip.

I went to church on Sunday because it was something I was supposed to do. I sang songs and listened to the preacher. I talked to people there sometimes, but usually I didn't get involved. I just listened to what the preacher was saying and didn't question, not knowing whether he was right or wrong. It was supposed to be true because everyone told me it was.

We went to a Baptist church, but I didn't really consider myself a Baptist, because it was just something I was supposed to do. After a while, if my mother hadn't made me, I probably wouldn't have gone. It was like I was programmed to go. I wasn't going because I wanted to, but because it was on my schedule. I wasn't really feeling God inside of me. I thought God was something in the clouds. If you were good you went to heaven and if you were bad you went to hell.

Sometimes I was afraid to go to church because I really felt paranoid, to the point where I thought people were staring at me. In fact, I didn't want to be baptized because I was fearful of getting up in front of others. Yet, at the same time, I was worried about what people would think of me if I didn't. I remember I was in vacation bible school when someone asked how many of us kids wanted to be baptized. We were told to close our eyes and raise our hands if we did. I raised my hand because I thought if I didn't, someone would try and

17

talk me into it or the preacher would get mad at me. So I was supposed to be baptized, but I got into an argument with my mother and she decided that I wasn't good enough to be baptized, so I wasn't.

When I went away to college, I was finally on my own. I thought by changing my environment I could begin relating to people and doing things which would be satisfying to me. I felt that, if I could learn to relate to people, then I'd be happy. I'd heard that drugs could make you feel real good, so I decided to get into them.

The first time I got stoned on marijuana I felt great. I went to a Grateful Dead concert and me and two other dudes were walking back to our dorms and a guy pulled over in his car and asked us if we wanted to smoke some dope. I got really stoned, laughed a lot, and felt good. I think the best thing about it was that I wasn't thinking about what was going on. I wasn't worrying so much, although I was pretty paranoid about the cops. But it was enjoyable. It just turned my mind off for that time and I had never had anything like that happen to me before.

After that experience I started hanging out with people who smoked dope. So, before long, I was smoking a lot of dope. When I was by myself I'd get completely stoned. I'd just lie back and enjoy it, although sometimes I'd worry about it too.

By the time I got into psychedelics I was really crazy so I thought maybe they would help to get me together. There wasn't anything controlled about the way I used them. I'd just take them, thinking that maybe the experience would be good or maybe it wouldn't. Maybe if I'd gone out into the woods it might have been better, but I'd trip during classes or in the middle of the night, then the next day I'd really be wasted.

When I took psychedelics I felt exhilarated but, at the same time, my mind would be operating in the background. I remember one time I took some LSD at a concert. At times, I really felt good, but then I'd look at people and experience separation. I'd wonder what they were thinking about me and would feel so paranoid I couldn't relate to them at all.

I also got into drinking, because I was trying to find something that would make my mind shut up for a while. Sometimes I felt a

18

little bit of peace, especially after thinking that things weren't as bad as I had thought. Then I'd try to go out and relate to girls and people.

When I was in my last year of college, especially when I was tripping, I'd go out to see someone and start thinking they didn't want to see me. And I'd even think about people driving by in their cars and worrying about what they thought of me. It seemed like my life was pretty well planned, that I was supposed to be unhappy for the rest of my life. Sometimes I felt good on acid, but it really never helped 'cause, when I'd come down I felt just the same, and, when I was tripping, I was just the same as when I was straight, which was really bad. I finally gave up psychedelic drugs because I got so freaky.

It's really hard to figure out how you are the way you are, but it seemed to me that other people were doing okay, and that I was the only one on the bottom. I wanted to be happy like everyone else, but I didn't know how to find happiness. I thought I'd try different things until I found the right situation and then everything would be okay.

I reached a point where I just couldn't cope with myself. I couldn't relate to anyone. A lot of times I'd talk just to be talking and I wouldn't say important things. I couldn't just be, because I felt the social separation so much. I even began thinking that maybe I was a homosexual because I couldn't relate to girls, but I couldn't relate to guys either. I was so hung up inside I didn't know who I was.

I went to see some psychiatrists, but they didn't help because I couldn't tell them what was really going on inside. They would ask me questions and sometimes I wouldn't say anything or I'd slur the issues, 'cause I had a lot of sexual hangups I didn't want to talk about.

I remember going to group therapy where there were some people just like me, who couldn't open up. Other people cried a lot and talked about their relationships with people and you could see a lot of what was going on with them was social separation. We were all just like a bunch of billiard balls bumping into each other. Sometimes I got so depressed I didn't even want to go and talk with them.

During college, I got into dealing drugs. When I saw dealers in action I thought there was a lot of excitement in it, so I started dealing. I began selling drugs and someone ripped me off, so I had to

19

sell a lot more to make up my losses. It seemed like I couldn't get out of it. Yet, I knew I'd have to because the cops knew I was dealing. After a while I got set up for a bust. Someone bought something from me, took it to the police, and they came and arrested me. At first I was supposed to get off if I didn't get into any more trouble. Then six months later I got busted again and I also got arrested a few other times for things like shoplifting and trespassing.

It seemed like I'd reached the point of no return. When I was in high school, I felt really sad at times, but there was the hope that, if I'd make certain changes in my life, I'd have a good life. But by the time I'd gotten busted, everything seemed out of my control, whatever happened to me I didn't have anything to say about. When I was happy it was no fault of my own, when I was sad I couldn't help it.

To get beyond the reach of the cops, I crashed at a place across the river, but, after two months, the people I'd been staying with decided they didn't want me around. I'd heard about this halfway house, so I decided to check it out. I'd read a newspaper article about it and it said to contact the Director so I went and talked to him. I guess he decided from the rap I gave him that I was hooked on marijuana or something, because he let me into the halfway house that same day. A halfway house is supposed to be a place where you go to get off of drugs, but I wasn't really hooked. I just figured it would be a good thing to do to make the cops think I was rehabilitating. So I went there and it was like going from the frying pan into the fire.

I moved in that night and the people there were mostly junkies, and a couple of alcoholics. They were all blacks from the slums of the big city. I'd never experienced ghetto life before and being there with those dudes was really heavy. One was violent, always talking about killing people and getting into fights. Then, he'd tell me that I'd better stay out of his way. You'd say one thing he didn't like and he'd burst into anger. I couldn't handle it because I was already so dark; I was already so crazy, being around more craziness just made me crazier. Those guys were supposed to be getting off drugs in that halfway house, but there were more drugs and better drugs there than they'd been getting on the outside. On the street, they might have

ALAN

been getting a fix that was maybe five percent heroin and the rest just crap mixed in with it. But in the halfway house they were getting pure stuff, so they had worse habits than when they'd come in.

They were into a Jesus trip, like they'd go around to high schools and tell the kids how they'd been on drugs and how they'd been saved. This one guy would get up and preach for a while and we were all expected to experience the Holy Spirit and really feel high on it. But, at first, I couldn't feel anything and I thought maybe they were experiencing something I wasn't.

The first time I went to the high school scene, I was supposed to be their expert on psychedelic drugs because they were all into downers. They got up and rapped about how bad heroin was and how they'd gotten started on marijuana and they said, "You better not mess around with marijuana 'cause you'll get hooked on heroin, 'cause we did." Then I got up. I rapped about LSD. I said I'd had some good trips and some bad trips, 'cause people have different reactions. Well, those guys didn't like that rap at all, because what they wanted me to say was that LSD was really bad and you shouldn't mess with it or you'd get hooked. They wanted me to put on a front.

After a while I started putting on the same front they did, like I'd experienced Jesus. I figured that if I didn't put on a front and play their game, I'd get kicked out of the halfway house and end up in jail. It was just loading up more crap on my back and it was getting heavier and heavier.

I was getting more and more depressed. I knew I was crazy, but those guys didn't know they were crazy. They'd gotten into heavy drugs, had committed all kinds of crimes and some had been violent. They didn't think they were crazy, but they really were and it was just making me crazier. I'd look around the place and all I could see was violence, jealousy, anger, and hatred. Some were stealing drugs from each other. Others were spying. I just finally reached the point where I didn't want to live anymore. I'd wanted to kill myself many times, but I guess I was afraid to die 'cause I didn't know what it would be like.

After four months at the halfway house I went to court and the

21

ALAN

Director testified that I was rehabilitating and getting better. But I wasn't really. I was just pretending to so I could get out of going to jail. It was just a big fake 'cause I was using drugs while I was there and, if I'd wanted to, I could have gotten hooked on heroin. Two weeks after I got my suspended sentence I split from the halfway house because I couldn't take it anymore. I moved in with a friend, got a job, and saved a lot of money. I was still very unhappy, although not as bad as in the halfway house.

I'd quit using psychedelics and was just smoking marijuana and drinking. I was trying to blot everything out, trying to turn my mind off, to shut it up for a while so I could be happy. Sitting around, smoking joints, drinking wine; that gets you to a place where your head isn't functioning at all and I'd get to feeling good for just a minute, then it would be like before. I was okay when I was by myself, but if someone came in I couldn't relate to them.

I had gotten to the point where I couldn't look anybody in the eyes. I couldn't relate to anyone, not even the people I knew. So I went to Boulder trying to escape from the past. When I got there, the first couple of days seemed okay, but then everything started to come around the same way as before. I couldn't relate to anyone there either.

I'd heard about Guru Maharaj Ji the first night I came into town, and, although I was a bit curious, I wasn't really that interested since it didn't mean anything to me. Then, one day, I was walking across the university campus and came across a group of students, some older people, and babies. I sat down 'cause I was curious to see what was going on. It turned out that they were giving satsang. I don't really remember their words, but just the feeling I got from them. It was really blissful. I guess it was such a sudden change from being so dark to feeling a little bit of joy that I knew I had to find out what it was all about.

I went to satsang again that night. In fact, I started going as much as I could and I began to hang around premies. During that time, I went to see Guru Maharaj Ji at the airport and at one of the Mission's programs. I felt I was being taken out of my mind, out of

22

my craziness, and into bliss. I knew that whatever Guru Maharaj Ji had to give was what I needed. I just knew. I just knew.

I went to satsang for about two months before I received the Knowledge. Once you're exposed to satsang, once you get the desire for the Knowledge and the desire to experience what premies are experiencing, then things start happening inside of you. I got to the point where I had to go to satsang, because it was the only good thing happening to me. I got to a point where, when I wasn't at satsang, I felt I should be. Whatever else I was doing wasn't anything in comparison.

I'd go to satsang and it would be very blissful, then I'd go home, back into the darkness. That was one of the things that made me want the Knowledge so badly, having to experience the joy of satsang then coming back into the darkness afterwards. I got to the point where I wanted to feel the bliss all of the time.

Not long afterwards I went to receive the Knowledge. I went in the afternoon and that night they had satsang. It's really hard to describe how I felt that night. There was so much energy and everyone was jumping up and down and laughing. I knew then I just had to have it. The next morning the Knowledge session took place. First there was satsang and then we were asked if we had any questions. At the time, I didn't really have any questions I could put into words. There was something in the background, like me asking myself "Am I really ready for this?" But I just decided it was now or never, so I went up. The Mahatma showed us the techniques and it was very blissful. I got completely wiped out.

By the time I received the knowledge I was so miserable that just feeling a little bit of joy and seeing what everyone else was experiencing, I knew it was what I had to have. All of those experiences building up on top of each other from way back in high school, when I first started feeling isolated, and then going to college, getting into drugs, living at the halfway house: all those experiences made it so dark and once I saw the light I just knew that was what I had to have.

I went to India about a week after I received the Knowledge. After I got there my mind started freaking out because I had to go

23

ALAN

through purification. The darkness inside of me started getting really shook up because it was being bombarded by the light and they can't coexist. Most of the time I was either totally blissed out or totally miserable, depending on whether I was into meditation or my mind. [Premies use "mind" and "ego" interchangeably.] The thing that makes you freak out is that your mind realizes it's not blessed, that it's about to lose the battle and it just fights for life. Once you start meditating and getting into that joyful state, with the light coming through, the mind freaks out and tries to keep a hold on you.

Some of the people who went to India had such strong minds they left the ashram and went wandering around India, going into town and doing lots of weird things. I was really freaking out a lot too, but I realized there wasn't any reason to go anywhere else because the ashram was the best place to be.

Sometimes I couldn't relate to other premies. I'd look at them and see them freaking out and think "Well, why are they freaking out, they're premies and they should be going forward," but, then I'd realize they were there for the same reason I was. They had heavy minds and they wanted to be devoted to Guru Maharaj Ji too.

The Knowledge is the strongest thing, but the mind is almost as strong and it can be very tricky. It can sometimes make you think you're getting into the Knowledge, but then it creeps in without warning. The thing about the Knowledge, though, is that it makes you understand your craziness. Before I received the Knowledge I knew I was crazy, but I didn't know why and I didn't know how to get out of it. Now, I still know I'm crazy, but I know why and I know there is no reason to be attached to it.

Before I received the Knowledge I didn't have anything but my mind, which was totally crazy, so I was totally crazy. Now I realize my mind is just something in the background. It's not really me. It doesn't matter. It can do whatever it wants, as long as I try to be devoted and meditate. My mind can go on and be crazy.

Being in India showed me that the Knowledge was the most important thing, that it's the one thing that makes us all the same, it's the one thing we can all experience. It wasn't that I grew so much spiritually, but I was shown exactly what I had to do and exactly what

24

devotion was and that I had to get myself together and do it. Compared to the two months before I'd received the Knowledge, Guru Maharaj Ji had taken a lot of heaviness off my mind. Before, I took so many things seriously, especially my ego because that's all I knew. I could still look out and see the separation between everyone, but even though those things were happening I knew it was nothing, it was just something we have to get over, to grow out of. But the times I did experience the oneness with everyone, I knew that Guru Maharaj Ji had saved me. Like, when I talk about being saved I mean being taken beyond my mind, 'cause that's the only thing that keeps us separate from God. Our mind keeps us separate. What we call "God," that energy or vibration, is in all of us and as long as we're ignorant of it we're going to be into our minds.

I'd gotten pretty sick in India and going through the change of going halfway around the world on the way back home really hit me. I started feeling pretty sick. So, I stayed at the New York ashram for a couple of weeks and went to the hospital for treatment. I was trying to get into doing service, but most of the time I didn't feel like doing it, not because I didn't feel well, but because my mind kept telling me I didn't feel like doing service. I just sat around and spaced out. Then I hitchhiked home to see my family.

I tried to talk to my relatives about Guru Maharaj Ji, but they wouldn't take it seriously. My uncle said I was hypnotizing myself. My grandmother talked about Jesus and, when I told her Guru Maharaj Ji was here for the same reasons, she wouldn't believe me. My relatives tried very hard to pull me back into my old self. They wanted to relate to me in the old way. So, I ended up doing a lot of things I'd done before, like thinking a lot, watching television, and just generally falling back into the old game. I also smoked some pot while I was there and my mind tried to convince me that it was all right but, at the same time, I knew it wasn't, because Guru Maharaj Ji had elevated me a lot and I could look back and see where I'd been.

My mother could tell that what I was into was good, that I had changed some and was more together than before. The last time I had been home I was so messed up on drugs I argued a lot, about

25

ALAN

drugs or whatever I thought was right. This time I didn't argue so much and was more peaceful. She could tell something had happened to me, but, of course, she didn't believe that Guru Maharaj Ji was the saviour and she didn't believe in Perfect Masters either. I guess she reacted like a lot of people, feeling that no one is perfect. I wasn't clear enough to give good satsang 'cause they didn't pick up that much from me. They just thought it was another trip I was going through, I guess. Like, I'd gone to college, gone through drugs and gotten kicked out, so I guess they figured this was just something else I'd gotten into. I'm sure my mother thought that what I was doing was better than getting strung out on drugs, but she really didn't think it was anything much.

I hung around home for a couple of months and I finally reached the point where I just knew I had to get back to the premie community, because I was falling away from the Knowledge. I felt if I'd stayed there much longer, I'd be the same old person I'd been before and I didn't want that to happen. So I hitchhiked back to Boulder.

The first thing I did when I got back was to go to satsang. I really started to get back into it, but it was hard at first because my mind was still trying to pull me back. But I began meditating again and going to satsang, so things began to happen. It was nothing big, just a slow growing process. I knew that Guru Maharaj Ji was the Lord and I knew this was the only way, the only thing I needed, the only thing I wanted. So I started trying to be a devotee. I haven't gotten any big flashes over night or become a super devotee or anything, but I've grown slowly. I can look back and see where I was at and see how far I've come and everything is coming together.

I moved into the ashram during that summer. It was pretty heavy at first because I wasn't used to living in an ashram situation. There were a lot of conflicts but they just had to be worked out and doing what Guru Maharaj Ji says really helped. You see, Guru Maharaj Ji is experiencing the Knowledge all the time and he can look at us and see what's wrong. He's the master psychiatrist, I guess you could call him, 'cause he can see our craziness and he knows what to do about it.

26

ALAN

In just these past few months I've been trying to be on the path of devotion as much as possible. When I get out into the world sometimes I stop and think about it and it seems like nothing is happening. I'll go out and do my job but I can't seem to meditate there. I can't remember the Word and it seems that I'm not devoted at all, but I know Guru Maharaj Ji says to just try and things will work out.

Looking back a year or more, before I received the Knowledge, it's hard to believe I was really that crazy. If I'd looked forward a year back then I would have thought I'd still be crazy. Maybe I would have killed myself or have entered a mental institution. There's no way I could have imagined this thing happening to me. I'd read about Transcendental Meditation and about different gurus. I'd hung around people who were into meditation and yoga, but it's hard to imagine that I could find something worth doing, something that would give me peace of mind and joy, which I'd never experienced before.

A few times before receiving the Knowledge I felt good compared to where I was at most of the time. Sometimes I'd even be a bit open in my relationships with others, but none of that compares to where I am now. Now, when I'm down I'm not really down, it's just my mind wandering around. I feel confused sometimes when my mind is wandering around, but I never really feel down 'cause I know that's just my mind. There's no reason to be crazy, because that's just illusion. Where I really am is with that Truth and Energy.

Guru Maharaj Ji's done so much for me. Before, I had no idea there was such a thing as peace. I'd hung out with some people from Students for a Democratic Society and we had big rap sessions about how we should withdraw the troops from Viet Nam. So I thought there'd be peace if we withdrew the troops. What I didn't know then is that peace has to be experienced inside and I'd never experienced that before.

I had to leave the ashram for a while because I had to pay off a college debt. Just being away from the ashram can do things to your mind if you let it, because you're always around people who sit around and smoke dope. That's what a lot of premies experienced who moved out. But, if you do everything Guru Maharaj Ji says it

27

doesn't matter where you are, whether you're in the ashram or not, but it's so easy for your mind to sneak in if you're not totally devoted. Like, I'm not totally devoted myself, 'cause when you are your mind can be going "yakkie yak" and you're not even hearing it. It's just something you can look at and laugh at, it's something that doesn't really exist. If I was completely devoted I could even meditate at work, but I can't and that's why it's important that I live in the ashram now. I still need the ashram because I haven't reached the point where I can go out into the world and still be into the Knowledge.

Before I received the Knowledge, I looked out at the world and saw people who were happy and people who were sad, but I wouldn't get involved with any of them. I came in contact, but never got involved. I was feeling completely separated from them. But now I can be separate and, at the same time, know I'm involved in something that's the essence of everything. I can go out in the world and give satsang or rap with people, but I don't get sucked into it. I know that the only reality is inside.

Before I received the Knowledge, if I was around people who were upset or having an argument, it would bring me down. Like, at the halfway house, people would start arguing and getting violent and I'd have to leave because I would start feeling bad. Now I can go out into these situations and be in that kind of craziness and give satsang and it doesn't bother me.

Sometimes it's a good thing to go out into this darkness and when it really starts to get heavy, you can get on the Word. If somebody starts to lay a trip on me, like, that Guru Maharaj Ji's a fake, I just get onto the Word. Whatever they're saying doesn't really matter, 'cause all it can do is affect my mind. If my mind latches on to what they say, it can make me feel bad, but if my mind is on the Word then it can't harm me. Guru Maharaj Ji has taken my downers away; he won't let those things happen to me anymore.

When Guru Maharaj Ji's around there's just no way your mind can convince you he is not the way, because when he's around you feel his Grace and you feel that energy because he's so pure. It just comes pouring through and you're absolutely positive he is the Lord and everything he does is for us. Whatever is going on is for our good, even if nothing is happening and we're just growing at our own rates.

I've reached a point now where I know there's nothing else for me to do than be devoted to Guru Maharaj Ji. If I find myself spacing out and thinking about things like reading the newspaper or just sitting around daydreaming like I used to do all the time, I find some service to do or try to meditate. Wasting time is such a waste of time and it's what made me go crazy in the first place.

It's very important for me to be devoted to Guru Maharaj Ji. If you just use the meditation techniques Guru Maharaj Ji gives you maybe you'll get high or maybe you won't. If you don't get anything out of them at first, you may just think the Knowledge is the techniques and say, "I don't really need Guru Maharaj Ji and I don't really need to do service." And, if you don't get off on the techniques, you're going to say, "Oh, there's nothing to these," and just throw them away. But if you just try to get into devotion something happens to you.

To me, being devoted means just doing what Guru Maharaj Ji says and just trying to do service for him. Whatever you do, you do it for him. There's just something you feel inside. He's the Lord and he's saved us and he's given us everything we need. He's given us this Knowledge that's so bright it just wipes out all the darkness. Devotion is learning to love Guru Maharaj Ji, learning to serve him and to obey him, 'cause we're like children and he's the school master who truly knows. He's the teacher who knows what we need.

Guru Maharaj Ji has experienced the Knowledge completely. He knows his devotees want the same things he has and the same things he feels, so he just tells us what to do because he knows how to get out of the trap of the mind. If you're not devoted to Guru Maharaj Ji, you must be devoted to something. If you're not devoted to him and his Knowledge, then you're probably devoted to your ego.

chapter
THREE
Helen

My family is of a fairly strict religious faith from up-state New York. Besides putting down drinking and smoking, our religion creates some up-tight feelings about sex. My parents gave me very little sex education. I can't really blame them because that was the way they were brought up, but the whole taboo on sex put me through a lot.

When I was a junior in high school sex became pretty important. My girl friends talked about how they'd been turned on sexually and that concerned me 'cause I'd never experienced it. In fact, I didn't know anything about it. I felt my body wasn't pretty and the guys who always liked girls for their bodies never paid any attention to me.

During my Senior year I had a hard time concentrating on my school work. Instead of studying when I got home, I'd take a walk. I got into the habit of staying up late and getting up early. So, I was tired all day long, almost sleeping through my classes and not really caring about them. People used to come up to me at school and tell me I looked too serious and somebody even told me I looked dull.

A lot of my high school experience was pretty unhappy. I didn't fit into the life style and I didn't know why. So, I started getting in-

31

volved in the political protest movement. I saw pictures of children who had been burned by napalm in the Vietnam war and my emotional reaction was just intense. I got really inspired reading about the war, but I couldn't get excited about my studies anymore. I'd take my American government book home and it would take me hours to get through the assignment 'cause it was so boring.

When I was a senior, Martin Luther King, Jr. and Bob Kennedy were assassinated. When Martin Luther King, Jr. died I felt called upon to do something more than I'd been doing about the race problem. I remember, I went to a friend's home to watch the television coverage of the tragedy and to pray together. And when Bob Kennedy died I just knew he couldn't have died in vain. It just made me want to do something with my own life.

I graduated from high school and enrolled in college. My first semester was much better than the experience I'd had in high school. For one thing, I started to date a lot more. I was happy to be appreciated and to be liked for my physical appearance as well as my mind. Yet, I was still sexually naive. In fact, the first guy I went out with I became immediately attached to. I thought, "Well, we had a date, so now we're supposed to be together." But, he really didn't want that, so he let me know very subtly. I remember being very upset about that. But then another guy came into my life.

It wasn't long after I'd arrived at college that I smoked my first grass. A girl friend of mine came up to me one day and said, "Helen, would you like to smoke some marijuana? You've gotta decide in ten minutes. If you want to, come with me and these other people, and we'll do it." I ended up going with them, even though I was scared.

Right before I was going to try it one of the guys said, "Sometimes people throw up the first time." So, sure enough, I was so nervous I got really sick and threw up. I should have known that grass and drugs were not my trip after that, for practically all my experiences with drugs have been very negative.

The first semester of college I was really outgoing, but then I got into a seclusion trip. I just wanted to be alone. I was so unhappy I decided to go see a school psychologist. When I was with him, I cried a lot and I usually felt better afterwards. I tried to tell him about my sexual fears and hang-ups. He gave me a book about sex and I read parts of it but it didn't help me that much.

I knew I needed help to figure my trip out but I didn't want to go back to the school psychologist. In fact, I wanted to get as far away from school as possible. I wasn't keeping up with my studies and I had fallen in love with a guy who wasn't responding to me, which was upsetting.

I finally decided to go see a psychiatrist. As soon as I sought outside help I felt relieved, for I had been feeling pounds of pressure to get it all together and I didn't see any way to do it. I told him what I was going through and he said it was just an identity crisis, that I didn't need to be too concerned but that I should go to some group therapy sessions. So, I went once a week for eight weeks. When I look back on those sessions now, they seem like they were nowhere. All of us talked about our problems but there were never any answers. There was never anything we could do to get ourselves out of the difficulties we were in.

I was sleeping about 10 to 13 hours a day then, because it was an escape from a world that was too painful for me to face. Usually I slept past the time for my classes, so I wasn't into school at all. And the dorm where I was staying got very depressing too.

With the therapy sessions going nowhere and my studies at a standstill, I finally decided to leave school. One of the things that helped me make the decision was a book about alternative education. It offered such a positive view of man's nature, that we are supposed to be free, creative people. It gave me the idea that maybe my problems at school weren't all my fault, that school was possibly expecting things of me I was not ready to give.

By the time I'd decided to quit college I was really ready to leave. In fact, I'd been so depressed there at times I even thought about committing suicide. I never came close to actually attempting it, but I told myself "If there's nothing better any place else, then forget it. Life isn't worth living. It's not worth all this pain and suffering."

A week after I left college I knew it was the best decision I'd made in my whole life. I started growing again. And this was the

33

beginning of a whole new set of changes. Even though I knew what I was leaving, I still had very little idea of what I was getting myself into. I had so little confidence, 'cause everything I'd tried to do just seemed to fall apart.

After dropping out of college, I met a girl, named Jean, who had been out of school a couple of years and who wanted to travel. So, we decided to hitchhike across the country to northern California to check out some communes we had heard were there. We stayed a week at a house where some people had just returned from a Hare Krishna meeting and they were really turned on to that. I remember them saying, "Don't do acid, don't do drugs, turn on to this thing we're into, it's the permanent high. It's the natural high that you won't ever come down from."

We began hitching again. We were picked up by a guy who played in a band and he took us to his place. Everybody was sleeping with each other there, which, the way I was brought up, was very foreign to me. One guy was very charming and, of course, I really dug him. But after a couple of days of being together, he started running after another girl, which really freaked me out. I was unhappy there anyway because I couldn't get into drugs that much and they were heavily into them.

Since Jean and I had come to check out the communes, we took off hitching again. Well, another band group picked us up and took us to this commune called the Old Cow Commune. There were two groups of people living there. One was into macrobiotic cooking and yoga. They wanted to get away from electricity, stereos, and the world at large. The second group was into drugs, music, and material conveniences.

A guy I'll call Sagittarius Bob, the leader of the second group, was open to us, while the first group was really uptight about strangers. So naturally we went with the second group. Five guys lived there, and another girl came while we were there.

I stayed at the commune a month and that is where I went through some of the biggest changes of my life. That's where I dropped acid twice and where I learned about karma and reincarna-

HELEN

tion from a guy I'll call Capricorn Bob. He told me about the soul's journey back to the source and that the soul was all things, like love, happiness, and joy. He told me that evil was just the absence of good.

I had told Capricorn Bob that I figured it was my fate to drop acid some time, I guess because my friends had gotten off on it. Well, one day he came along and handed me some LSD. I didn't feel I was really ready to do it, but it was there and he wanted me to, so I did. Well, that day was the longest day of my life. As soon as the acid started taking effect it felt very unnatural and really horrible. The whole day was a struggle to keep control.

Capricorn Bob spent the day with me. I don't know if he was messing with my mind, but there were times when he personified the devil. He showed me a book which had some psychedelic pictures in it and he pointed to a name written in French and the last name of the person was "devil." It sent a horrible fear through me. At the same time, the record player in the room was playing Santana's "You've Got to Change Your Evil Ways."

We went for a walk and I hallucinated that we were surrounded by cactuses. At one point I even tried to walk away from him when I was sitting under a tree and the tree started turning into snakes. We went down the hill after a while to a little house and we talked. He kept wanting to leave but I was frozen and couldn't move I was so paranoid and uptight.

Later on, we went to the little adobe house where I was staying. I laid down on the bed laughing hysterically, not a happy laugh, but a miserable laugh. I was laughing desperately because there was nothing I could do. I remember him handing me a little candy lifesaver, which was ironic because what I needed more than anything was a feeling that something would save me. I felt as if my very life was being threatened.

Later that night when I could talk, I said, "You told me that the soul is love, happiness, and joy." And he said, "Yeah." But, when he said those words, they were very far away from the actual experience I was having on acid. I only experienced love on that trip one time,

35

which was when Jean came up to me and said, "Helen, I've been wanting to tell you that I love you." I just felt a beautiful rush of love. But I didn't feel that at any other time during the trip.

The next day I told Sagittarius Bob my acid trip had been bad. He said, "Now you've seen the bad and the next time you can take note of that and get into the good." Before I did acid again I figured I would learn a little bit about it, so I read *Psychedelic Experience* by Timothy Leary.

It was a week after the first trip when Capricorn Bob came up to me and handed me some more acid. So I took it and I went on my way thinking, "Far out! This is going to be a good trip!" I took a walk by a beautiful stream, but then on the way back I came to the tree I had been under during the first trip and it started turning into snakes again. I thought, "Oh, no, not this again. I've got to go for help."

I went back to the commune and walked into Sagittarius Bob's room looking for help. I was told that he had died. I knew he was sick because he had been coughing up blood. In fact, just the day before he told us that maybe it was his time to go, and that night he was taken to the hospital.

When I heard that Sagittarius Bob had died it hardly affected me because I was going through a life and death struggle of my own. I was having very heavy hallucinations and I was taking it seriously. Like, I'd look at a guy and his face would become terribly distorted, like a werewolf's. Finally, I asked one of the guys, "What do you do when you see strange things outside of yourself when you're on acid?" And he said, "Well, you see those things because of a misunderstanding inside yourself." But, I couldn't relate to that. We had a few more exchanges and another guy in the room said some crazy things which didn't help me either. So I just got up and left.

I'd read that, if you started feeling weird, you were supposed to lie down flat on your stomach. So I went to the teepee where I'd been staying for a couple of nights and I laid down flat, but when I closed my eyes I saw horrible black patterns that had bad feelings connected to them. Then, I'd open my eyes to escape from that and the tent would start becoming black. I remembered then that Jean had helped me during my last acid trip, so I thought I would go find her.

36

HELEN

I went to the place where she was staying, threw my arms around her, and cried. I just released a tremendous amount of tension and frustration. After crying heavily, the whole thing was brought down to a level I could handle. Capricorn Bob came in, because he was really concerned about me, and I saw him as a handsome prince.

We went to the place where all the people were gathered because Sagittarius Bob had died. There was a very meditative atmosphere there. I sat down and, I don't know how it happened, but I went into the deepest state of meditation I'd ever experienced. Knowing I couldn't get help from outside, I realized that everything I needed was inside of me.

I slept in Sagittarius Bob's bed that night and I woke up in the morning saying things like, "We are all one," and "Everything you need is inside of you." I had such a deep faith in God and I knew Bob's body had passed away but his spirit was still living. That whole feeling of faith and deep understanding of myself, life, and other people stayed with me for days afterwards.

While I was in California I took part in some yoga classes, although I really knew little about yoga then. Afterwards I went back home to tell my family and friends what had happened to me. From there, I went back to New York City, then to Denver with a girl I had met.

In Denver, I met a guy who was into yoga seriously. He told me that it was beyond drugs, so I decided to really give it a try. In fact, after I turned on to yoga and meditation I quit using drugs. Not long afterwards, I moved into the Integral Yoga Institute in Boulder to practice yoga under Swami Satchidananda. I lived there about ten months, tried to get into the yoga practices, and received my mantra from Swami Satchidananda.

One day I noticed a picture of Guru Maharaj Ji on a store across from the Institute, announcing that he was coming to the United States. The poster said that he was a Perfect Master. My first reaction was that he was probably far out, but I already had a guru and I was trying very hard to be into him.

After spending that summer at a yoga retreat, I didn't know what

37

to do with myself. I was tired of drifting around in the world. In fact, I was even thinking about going to a monastery. I went to talk to my first yoga teacher and I asked him what I should do. He was living with nine other people in a yoga house in Denver and they weren't into any specific master at that time, so I decided to move in with them.

I moved into the yoga house and then I went away for a few day's vacation in the mountains with a girl friend. At that point I had substituted the mantra I had received from Swami Satchidananda for a Jesus Christ mantra, 'cause I really felt the power and peace of that. I prayed all day and night to Jesus.

When we returned there was a note on the door of the yoga house saying that everybody was up on Wall Street in the mountains to be with Guru Maharaj Ji. The note concluded with the words, "Come and receive the true Knowledge." We sat down on the porch and a guy who had already received the Knowledge came by and said incredible things about how his mind was blown away 'cause he had seen the divine light. He kept going on and on about how beautiful an experience it was. Then a girl came by who lived at the yoga house and she said the same thing, but even more deeply. I knew something far out was happening, but I wasn't sure what.

After my friend left, I decided to go up to Wall Street. On the way, I stopped at the Integral Yoga Institute. About twenty people had been living there but almost everybody had gone to follow Guru Maharaj Ji. In fact, they had called Swami Satchidananda and told him of the possibility they might follow Guru Maharaj Ji and asked him if that was okay. He said that the only important thing was their spiritual growth. I guess he just gave them his blessings. That really blew me away 'cause I was somewhat attached to Swami too and I would have felt awkward if he hadn't approved of us going to follow Guru Maharaj Ji.

When I was up on Wall Street, Guru Maharaj Ji came out and gave satsang. I saw a 14-year-old boy, but I knew he was very high and there was no doubt in my mind that he was very far out. He spoke, then people asked him questions. I said, "How can I remove the blocks that keep me from being totally receptive to the Knowl-

38

edge?" And he told me to just stay in the atmosphere of satsang and feel the vibrations, that satsang would act like chlorine on my mind to remove all my doubts and fears.

Everybody in the yoga house where I'd been staying received the Knowledge, but I didn't because I wasn't sure I was ready. For the next week I listened to satsang. It was strange 'cause most of my life I'd been very serious and not all that happy, not the bubbly, joyful type. Yet, the week before I had been really joyful. But premies were telling me I had to really be desperate to receive the Knowledge. I kept hearing them say that, before they'd received the Knowledge, they couldn't sleep for nights, that's how badly they wanted it. So I thought the same thing should be happening to me. But it wasn't and that confused me.

I turned to the I Ching for guidance. I asked it whether I should receive the Knowledge. It indicated that I should. Then, a girl read the Tarot cards for me and it, too, said I should. Everything was telling me to receive the Knowledge. But, inside I just didn't know. I was so confused, because I just didn't know if I was ready.

Guru Maharaj Ji spoke in Boulder. He said, "Don't get lazy, 'cause I'm gonna go and I might not leave a Mahatma here." After hearing that, it hit me that I'd better receive the Knowledge while I could. So, I finally got up enough courage to go to Guru Maharaj Ji's room that night to ask him if I could receive the Knowledge. I was afraid and confused, almost to the point of tears, but also happy and excited to have an excuse to talk to him. He said yes, so I knew that the next day I would be going to the Knowledge session.

There were maybe a couple of hundred people waiting to receive the Knowledge the following morning. Some disciples were screening out people and selecting those who they thought were the most ready. One guy who was doing the screening asked me if I was ready to be 100 percent devoted to Guru Maharaj Ji. I was unsure, so I told him I didn't know if I was ready to do that. So, he said that I'd better wait. I told him that Guru Maharaj Ji had given me the okay to receive the Knowledge that day. He responded by telling me the day wasn't over yet.

Guru Maharaj Ji was giving satsang at another place, so I went over there, crying and confused. When I got there I got up enough courage to tell him what had happened. I told him he had said I could receive the Knowledge but they wouldn't let me in. He said that I should go back and get in and, if they didn't let me in, he would come over there personally. When I got back, the same guy asked me again if I was ready to devote my whole life to Guru Maharaj Ji and, again, I hesitated. But he let me go in anyway, so that was a relief.

Each of us brought a flower or some other offering, then we were led up to a little room to wait for the Mahatma. I was still confused. Then the Mahatma came and the Knowledge session started. We were supposed to ask questions if we had any doubts. A couple of people did, but not me. The Mahatma showed me the light technique and I saw just a very vague pattern of light.

When the session was over I felt there were a lot of people who didn't pick up on what was happening and I was one of them. I walked out of there with the same deep feelings of depression I used to get when I wanted to commit suicide. I felt like everything had been building up to this and I had experienced nothing. I felt bad 'cause a lot of times when people come out of the Knowledge session they're really blissed out. I really wanted to be blissed out too, for those people who would come to me and ask me how it was.

It is one of Guru Maharaj Ji's commandments that you should "Never leave room for doubt in your mind." One way to deal with a doubt or confusion is to tell someone and that's supposed to clear it up, to help you see it's nothing. The Mahatmas had all left town, so I didn't have a chance to clear up my confusion. I cried and cried that night. In fact, I was really unhappy for the next several days. I never really had any doubts that the Knowledge was real or that Guru Maharaj Ji was a Perfect Master. My doubt was that I was not fertile soil for the Knowledge. I felt I'd really blown it.

A few days later one of the Mahatmas came back and I went to talk to him right away. I told him my problem and he went over the meditation techniques with me. He assured me I had them and that I should just keep on meditating. So that was a real relief to me.

HELEN

A lot of people were already talking about going to India, but I thought I couldn't because I didn't have any money. Then I heard that the best service one could do was to go to India. All of a sudden, I realized how I could get the money. I consulted the *I Ching* and it said I should go. So I knew I was going to India.

When we got to New Delhi, there was a big festival in honor of Guru Maharaj Ji's birthday. There were huge tents, hundreds of western premies and thousands of Indians. Right away, a lot of my friends started freaking out. A bunch of them eventually left, some to follow other gurus. That really affected me and, at times, I wanted to go with them too, but I didn't.

After a while, we all went to the Prem Nagar ashram. I could sense the high vibrations there, for it was very peaceful and you could almost feel the devotion. A lot of my time centered on satsang, service, and meditation. But a dualistic thing happened to me. I'd sit and listen to satsang and be taken in by it, but when it came to actually practicing what was being said I didn't do very well. For example, there was this little town a couple of miles from the ashram and some of us started going there in the afternoon to eat at a restaurant which served American food. But then I'd come back and listen to satsang and I'd say "Yeah, that's right." I finally realized that I had to get into the thing all the way or not at all, because the going back and forth was driving me crazy.

The time came for us to leave Prem Nagar. I had been counting the days 'cause I wasn't happy there and I wasn't meditating or doing service that much. I'd listen to satsang but it just made me feel badly because I wasn't doing the things they were talking about. The very best moments were when Guru Maharaj Ji was there and almost every time he gave satsang it was far out.

On Christmas Day, I was reading the section on gurus in *Be Here Now* by Baba Ram Dass. He said that when you get ready to meet your guru you'll find and recognize him. I read that at a time when I was concerned about my relationship to Guru Maharaj Ji, wanting to be devoted but unable to complete my surrender to him. It was comforting to me when Baba Ram Dass said not to worry

41

about holding back, that if you did it was just a sign that you weren't ready for complete surrender and you should relax and trust the process.

I left India for home. We were told, "Okay, you've been to India and received grace, so now it's your duty to propagate the Knowledge and tell everybody about Guru Maharaj Ji." At that point, I wasn't ready to do that and I was pretty upset because I didn't feel like I had realized much of anything for myself.

I roomed with a girl in India who had been a follower of the Tibetan Buddhist teacher, Trungpa, Rinpoche, and she said some really positive things about him. Then one night I had a dream that Guru Maharaj Ji changed into Trungpa, Rinpoche. So, I decided I would come back to the United States and, somehow, I'd find a teacher I could learn from. I knew I was a seeker after Truth. I wanted to love and know God and I felt the way would be shown to me, if I was sincere. Soon after my return to Colorado I went to a class Trungpa, Rinpoche's followers were teaching and I was very impressed.

I decided to move to Boulder then because Trungpa, Rinpoche was there, plus I had a friend living there who said I could stay at her place. She had also just come back from India and was kind of upset and confused the way I was. She was taking Trungpa, Rinpoche's class at the University of Colorado. I immediately got into a couple of his books, *Meditation in Action* and *Born in Tibet*, and both were impressive. Then I had an interview with him. I learned that his meditation techniques were about the same as Guru Maharaj Ji's. After the interview, I quit doing Guru Maharaj Ji's techniques and I started using Trungpa, Rinpoche's instead. For three or four months that was the case.

The thing about Trungpa, Rinpoche which impressed me was that he didn't want to relate to people as a guru, but as a spiritual friend. But I had the same problem with him as I had had with Guru Maharaj Ji. I looked at both of them as big, authoritarian, cosmic figures and at myself as lowly and small. I found myself not being able to relate to Trungpa, Rinpoche, 'cause I was afraid of him. So I finally realized his trip wasn't mine either.

42

HELEN

Once again I got into drinking, smoking, and sex. I thought I'd try the sex trip again, but it didn't work. It was obviously not right for me to be doing that. Also smoking had unusual affects on my body, so physically I was pretty low those four months. But there was one thing I was still into.

When I was living in the Integral Yoga Institute I'd gotten into Johrei, the channeling of divine light. It's a practice used in The Church of World Messianity, a Japanese movement. During those four months I was going to Johrei meetings and being channeled to and channeling to others, which is a form of spiritual healing where God's light is transmitted through the hand. And through my Johrei activities I kept in contact with premies 'cause a lot of people in Johrei were also in Divine Light Mission. It was through Johrei that I met a couple of premies who helped me.

I was led to this house where Sam lived because I wanted him to channel to me. I sat with him and told him how confused I was and how nothing was coming together for me. One thing had been hassling me since I'd taken acid and that was black magic. Even when I was living in the Integral Yoga Institute I was vaguely afraid of evil spirits. I didn't know how to deal with those fears. In fact, I had some trouble sleeping nights from time to time. So, I told Sam and he said that I should see Julie. A few days later I talked with her and she told me she had gone through similar trips and that Guru Maharaj Ji had helped her out of it. I could see how he had changed her life and how beautiful it was.

Both Sam and Julie were very deeply into meditation, which inspired me, so I began meditating with both of them. Being around Julie was very inspiring for me. She talked with such conviction, saying things like Guru Maharaj Ji was the same spirit as the Christ and that this time, instead of being crucified, he would be exalted. She said Guru Maharaj Ji was the embodiment of love the same as Christ and he'd come to save and uplift humanity just by the vibration of his love.

I went through a very heavy experience about that time which turned my life around. Guru Maharaj Ji's mother, Mata Ji, was going to give satsang in Denver so I decided to hitchhike in to hear her. I

43

HELEN

was picked up by this guy on my way to get a ride from some pre-mies. If I hadn't been so naive I would never have gotten in with him, 'cause he was going the opposite direction and he turned around, came back, and picked me up.

The first thing he did was to turn instead of going straight, where I told him I was going. And I said, "Oh, this isn't the way." I had a hold of the car handle and, if he wasn't going to turn around, I was going to jump out. But he said, "Oh, I thought you meant this way. I'll turn around." But then, instead of turning around, he went onto the freeway toward Denver.

I decided I wanted to go to Denver anyway, so I thought maybe that was my ride. But when we got close to Denver he told me it was getting late and he had promised to stop by and see his sister and asked me if I minded. I said okay. He kept driving and driving and I told him it was sure taking a long time to get there and he replied that there was a road coming up he planned to turn off on. Sure enough, there was a road, but pretty soon we were on dirt roads and he told me it was just three or four miles and he went at least ten. By this time, there were very few cars and hardly any houses and I thought about getting out and hitching back.

I started praying to Mata Ji and Guru Maharaj Ji and chanting a prayer from Johrei which has a very high vibration. I thought a mira-cle might be necessary, because, even though I was trying to have a positive outlook, every once in a while I'd have flashes of the rape trip. Finally, he turned into a field and said, "This is where my sister lives."

In my naive trust, I half expected to see a house there. Of course there wasn't. He stopped the car, turned off the key and then he lunged for me yelling "You're going to die!" I started struggling with him, but I was helpless out there in the wilderness. So I just cried out, "Guru Maharaj Ji, help me please!"

As I was struggling, the guy got into the back seat of the car and put a noose around my neck. He tightened it and tightened it. At that point, I quit struggling, 'cause I knew there was no point to it.'

As he kept tightening the noose, I was saying something like "Guru Maharaj Ji, if it's your will for me to die, then take me, but

44

please take me to your lotus feet." The noose was getting so tight I was beginning to see white spots and my voice was sounding far away. Then, all of a sudden, he loosened it. He told me if I didn't struggle, he might let me live. So I sort of went "Whew, maybe Guru Maharaj Ji wants me to live."

He came around to the front seat and that's when the miracle happened. In ten minutes time he changed from a person who was telling me I was going to die into someone else, 'cause he started asking me questions. He asked me if I'd been raped before, and whether I was married and had kids. I said no and told him I didn't want to get pregnant. Then, pretty soon he said, "Well, you're nice and you're honest, so I won't do anything to you." I told him God would really bless him for not having hurt me. Then, he drove directly back into Denver and I got out.

It was definitely a miracle. It was sort of like being taken into the wilderness to face demons and having them overcome by the grace of God, by Guru Maharaj Ji, and then being taken back to civilization.

When I got into Denver I went to where Mata Ji was speaking. When the program ended I ran to Julie and threw my arms around her and cried. She picked up on the heaviness of the situation and poured out her love to me. We drove back to Boulder, meditated and chanted together. She fed and took care of me. She let me sleep in her bed that night and told me I could stay at her place for a while 'cause she wanted me to have a speedy recovery.

That experience deepened my faith in Guru Maharaj Ji so much. In fact, it was one of the first experiences I had which made me start feeling inside that "Yes, Guru Maharaj Ji is the way."

Because of that experience and my talks with Sam and Julie, I found service, satsang, and meditation taking on new meaning for me. Shortly afterwards, I went to my second Knowledge session for a review. The second time was definitely better. I sat there and could feel the energy and love coming through the Mahatma. Rather than be uptight about whether I would get the techniques right, I just sat there trying to be as open as possible to the love. Also, the second time I saw more light than before. I was just less confused because of all of my experience.

45

HELEN

After the Knowledge review I started thinking that maybe I would move into an ashram again. I sought out Julie's advice on the matter and shortly thereafter I moved back in. Right away I felt at home with the premies living there.

chapter
FOUR

Matthew

I grew up in a good family on a farm in western Colorado. My parents are very simple and good people. Their philosophy is that everybody should be going to church 'cause that means good up-bringing, but they aren't dogmatic about that. They are active in the Methodist church, but without much conviction. I became a member of the church against my wishes when I was in high school. My own religious education was pretty much on a surface level, but, nonetheless, I acquired a feeling for spirituality.

Later, I began to question religion. In fact, I reached the point where I was convinced I was an atheist and that I didn't see anything at all in the Bible, which upset my parents. I let them know I had no interest in religion whatsoever, even though I attended church with them once in a while. Then, I asserted myself and told them I didn't want to go to church at all, so I quit. The church was something I had to get away from because there was no substance to it. It was only a social thing.

Living on a farm, there were only a few kids to play with. So, I spent most of my time alone or with my brother. Only on special occasions did I play with my cousins and other members of my family. Basically, I learned to relate to the world as a loner.

47

MATTHEW

When I started school, I felt shy, scared, and somewhat inadequate. I had a feeling of being separate from the other kids. My basic pattern was to withdraw, rather than to jump in and try to conquer my social fears. Like, it was a year after I started school before I would go down the slide. It wasn't that I didn't like school, but only that my relationships with other kids weren't that good. However, I made some decisions which really affected the course of things.

One of the biggest decisions I made was in the seventh grade. Until then, I hadn't been into studying that much. I wasn't a bad student nor a good student. But I hated doing assignments because they bored me, so I rebelled against them. Then I looked at the situation and decided that, if I had to do them anyway, maybe I should just get them over with. So I began doing my assignments as soon as I got them, which improved my grades and self-image. It gave me the feeling I could accomplish something. So I quickly developed a commitment to being a good student, which led to an interest in science. That mushroomed until I reached the point where I decided I was going to become a physicist. So, I started saving my money for college. I wanted to go away to college in order to get away from the farm situation and to find some people I could relate to, since I was not able to relate to the kids in my high school very well.

I wasn't completely aloof from others during high school. I was friendly with everyone, but outside of school I had some limits 'cause I was so isolated on the farm. I just wasn't in a situation where I could easily see my friends. So, I stayed home and read most of the time. If there was a social gathering I normally went, but my usual entertainment was reading and taking walks.

I found out I could run pretty well, so I became active on the high school track team. Track is an individual sport, so I found that, like studying, if I applied myself I got a positive result. The harder I pushed myself the more exhilarating it was and there were times when I was the only person to represent our school at the state meet.

Some of the activities I became involved in had indirect rewards. If you were good enough in track, then you might go to the state track meet. If you were good enough in debate, then you could go to the state debate tournament. It wasn't just going to those events

48

which meant something to me, it was the chance to visit the eastern slope of the Rockies to see what was there. In fact, I came to Boulder when I went to the state debate tournament, became captivated by it, and decided I wanted to go to college there, partly because I'd heard that they had a good physics department.

It was pretty traumatic for me to go to college in Boulder, because I'd never lived in a community the size of the University of Colorado. I found the only way I could relate to the university community was as a loner. I just got totally into that role again, going to events, standing off to the side and watching, and not being a part of things. I couldn't relate on a social level with anyone, although I did strike up some friendships quite by chance through dormitory living.

I really didn't have any ego to project in social situations, so I just followed people at first. But I got tired of that after a while and decided to do my own thing, so I went on my own way. The friendships I'd hung onto for the first semester I conveniently ducked out of and I tried to pick up on something else.

One of the ways I tried to free myself from those social relationships was to hit "The Sink," a hangout near the university. That was in the spring of 1967 and there were some exciting things happening then. People were beginning to grow their hair long and they were smoking dope and dropping acid. Songs were coming over the radio about San Francisco and the press was splashing stories about the hippies of the Haight-Ashbury district all over the newspapers. And an antiwar group was emerging.

I noticed that the people I could relate to the best were either in the dope scene or in the antiwar movement. So I began wearing long hair and thinking I'd like to try LSD. I also wanted to get involved in the antiwar movement, so I made contact with a person I'd met through the Student Peace Union and in the second semester of my freshman year I started attending their meetings.

During finals week of that semester I scored some acid. I'd made some friends, but not anyone I wanted to take it with. So I dropped it at my older brother's place in Denver. It didn't blow my head away, but it did something very subtle in terms of my self-awareness, for I was seeing myself at the same time I was experiencing. I wasn't really

49

MATTHEW

awake then. Sure, I was a reflective person, but I hadn't yet deeply considered the meaning of my existence or the nature of my own being.

That summer I went home and worked at an oil shale plant as a lab technician. I had a few conflicts with my parents about my long hair, which I eventually had to cut because of my job. It was a quiet and lonely summer. I couldn't relate to people there, even those, like me, who had gone to college and had come back home for the summer.

When I returned to college the next fall I was determined to find some marijuana. I'd arranged to live with my former roommate and two other guys who'd lived in the same dorm with me. We all had something in common, in the sense that we were searching for something more than just superficial things. So, after I'd found some grass, I assumed the responsibility for turning them on.

Students for a Democratic Society was a brief political explosion on campus about that time and I got into it. I agreed with its philosophy. Well, not all of it, but I agreed with what was wrong politically. So, I got into what was called the "CIA demonstration." I helped to block the door to the CIA's recruitment office for a day. Because of my role in the demonstration I was suspended from school and then readmitted on probation at the same time. It didn't harm me academically, but a copy of the charges against me were sent to my parents which really upset them. That was the first really big freakout they'd had over their aspiring son who had gone off to college with bright hopes of becoming an intellectual. So they came over to Boulder for a showdown.

They talked to the dean first, then to me. I laid out my political philosophy which provoked and infuriated them. It wasn't a calculated rebellion against them, but against authority in general.

My political interests came to a stop after the first semester of my sophomore year, and I tried to get back into my studies. I changed my major from physics to sociology and I took a number of philosophy courses. But, during that time, I was still heavily into dope and listening to music. Then everything began to open up that summer.

I went home to get a job for the summer but I couldn't find any-

50

thing. So I returned to Boulder and got a job as a janitor at the university's student center. During the summer, a spiritual urge began welling up within me. I stopped smoking dope but I dropped acid twice for purely spiritual reasons, which were the deepest experiences I'd had on drugs.

My spiritual urge developed through a lot of chance things. During the second semester of my sophomore year I read *Siddhartha* by Hermann Hesse and it lit a spark in me. From there I got into the works of Carl Jung. His books inspired me to meditate. In fact the urge became so strong I had no choice. One day while I was meditating outside a butterfly landed on top of my head. It sat there for a minute, then flew away. I've had butterflies land on me since without attaching any meaning to it, but at that moment it was symbolic. It was a sign that something powerful was happening. So I started meditating regularly, which helped me pick up on some inner truth.

That fall I enrolled in school in order to avoid the draft. I took courses that were deeply interesting to me, like Chinese philosophy and ancient history. But there just wasn't anything there for me so I stopped going to classes. I was meditating regularly and was reading a lot of spiritual books.

Spiritual books explained what was happening to me. I saw something that definitely related to the experiences I was having in meditation. It was always that way. I didn't read the books first, and then try to experience what the books said I should be experiencing. I experienced things first, then went to the books to see how they would explain it.

I began to feel that, previous to that time, I'd never seen, felt, smelled, tasted, or heard. I was coming into the here and now, becoming more self-aware. Previously, when I walked down the street I thought about where I was going, what I'd been doing, and what I would be doing. Now I was walking down the street really seeing things, street signs, cars, expressions on people's faces. Visually, I got a sense for what artists see. I tapped a level of awareness then I can never lose.

Acid hadn't answered my questions, but meditation was getting me somewhere because I experienced definite changes in myself over

51

time. So I decided to forget drugs and go with meditation. I was entering a new stage.

I was hanging around Boulder at loose ends, not really knowing what to do. I'd meditate, go out and hang out somewhere, have a cup of coffee and observe people. But there was no way for me to relate to people on a spiritual level, except with a few friends. And I was waiting for something to happen with the draft.

The next summer I received a notice to take my induction physical and, of course, I passed with flying colors. But I had no intention of reporting for duty. I told my parents that. I don't think they really believed I would refuse to go into the Army, but in December 1969, I went to the induction center on the appointed day and told them I wasn't going and then I walked out.

I didn't hear from the authorities for six months. A friend of mine was reading a list of indictments in the newspaper one day and my name was there. So I got a lawyer who had handled draft cases and he took mine for a really low price. The process of going to court lasted about six months.

I had confidence and faith that what I was doing was right, and prison didn't scare me. When I went before the judge, he couldn't ruffle me. I didn't care what he said. I was under his power, yes, but in a sense I wasn't. They could take me away physically, but not spiritually. Because my philosophy was not heavily political, the probation officer put through some favorable words for me and, with a liberal judge, I got a sentence not many people had gotten up to that time. It was six months in a low security institution and then probation for a year and a half doing some sort of alternative service. So, in December 1970, I went to jail. I spent three weeks in the Denver County Jail and then the rest of my time in a minimum security prison camp in Arizona. I had no problems there. I meditated a lot. It was a good experience and it was even fun getting hauled around in handcuffs.

After being released from prison I got my job back at the university. They knew I'd been in jail but they treated me fairly just like the courts had. I didn't really have any negative feelings about that whole trip. In fact, to fit the conditions of my probation I worked at the local free medical clinic. So it wasn't bad at all.

About that time, I heard that Guru Maharaj Ji was attracting a lot of people up to Wall Street where he was staying. I talked to a person I worked with about going up there to see him but that didn't come together. Later, I saw some posters saying he was going to be speaking at the university, so I decided to go and see what it was all about. Generally, I checked out spiritual people who were in town, so that wasn't an unusual thing for me to do. But I had a sense of greater anticipation than I'd felt about other people who had spoken.

I went to the program and the energy seemed to be very high even before the program started. It showed in the way people were bustling around fixing up the stage and putting flowers around. You could feel the enthusiasm of the devotees.

The program started with people giving testimonies. It continued in that vein for some time because Guru Maharaj Ji hadn't shown up. A number of people walked out disgusted, but it didn't bother me a bit. I was willing to wait, however long it took. I wasn't sure what was going to happen, but I was attracted to the energy I felt there. Then people started chanting and that developed into some really high energy. Everybody was standing, chanting, and clapping for a long time. I even got into it which was something I didn't normally do. Usually, I would enjoy something like that as an observer, not as a participant. However, I got into it and a good feeling came over me.

Eventually, the chanting dragged out for so long some people got turned off by it and left. Pretty soon the only people in the auditorium were those who were definitely interested in hearing Guru Maharaj Ji and his devotees. Then he came. We were standing up at the time and the feeling I had when he walked in was definitely a rush of energy all over my body. I felt I could hardly stand on my feet it was that intense.

His Mahatmas gave satsang. It was interesting, but that went on and on too, although it didn't really bother me. I wanted to stay because I was still getting high off of it. When Guru Maharaj Ji gave

53

MATTHEW

satsang he spoke simply but with a high degree of certainty. I wasn't
sure what to make of it, but I was entranced. I was beginning to think
that I wanted to receive the Knowledge. As the program ended I was
really high but a little bit confused about what to do. We were told
the Knowledge sessions would be the next day in Denver. I didn't
have a car and all sorts of things went through my mind trying to
convince me it was a hassle to go into Denver and that I didn't know
how to find the ashram. I could have gotten it together to go, but I
was holding back and I knew it.

Holding back was definitely an ego thing for me. You see, I'd
spent most of my time observing spiritual groups while sticking to my
own path. I felt a certain sense of satisfaction with the way my spiritual trip was going. I guess I'd developed some sort of spiritual ego
'cause I couldn't get into Guru Maharaj Ji that easily. I felt I knew
something already and I had to satisfy myself that what he was saying
was really what I wanted before I could let myself go into it.

I had watched all sorts of spiritual groups, even Christian ones,
but I stayed back. Those groups were saying, "Come on over. We're
here if you want to learn about what we're doing." But Guru Maharaj Ji was saying, "I want you! I'm calling you. Come! I have
something I want to give you." And that struck a responsive chord in
me.

Two weeks later, I noticed that a Mahatma was going to be
speaking at the university. I really didn't know who the Mahatmas
were or what their relationship to Guru Maharaj Ji was, but I sensed
they were more than devotees and that it would be something special
to see and hear them. When I saw the announcement I didn't definitely make up my mind to go, but I just happened to be around
when he was going to speak and went to hear him. Again, I felt a lot
of intense energy there. It reminded me of something I'd felt in meditation. There was a level of consciousness behind satsang that was
definitely affecting me. There was to be a Knowledge session in
Denver the next day and, again, I wanted to go, but I didn't.

I spaced out the whole thing for a week, then I noticed another
announcement that there was going to be satsang in the student

54

center that Sunday. So I went and it turned out to be a business meeting, since premies were getting things together to make the trip to India. That fascinated me, because I thought it would really be something to go to India. It made me want to check it out more carefully.

People were obviously very excited about the trip and again I sensed something was there, that those people knew something mysterious that I didn't know. I definitely sensed something in them, maybe it was the look in their eyes. And again I felt in tune with that, just as I had felt in tune with the Mahatma who had spoken at the university a while before.

After the meeting, premies sang for a while and I got the feeling from their singing how blissful and enjoyable the experience was that they were receiving from the Knowledge and their meditations.

The premies who gave satsang at the different programs I'd attended were people I'd felt in tune with, who were on a spiritual path similar to mine. I'd never talked to them, but I noticed they were leading the people they were with. I respected them. Every time I came in contact with Divine Light Mission I saw somebody else I'd felt in tune with and, because they were in the Mission, I began to feel there might be something to it.

After satsang I went up to a premie and told him I felt I wanted to receive the Knowledge. That was the first time I'd really declared myself and drawn anyone's attention to me. He responded with compassion and told me I should listen to satsang as much as possible and the next time a Mahatma was in the area I should receive the Knowledge. That's all the explanation I received, but I walked away feeling good.

Up to that time, I was teetering back and forth and I think that satsang is what made the difference since it forced me to declare myself. Neither Mahatmas nor Guru Maharaj Ji were there. There were just people like me, yet I was picking up intense energy from them. I sensed that they were not just fooling around. They were really in it together and they were going to India. I knew then that I had to share their excitement and the level of their involvement in

55

the spirtual life. I realized I could go a long time with my own medi-tations and not get very far; whereas, they were moving along rapidly. There was really something behind them.

My normal mode of behavior had been noncommital up to that point. I'd watch a spiritual trip, check it out, and get to know what was happening. I didn't really feel a strong need for companionship. I was happy just the way I was going, except I knew that at some point my spiritual quest would have to become stronger. I wasn't frustrated about this though because the changes I'd made had usually come without being forced. Getting ready to receive the Knowledge was just the next phase and it was slowly taking me away, just like my first meditations had done.

After I'd declared that I wanted to receive the Knowledge, a re-ally strange set of events took place. From that moment on, I was caught. Instead of waiting to run into satsang, I began looking for it because they told me I should go. First I looked for it half-heartedly. I sort of meandered over to where it was supposed to be, looked into the room quickly, saw that nobody was there, and left quickly. That happened for a while until I decided that maybe people were coming late. So I started sticking around a little longer, but nobody came. Then I checked out several places where they had posters up to see if I had the right information. Finally I went to the Divine Light Mis-sion office hoping that I might find something out there, but it was locked. I developed the distinct feeling that premies were hiding from me, that I was being tricked.

I stopped and took stock of the situation. I knew I'd never done such a thing before, running all over the place looking for satsang. I realized I was hooked on Guru Maharaj Ji and that he must be lead-ing me on some sort of chase. I puzzled over why I had to go through it, then I realized that the people in the Mission expected commit-ment, so I followed through.

One day I ran into a premie who was manning a booth on campus and I asked him why satsang wasn't happening. He told me that everyone had been working hard to raise money for the trip to India and they hadn't been able to hold satsang. So at least I knew

MATTHEW

they weren't hiding from me. I also learned from him that a Mahatma was expected in Denver that weekend.

He told me that when the Mahatma came I should go and just hang out at the ashram. Somehow during the process of hanging out the Knowledge session was suppose to happen. How you ended up in the Knowledge session I didn't know, except you really had to be open and sincere. I was also told that the Mahatma would probably question me to see how sincere I was. Yet, I didn't have any idea what questions he would ask and how I was going to be tested. So with that scant information, I was ready to go to receive the Knowledge.

I got off work on Saturday morning, got cleaned up, had some breakfast and took the bus to Denver. When I got to the ashram I started listening to satsang and learned that a Knowledge session was already under way. After quite a while, the people in the first Knowledge session came down. I watched them closely and it was obvious from the look in their eyes and from their facial expressions that they were all pretty blown away. It looked to me as if they'd all gone through something which had affected them deeply. Some appeared to be puzzled, while others were very exuberant and joyful.

The Mahatma came down and his expression was very blissful too and I felt very attracted to him. I continued listening to satsang all day. People would go out for lunch but I just hung around there waiting for more satsang. Evening came and I was anticipating what was about to happen. By then, I was very blown away by all the satsang.

In the evening another Knowledge session formed. I was pretty tired, along with everyone else. I spent so much time sitting and being uncomfortable I began to feel I was being tested again, like when I was running around in Boulder trying to find satsang. I felt they were putting me in those cramped situations just to see if I'd get so physically desperate I would leave. But I knew I was definitely going to stick it out. I didn't necessarily agree with everything they said in satsang, but the sensation I had of the Knowledge was beyond words and I knew I wanted it.

57

MATTHEW

The Knowledge session finally started. It was very cramped and stuffy and it lasted eight hours. I was really tired, so I was lucky the Mahatma didn't ask me any questions. He did pick out some people he felt were tired and told them to come back at another time. I knew I was exhausted but I wanted to stick it out, so I stayed very open to the Mahatma. I glued my attention on him so he wouldn't sense any conflict in me.

I was shown the techniques of meditation and the Knowledge was revealed to me. It was so close to me and so simple, yet I knew it was very profound. But it was a little too simple so I was puzzled. Is this all, I wondered. Is this what they were talking about? So I walked out of the session confused and puzzled.

I walked downstairs and there were a number of people trying to pick up on the vibes of everyone coming out of the Knowledge session. One guy was looking up at everyone with a broad grin on his face and checking everybody out as they came down. That really frustrated me because I couldn't walk down with the feeling of "Wow, now I know. Yippee!" I was puzzled and it bothered me that he was there trying to pick up on my vibes.

The next day I went to a premie satsang at the university. There, I got drawn into the Mission, as if it were made for me. But it happened in a very strange way. I wasn't sure about the Knowledge. I didn't know what the Mission was or how the people in it ran their affairs. But that day everybody was getting ready to go to India except for a small number who were supposed to stay and keep the Mission together. However, heavy satsang came down that day saying that everybody should go to India. So, as things turned out, the premies who were supposed to stay changed their minds and decided to go and they laid everything in my lap.

The reason I ended up with the responsibility was because I had spoken up during the meeting to say that I could donate a little money for a down payment on an ashram. From that small gesture of support, I ended up with my name on the Divine Light Mission checking account. I didn't even know the people in the Mission, or its purpose. But that little place was put there for me and, even though I was still confused about the Knowledge, that connection

58

with the movement kept me from spacing out the Knowledge over the next few weeks.

Service and meditation began to have a very intense effect on me within a few days. I still had a lot of uncertainties, but I began learning and became familiar with the meditation techniques. Since then it's been a very slow progression in my understanding. It's been a gentle evolution and yet its been amazingly intense and the changes have struck deep. Now, I'm more accepting of myself and the world. I'm learning how to function in our society rather than dropping out, yet I'm not being trapped by it the way most people are these days. Now I'm just playing with the system and enjoying it.

chapter
FIVE

Marc

My most vivid memories begin in elementary school. About the second grade I was given an I.Q. test and I scored about 145. Through those tests I was placed in advanced classes. By the fourth grade I was doing well in science and I liked math a lot. And at home I played around building things, like radios. In junior high school I was placed in advance math and science, was elected Student Body President, and ran with the track team. In high school I also moved ahead in my education as far as I could, even to the point where I was taking a college course in Physics.

Most of my friends lived in my neighborhood. We had lots of parties, but I don't think we were getting drunk very much. We just played around having our make-out parties and things like that. My first long romance started in the eighth grade and lasted until the eleventh. After almost four years, I began feeling the pressure of our relationship, that I was tired listening to what she wanted and needed. I got to the point where I just wanted to live for myself, so we broke up.

I went to Hebrew school twice a week in addition to public school. But, instead of getting into the essence of the Torah, we learned how to speed read. I'd study a prayer in the Torah, go to class, and the teacher would give us the go sign and we'd read as fast as we could. Then he'd count the mistakes and give us a score. It was intense competition. Sure, it was probably good for the ego, because I was the second fastest, but it didn't show me the meaning of what we were supposed to be there for, which was to get into the Jewish religion.

During my high school years I used to go to the synagogue on holy days, sit there, and freak out. I'd just get hot and tired. Sometimes I'd fast because it was the thing to do, not for the spirit of it.

My mother and father weren't getting along very well during my high school days. They weren't yelling and screaming at each other all of the time, but there were fights for sure. Finally, they told me they were going to get a divorce.

With my parents going through changes of their own, they weren't too concerned about whether I wore long hair or dressed differently. They had complete faith that I knew what was good for me. They seemed to be aware that they were of their time and shouldn't lay their trips on me. They knew it was my life and that I had to experience it for myself.

During all the confusion of my parents' situation, with my father sleeping one place and my mother another, I had to choose a college for myself. My high school counselor recommended a small, private college and told me not to worry about getting in, because I had good college board scores in math, although my English score was not so great.

As time passed, everybody else I knew had been accepted into college but me. I had an application for a large, urban university, so I decided to apply there and a week later I was accepted into the Engineering School.

During high school I was seldom absent or late to school, because I took it seriously. Well, I got to my first university class at eight o'clock in the morning, having walked a mile in the freezing cold, and the professor didn't even show up. That was my first impression of college and it lasted. I soon began to find ways of getting around the college system and making time for social things.

I was rushed to join a fraternity. I found some guys who seemed to be doing the same things I was and I felt comfortable with them. That's how twelve of us first came together, as pledges of a fraternity. It was a wealthy, Jewish fraternity and the twelve of us went through an intense pledging period together for about five months, until we banded together and revolted. It was disgusting what they wanted us to do. We were supposed to go through a session where they were going to dunk our heads in "brew." It was a mixture of piss, peppers, and shit. We told them we didn't want to hear about it. Through our struggle, the twelve of us became stronger as a group.

During that time, drugs started floating around. We had said that we'd never touch marijuana, but, before long, some of the guys fell by the wayside, and of course, I finally did too. I had had a fight with a girl I'd been dating steadily and when she went on vacation that was my excuse to smoke my first grass. I didn't get off on it the first time, but a few times later I got high with the brothers in the house and the music was doing amazing things to my head as new dimensions were opening up for me. That showed me something new, so I started becoming heavily involved with drugs.

During the spring of my sophomore year I was living in the fraternity house with those twelve brothers, but we were becoming different from the other guys in the house. We were beginning to grow our hair long and to deal drugs a little. That was about the time I started tripping on psychedelics.

I'd see my straight girl friend after school, from about six until eleven at night, then I'd go home and trip with a friend the rest of the night. We'd just sit around and go through astral trips. My mind would just leave my body and go somewhere else. With my girl friend, I was one person but later that night I'd be another. Yet, I didn't tell her I was doing drugs. I realized something had to be done, so I broke off from my girl friend.

I tripped on psychedelics a lot after that summer. I'd walk around the park with a friend and we'd realize how all of our words and actions were meaningless. We saw how ridiculous the means of communication were, how you could attempt to say what your eyes were seeing, but you could never communicate the essence of your experience to another person. So, we decided we wouldn't talk when

63

MARC

we tripped together, except to say things like "Wow!" or "Beautiful!" There were times when we'd see something and feel the same emotions about it. We'd just look at each other and realize we were experiencing the same thing. There was no reason to put it into words.

The twelve of us were getting tighter as our drug trips evolved. Other people had tripped a year or two before us and they seemed a bit further along the path, so they were telling us about books to read. I began reading the works of Carl Jung. I really got off on him. In fact, I went to a psychologist at the university to see if he would sponsor me in an independent study dealing with Jung's work, but he told me he couldn't help me. I went to everyone in the psychology department I could think of and not one of them knew enough about Jung to sponsor me. At that point, I realized those professors couldn't tell me anything, and I wondered what I was going to do.

It was about that time that I took a course in eastern mysticism, 'cause I'd come to feel I had had mystical experiences on drugs. I'd read a little of Timothy Leary's views on the clear light, which he translated from *The Tibetan Book of the Dead* into psychedelic experience. He talked about how you go through levels of illusion, until you get to the high level when you free yourself from evil and burst into clear light.

LSD had been a beautiful thing in my life, but I knew it couldn't keep me where I wanted to be. You come down from a trip with such an energy loss you gotta sit around for a while until you get your strength back. At that time, I wasn't calling the levels I'd experienced God, 'cause that was religion and, from the experience I'd had with religion, it wasn't much. It hadn't taken me, or anyone else I knew, into higher levels of consciousness.

Alan Watts came to speak at the university and I went to hear him. Here was a man who had experienced something I had and he was walking around without doing drugs and relating to people. He sat down and said: "Your mind is doing things to you. What goes on in your mind is one of two thoughts, either something that's going to happen or something that happened yesterday."

He started opening me up with that thought, because he made me aware, for the first time, that everything important is right here,

64

right now. I thought to myself, "This is a man who has been somewhere and really has something." I wanted to go there too, but I was
still dealing drugs.

Dealing drugs really puts your head into a different place. Let
me tell you about the paranoia of dealing. You see a policeman in
uniform and you fear and hate him. You find yourself thinking,
"That man is bad; he's got no business telling me what to do. He
can't tell me to stop dealing drugs. Dealing drugs is fine. I'm making
people happy, man."

After a while I began to feel guilty about dealing drugs. I would
sit home and read eastern religious books and study the works of
Jung, then I'd have to go deal again. I'd have to hide and be careful
on the streets, all the time becoming entangled in the incredible
illusion that I was doing people a favor by giving them the drugs they
needed.

By that time, four of us had moved out of the fraternity into an
apartment. One morning I was lying in bed when, all of a sudden, I
heard "Bam, bam, bam." At first, I thought someone was walking up
the steps and I said to myself, "What the hell's going on?" Well, it
was the police and they were using an axe to break down our door.
They had come to arrest one of the brothers for selling LSD. They
threw another brother up against the wall, and checked out the third.

They finally looked into my room. I was lying in bed and, luck-
ily, they didn't see me. When they closed the door to my room, I got
dressed, threw my drugs away, took my money from the dresser, and
rolled out the window. My friends went to jail. At that point, I
realized I must be doing something wrong. I told myself that I
shouldn't be dealing, that I definitely had to stop.

After the bust, we moved out to the country and my diet started
to change. A couple who was living with us were doing Transcendental Meditation. They ate macrobiotically, so they started cooking
for us. I soon became addicted to rice, feeling it was good for me. In
the beginning I was eating rice and a little bit of turkey, but eventually I gave up eating meat entirely. I got to the point where, every
time I looked at meat, I felt guilty and sick to my stomach.

About that time, I went out to Colorado to see a friend of mine.

65

MARC

He'd gotten into spiritual things through drugs and was doing yoga and eating health foods. My friend questioned whether it was necessary to follow a guru, since the books he had read said that, if you remember the name of God in your last breath, you become one with Him. He felt he could do that himself without the aid of a guru, but I wasn't sure. It turned out that he received Knowledge soon after Guru Maharaj Ji arrived in the United States.

I traveled around the mountains for a while, then went to California. I met a girl there who told me to come up to northern California and visit her for a while, but when I got there she wasn't home. It turned out that the guy who lived next door to her was a teacher of Transcendental Meditation. He asked me if I was interested in helping him build a cabin, so I stayed on and helped him, which was my first experience with carpentry work and the continuation of my spiritual growth. That guy seemed completely in tune with the spiritual world. He gave me satsang all day and in the evening he played his sitar for me.

By the time I returned to Boulder, the dealing family I had lived with in the east had moved there, so we got a place together. We were still dealing, but people were getting into heavier drugs like cocaine and heroin. My desires were somewhere else, but I also had the feeling I'd been with those guys for such a long time that maybe I would just stick with them in hopes that I might make them a little more enlightened. I wanted to be a spiritual guide for them.

People would ask me why I was into the dealing trip and I'd say, "When it's my time to leave I'll be ready to go. I'm here right now and I think maybe I can help these people, so I'm going to stay." Each day I was torn between dealing and my spiritual path.

One day I was standing on the street with some friends and a girl came running up to us and said, "There's a 13-year-old guru up in the mountains who's opening up everyone's third eye. He's just beautiful." So we got into our car and headed up to Wall Street. There were hundreds of cars parked on the street. When we got out of our car the first thing we saw was a picture of Guru Maharaj Ji with the words "Bull Shit!" written across it. So, my first impression was, "This little kid's come and all these freaks are doing drugs with him, like a side show in the circus."

66

MARC

When we got to the cabin a bunch of freaks were milling around, some were sitting and others talking, some playing music, others playing with their dogs. There was a circle of people there and two guys were talking, so we sat down with them. One of the guys was saying that he had been searching for the Truth and hadn't found it until he received the Knowledge of the 13-year-old guru. He went on to talk about higher consciousness things. I thought what he had to say was really beautiful, but my friends weren't even interested. I had been reading *Be Here Now* by Baba Ram Dass and he had said that when a person was ready for a guru, he would appear. So, I was sitting there wondering whether it was my time for a guru or not.

We walked over to the cabin and it was nice and peaceful inside. Then, all of a sudden, some people shouted some words in Hindi and a bald-headed Mahatma came walking out of a back room, then three other Mahatmas followed. Everybody fell down on the floor completely prostrated at their feet. I remember thinking, "What's going on here? There's something these people are bowing down to that must be incredible. This is America and people just don't go around doing that kind of thing."

I sort of got down on the floor with the others, but I was looking up to see what was going on. I saw the Mahatmas walking out and in the middle of them there was a small figure floating along. I'd never felt such a powerful feeling before, just seeing someone pass by. "He's coming to talk with us," was the word going through the crowd. But, before I knew it, the guru was getting into a Cadillac and was driving off.

At that point, I thought, "What's going on there? If this guy's such a beautiful person, why's he driving around in a Cadillac?" But the vibration of his purity had been the most powerful thing I'd experienced. I was just amazed by it.

Every once in a while, somebody's name was called off to receive the Knowledge. I didn't know how to get my name on the list and I didn't even try. I just left and I did not see Guru Maharaj Ji again for almost a year.

I continued to deal drugs in order to make money. My dealings took me all over the country. Each time Guru Maharaj Ji was in Boulder I was in some other state, so I missed seeing him each time.

67

MARC

I began to think I must be doing something wrong, that if he was my guru, then I'd better get it together and see him. But, meanwhile, I continued living with those dealing people in a large mansion.

I still had it in my head that dealing was no good, that I really wanted to become more spiritually oriented. So, I decided to take a course at the Free School in Integral Yoga. I began getting up each morning at 7 A.M. for an hour of Hatha Yoga. It really made me feel good. But I needed some kind of meditation technique, 'cause I felt that, while Hatha Yoga was good for my body, it couldn't get me to the higher states of consciousness I'd experienced doing acid. I had some friends who had become premies by then and I kept asking them to tell me their meditation techniques. The best they would do was to give me something to read. And of course they gave me satsang, that Guru Maharaj Ji was a Perfect Master and that he could show me the way out of the darkness and into the light. So, after a time, I started to get a feel for Guru Maharaj Ji as a very high person. The *Boulder Magazine* had a centerfold picture of him and I cut it out and put it up on my wall.

One day I was walking on the university campus and I met a girl and there was a strong feeling between us, and that girl was Lisa. Up to that moment, I had gone through many physical relationships with women, but I'd been reading in some eastern spiritual books that you should try to refrain from sexual relationships. I'd been trying to do that because I was convinced that's what should be done, until this temptation arose. I fell right back into sexual attachment when I saw Lisa. It was the "perfect love" we all dream of and we started living together almost from the beginning.

My discipline for doing yoga early in the morning disappeared as I channeled my energy towards Lisa. I'd stopped getting high before I met her, but she was into it, so we started getting high together. Yet, my spiritual interests were still strong. In fact, about that time, I asked to receive a mantra at the Integral Yoga Institute. But they said they couldn't give me a mantra because only Swami Satchindananda could do that, and he'd only been in Boulder from time to time. I went away thinking, "I want to start on a spiritual path immediately and it may be a year before I can get my mantra."

MARC

Lisa began to do Hatha Yoga with me. And, like me, she too became frustrated with it. We knew it was good for our bodies, but our minds stayed in a state of confusion.

Lisa was not happy having me dealing drugs. She would say, "What are you doing, you're on a spiritual path and you're still dealing. When you're dealing all you do is talk about drugs, bullshit about drugs and more bullshit about drugs. It's totally nowhere." Well, something happened which finally forced me out of the drug scene.

I was supposed to go on a ride with my friends to the airport but I stayed behind instead. On the way to the airport, they were smoking a joint, after we had just finished a deal. The police stopped them for smoking a joint, but when they opened the trunk they found a suitcase with drugs in it and one containing money. When they got busted, I realized that I had two strikes against me, the other one was when the police walked into my bedroom and didn't see me. I knew if I didn't get the message right then I'd be lost for a long time. So I quit dealing.

Lisa and I packed up that day and eventually we moved into an apartment. And, because I wasn't dealing any longer, I needed to find a job. Well, the managers of our apartment turned out to be the owners of a construction company and a week later they hired me to do carpentry work for them.

Herb and Peter began working on the construction site with me. They were both premies and they'd just gotten back from India. Herb mentioned Guru Maharaj Ji to me one day and I told him to tell me more. Well, before long he and Peter were coming over to our apartment for lunch every day, so Lisa and I were getting hot and heavy satsang. I began to really feel their satsang, not so much what they said, but the energy coming through them. It was knocking me over. Slowly they were getting me into the whole thing. I began to think that Guru Maharaj Ji really had something and I wanted to know and hear more about him.

I began going out to the farm where Herb, Peter, and a few other premies were living. I felt comfortable being there with them and listening to their satsang. Their energy made me want to see

MARC

Guru Maharaj Ji again. So, after a while, I was moved to quit Hatha Yoga 'cause I knew I wanted to receive the Knowledge.

There were always rumors flying around that a Mahatma was coming, but there were none around to give the Knowledge. So, there was nothing to do but sit around and wait. Lisa and I did a little Hatha Yoga every once in a while and we partied and got high, because there wasn't anything to discipline us. Finally, we got word that a Mahatma was coming and that a Knowledge session would be held out on the farm.

The day of the Knowledge session Lisa and I were at the farm about seven o'clock in the morning ready to receive the Knowledge. Since we got there first, we were way up front. There must have been about ninety people crowded together in one little room when the screening for the Knowledge session began. We were told that anyone who had listened to satsang more than five times could go into the meditation room for the Knowledge session. We'd listened to satsang at least twenty times, but we thought we'd let the people in the back of the room go in first since it was more convenient for them. We thought the Knowledge session would only last a couple of hours.

Fifty people went into the Knowledge session and we started wondering if it would last longer than we had thought. We were beginning to think we might have to wait a long time and we were already pretty tired. Finally, a call for ten more people came out from the meditation room. We looked at each other and knew we had to try to get in. I think we were about the last two or three to make it in. It was great faith that we got into the session because it lasted from eight o'clock in the morning until four in the afternoon. Physically, it was the most uncomfortable situation I'd ever been in. But I accepted the fact that I should go through some pain to receive the Knowledge.

There was a great fear in everyone that the Mahatma would throw them out, would look at them and say "You're not ready." But I knew I was ready. I was saying to myself, "I just want this Knowledge. So many people have it and I can see what it's doing for them and how much progress they've made. I just want it."

MARC

I think two people walked out of the session. One was a follower of Baba Ram Dass and one of the questions the Mahatma asked was "Do you have another living master?" That person thought that maybe Baba Ram Dass could give him the Knowledge, so he very beautifully got up and left.

We learned from the Mahatma that, if Jesus Christ was our master that was fine because Guru Maharaj Ji, in essence, was no different from Jesus Christ. We were told that, if we were Christians, the Knowledge would not interfere with that because what Guru Maharaj Ji reveals is our essence. But we were told that, if we were following a living master, then there was a conflict, 'cause "You can't serve two masters at the same time."

The other kid who left was from the Rainbow Family. The Mahatma asked him if he had another living master and he said, "Yes, the Holy Father." The Mahatma asked: "Who is the Holy Father?" The kid responded: "The *Holy* Father." That guy was acting like he knew all the answers and that he couldn't be told anything. He was so into the fact that he'd found Christ he couldn't humble himself to speak to the Mahatma. It was sort of upsetting.

What was really sad about the situation was that, when the kid got up to leave, he turned to his girl friend and nodded to her and she got up and left too. It wasn't as if she had come on her own.

The first part of the Knowledge session is when you receive the light, when the Mahatma touches you and you see divine light. I was at the back of the room and between the time he touched the first person until he reached me took over an hour, with me just sitting there concentrating on my third eye. When he finally touched me I saw flashes of energy flowing this way and that. Sometimes I would see a pinwheel and a little black dot with flashes of light coming out. That lasted for a minute or two.

After concentrating on the third eye for so long, my first experience of divine light was beyond words. I got the feeling that this 14-year-old boy, who could show me that simple way of seeing the light, must really have something. It's such a subtle way of experiencing the light, which is in all of us, you don't have to use a mantra or anything else 'cause its always right there inside of us. You get the feeling that it is something real being shown to you, that it is the Truth and is beyond words. At the moment you concentrate on the light you have no thoughts and you realize that, if you could be in that light all of the time, it would solve all of your problems.

Then the Mahatma taught us how to listen to the celestial music. Some people said they heard drums, others flutes. I just heard harmonious tones flowing through me. If you go deeply into the tone it takes you to other levels and you begin to hear different frequencies and higher pitches. It's such a subtle sound, even a child in the womb hears it.

The next thing we learned was how to drink the nectar that's flowing within the body. It's not a new thing, but something that's been with us since we were born and will be with us when we die. And if you can drink the nectar while you're on earth, you can realize God that much faster.

The last thing we learned was how to tune into the Word, which is a subtle vibration of life that flows throughout the body and is the beginning and end of everything.

Coming out of the Knowledge session was like a birthday of my soul. I'd been reborn. I had no relationship to what went on before. I didn't have to search anymore, for I'd found the Truth. Not having to search anymore takes a lot out of the trips you are into and having found the Truth puts you automatically at ease.

I had no let-downs after receiving the Knowledge. It was exactly what I'd hoped it would be. I knew if I followed the five commandments that were laid down in the Knowledge session I could realize God in my lifetime.

After I received the Knowledge I wanted to realize it as quickly as I could. I began attending satsang almost every night and I did as much service as I could around the ashram. Every morning and evening I meditated and soon I found myself wanting to see Guru Maharaj Ji physically and to become a part of him spiritually. I began to dedicate all of my actions to him, because it's just so natural to serve that energy which is making you do the things you do.

Lisa's reaction to the Knowledge was similar to mine. She Realized it was all there was, although maybe it's taken her a bit more time to realize the power of the Knowledge.

Lisa went to New Orleans for a two-week vacation and, during that time, I lived in the ashram. I was doing service there all the time. During that period I tasted nectar twice. I felt: "I can't wait until I feel full love, full Truth, full understanding of who Guru Maharaju Ji is. Each day I want to feel that more and more."

It's beautiful to get into physical things, but it doesn't bring you to the point of being one with God. There are even times when my mind says, "Give up everything and just become attached to Guru Maharaj Ji. Just become one with him and you'll get to the point of realization much faster." But, for 23 years I've become so attached to those things that it's not easy to let them go.

The Knowledge is like an axe cutting down a tree, the ego, that has grown for so many years. The Knowledge hits the tree and knocks it most of the way over. But the tree starts to grow back and fights back as doubts. Doubts are your mind telling you "He's laying a trip on you man, don't listen to him. You know how to take care of yourself. You know where you're going and you know what you want."

If you're entirely devoted you realize you're only a little bubble and that Guru Maharaj Ji is directing you. If you just let him take direction, you'll flow much more perfectly. When you know in your heart that he's the Perfect Master, then there's really no room for doubt.

Looking back, nothing has ever pressured me to change. When the time was right, and I hesitated each time, I wasn't knocked down but was allowed to linger. When I was ready to stop eating meat or dealing drugs, I stopped. When I was ready for the next step, it came naturally.

Part
TWO

Evolutionary Change

W hile thoughts of conversion normally bring to mind images of a sweeping change, the fact is that both conversion and commitment are gradual in their development. Small steps, not giant strides, are the normal course. In the following chapters, the pattern of this evolutionary process will unfold as each step in the developing conversion and commitment of premies is revealed in the lives of Walt, Mary Anne, John, and Tina. Passages of Guru Maharaj Ji's satsang are inserted in order to exhibit his teachings and to suggest their appeal for these young people.

chapter
SIX

Growing Up

At the turn of the century, Edwin Starbuck published his pioneering work on religious conversion, *The Psychology of Religion*, [1] a study so rich in information and theoretical insight that William James drew from it almost exclusively when he turned to the issue of conversion in *The Varieties of Religious Experience*. [2] And rightly so, for it was Starbuck who made the claim, bold for the time, that conversion was primarily a feature of adolescent development and should thus be considered a normal phenomenon. His view opened the way for a large body of psychological research on the subject, which operated from the assumption that conversion was basically a healthy development which increased personal integration and altruism, even when it had pathological origins.

Although Starbuck's theory does not suffice as an explanation for the conversion of these eighteen premies, it has enough power to be useful as we pause to reflect on the preceding four case histories and before we analyze the conversion and commitment of several other followers. After fifty years, Starbuck's theory is still the major source of intellectual inspiration for psychologists studying conversion and, for that reason alone, it is well worth extensive comment.

Through an exhaustive case study approach, Starbuck saw a pat-

77

tern to conversion which he called "unselfing." Unselfing was basically an adolescent attempt to break out of the confinement of early childhood egoism. When the child reached the first part of adolescence there was a stirring of the will to know and embrace a larger, spiritual conception of life. He saw this need to locate oneself spiritually in the grand order of things as the basis for sudden conversions as well as for more gradual lines of spiritual growth.

Adolescence is the optimum time for conversion, according to Starbuck, because it is during that period when physiological, psychological, and social discontinuities are strongest, and youth look for a new sense of order and meaning in their lives. This was borne out statistically in his study by the fact that the highest frequency of Christian conversions among males was at 16 years, while females, who mature earlier, tended to convert at 13 years of age. It was supposedly during those years that the spiritual search was begun. As the adolescent reached out for universal truth, Starbuck said, a new ideal emerged to compete with the old self and its bad habits. The ensuing conflict left the teenager feeling full of sin, thus emotionally ripe for a drastic change.

Caught in the conflict between the old self and the new ideal, the adolescent often retreated into the security of old habits, and sometimes even avoided spiritual influences in order to keep the self intact and thus maintain a degree of self-consistency. This period of reluctance, as Starbuck called it, persisted until the time when complete psychological exhaustion eliminated the power of the individual will, thereby unleashing the forces of transformation.

Experiencing a collapse of the will, the individual was ready to surrender to higher powers. Conversion was thus an experience of giving in to those powers and allowing the new ideal to be realized. The deep sense of sin gave way to harmony, joy, and peace, often spoken of as "rebirth." The old life of sin was forgiven; the new life of oneness with God or Jesus Christ awakened a new feeling of freedom, power, and well-being.

In the aftermath of the conversion experience, the reborn plunged into their new faith, found great pleasure exercising their newly acquired power, and identified strongly with others in the spiritual community.

Four Stories

In the brief accounts which follow, you will get a glimpse of the experiences of Walt, Mary Anne, John, and Tina in the realms of family, church, school, and friends.

Walt
Walt was estranged from church, school, and people in general while growing up, although he was fortunate to have a fairly supportive family. "I had a very good family life compared to most people. My mother is really a very wonderful person. But she's always laid her Jewish mother trips on me, like wanting me to be a big success. She definitely wanted me to get good grades and go to college. She wanted me to become a scientist or lawyer 'cause I had tendencies in that direction when I was a kid. But she could see I wasn't going in that direction, so she used to hassle me about it. She laid some heavy guilt trips on me which I had to work through. That was one of my hangups, always thinking there was something wrong with me."

As guardian of the Jewish faith, Walt's mother made sure the rituals of the faith were respected and observed, although, according to him, the spiritual aspects of Judaism did not make their way into her everyday life. Through the insistence of his mother, Walt went to the temple each week until the eighth grade.

When Walt became depressed during his high school years, he turned to his temple for direction. "I went to my temple a few times hoping to get something out of it, but there was nothing there for me. There were times when my whole family got together for services and I really got off on the rituals, but there was no spiritual experience whatsoever. It was just a cultural thing. Once, when I was pretty young, I told a guy I didn't believe in God. But what I was really saying was that I rejected the religious bullshit of the church. Ac-

79

tually, I've always believed there was a God, although I never knew what it was. I used to pray to God, like I'd say, 'Oh, God, please may this girl not reject me.' I didn't have a conception of God but I knew there was something there."

While Walt's experience with the Jewish faith was disappointing, it was far less devastating than the effect of school and social relationships on him. "When I was little, my relatives fawned over me all the time, treating me like a king. That really had a very serious effect on me because it made me kind of crazy. When I was in nursery school, everything was okay, but when I got into public school, thinking I was the king, I encountered immediate rejection by my classmates. I had a reputation for being intellectually smart, but everybody hated me, or so I thought. I don't remember having any close relationships with people. I was always pretty isolated from the world. When things got really bad later on, I couldn't even force myself to look another person in the eyes. I had a really painful, paranoid feeling whenever I did it."

By his senior year of high school, Walt was retreating more and more from social contact. "I got to the point in my senior year where I slept through most of my classes. I kept my conscious mind tuned in so finely that, if the teacher asked me a question, I could kind of respond and give a foggy answer and get by with B's. Generally, I wasn't motivated to try to do well in school. And after school I usually went home and fell asleep, or got stoned on grass. When I wasn't asleep or stoned, I read. Or I got lost in my fantasies. When I was in the ninth grade, I'd take out a piece of paper and draw imaginary countries and then I'd pretend to be a General and lead important battles. All of my fantasies were about me being in a very important position. I could never accept compromises. They just disgusted me, for all I wanted was the highest thing. That's one thing different psychiatrists told me, that my goals were set way too high, and that was why I was so frustrated. They told me if I'd just find a girl I liked and have a nice relationship with her it would be okay, but instead, I wanted to be the supreme lover of every girl in the world. I was always looking for the ultimate experience every moment. It was very natural that, by the age of fourteen, I began to devote myself to getting stoned and drunk all of the time. I also got into sniffing glue, drinking cough syrup, or just about anything I could get my hands on."

Mary Anne

Mary Anne's life was not easy before her initiation into the counter-culture. She had turned to the church for spiritual inspiration and help, only to come away disillusioned. She had a fairly successful academic career, although her social life was difficult, and home was far from sweet. "As long as I can remember, my father was an alcoholic and gambler. In fact, he was partially crippled as a result of his drinking problem. He never worked, so he was always around the house. And it was heavy having him around so much because he was so violent. He always beat up my mother or me, or my brother. If he wasn't beating up someone, he was screaming at us. He was just a very ugly person to be around. And my mother was always tired 'cause she was the one who worked to support the family, and she was sick a lot, too. Her marriage was so unhappy that the only thing she felt she had out of life were her two children, my brother and me. She kind of put her hope in us to fulfill her own desires for happiness and success."

Mary Anne was not required to attend church because her parents did not believe in God. Yet, desperate for love, she created spiritual friends who could fill that void in her life. "I had friends who were angels. They were very light astral bodies, glowing and very gentle. They were always so sweet and really full of love. Everybody told me it was my imagination, but they were real to me. They came to visit me and I was totally awed by them because they were so beautiful. My friends and parents were just gross in comparison to my angel friends. But I forgot about them when I started going to school."

Receiving no spiritual guidance from her parents, Mary Anne drew a religious viewpoint from outside her family. "All my school teachers talked about God, and we used to say the 'Lord's Prayer' until it was outlawed. I had the feeling then that, 'Well, since all these people believe in God, maybe there's something to it.' So, I

81

guess that's when I got the idea of turning to God for help when my family situation got rough. In junior high school I began reading religious books and they just confirmed what I had come to believe, that there was definitely a God to base my life on."

For a long time, Mary Anne's religion was a private affair between her and God, until she decided to attend a Presbyterian church on her own seeking the spiritual companionship of others. "I only went to church for a couple of months 'cause I didn't really enjoy it. All I saw were people who'd gotten dressed up to go to the sermon, and who stood around afterwards drinking coffee and punch, talking about things which had no relevance to God at all. All they did was go to church on Sunday because they thought it was the right thing to do. In their day-to-day lives they didn't seem to be living what they said they believed in. They talked about Jesus Christ, but they didn't seem Christlike. Even the ministers didn't seem like holy people and they didn't look particularly happy either. They weren't like those angels of light I remembered seeing as a child."

There was no one Mary Anne could turn to for help. Her brother was not someone she could confide in, and she had few friends. "I was just never outgoing with people. I always thought other people should make the first move as far as friendship went, so I never had many friends. But it never worried me that I didn't have any. I just thought that's the way it was, so I accepted it. A lot of times I preferred to be alone anyway, and I'd shut myself in my room and read or just let my thoughts go by."

School probably provided Mary Anne's most pleasant experiences while growing up, for she was generally a good student, especially in foreign languages. Yet, even though she received good grades, she was bored with many of her classes and disturbed that students were so preoccupied with their social lives. "During high school, I was getting more and more confused. Part of it, I guess, was because I didn't really have a close friend to talk to, so I couldn't express my feelings to anyone who might have understood. Although I had a few pretty good friends, they weren't relating to me on a spiritual basis. I began to look at all the things that were happening in the world, like the Vietnam war, and I started getting really depressed. I didn't have a deep enough understanding of what people were doing in the protest marches or with LSD to know whether things could be changed that way. I kind of lost hope. After I graduated from high school, when I had more time on my hands, I got really, really depressed. I didn't have any specific goal, except to be happy, and I didn't have any idea how to find happiness. Everything I tried just seemed like vanity. I got more and more depressed, to the point where I decided to take a bunch of pills and kill myself. I sat there and my body started to die and I freaked out 'cause I realized I wasn't together enough to know where to go when my body was gone. I realized I didn't want to die after all, so I called for help."

Help arrived in time and Mary Anne was pulled back from the abyss. As a result of her attempted suicide, she was sent to a mental hospital for a short time, which became a turning point in her life.

John

John was somewhat introverted while growing up. His family and church experiences were positive, whereas school was less satisfying, partly because he had a rather difficult time relating to others. He tended to be a loner with only a few friends, yet, unlike Walt, he was not terribly depressed or unhappy. At home he was aloof and withdrawn. "When I was home I would usually sit in my room and read or listen to the radio. I didn't get too involved in home life. My mother would come into my room sometimes and ask me why I was just sitting around. I guess I was the only one of the kids who just sat alone a lot. There's a total of eight children in my family and we got along fairly well. No one in the family had any big arguments. I just went along with the flow of things and didn't question. I just did what my parents told me to do and didn't think much for myself. I never really knew my father very well, being that it was such a large family. But I really liked him. My mother was probably a lot more pushy and cautious. She always worried a lot about her children. She was the core of the family as far as bringing up the children, and my father's major responsibility was bringing in the money."

Being strong Catholics, John's parents insisted that he and his sisters and brothers attend Sunday mass regularly. True to his pat-

83

tern, he conformed to his parents' wishes, even though he had misgivings about the church. "When I reached my junior year in high school, I realized I wasn't getting much out of the Catholic faith. I felt I shouldn't really be going to church, but I stayed with it because of my parents, especially since I was living at home. I knew they'd freak out if I left the church, so I waited until I moved away to college and then I quit going. I just had no interest and no desire to go. At that point I didn't have any religion or anywhere to turn to find a new spiritual direction."

Due to his moral training, John found it hard to conform to the social pattern of his high school peers. "During my senior year, I didn't have too many friends because I couldn't accept what a lot of kids were doing. On weekends they'd go out and get drunk, and I couldn't relate to that. Early in my high school experience I tried to get everybody to be my friend, but during my senior year I realized there were a lot of people I couldn't be friends with because of the things they did."

College was a replay of John's earlier pattern: He continued his solitary existence, a loner, shy with girls, but not excessively unhappy.

Tina

Tina was raised in Cleveland, Ohio, in a strong Catholic family. She was expected to attend mass each Sunday and participate in the rituals of the church. She was a good student and was popular among her peers. School was a place she liked to be, not just because she was successful there, but because it was a refuge from the conflicts at home. "I can objectively say that my childhood was more intense than that of just about anybody I've met. My parents are strict Catholics. Yet they always fought. They threw things at each other and sometimes beat each other up. My older sister and I couldn't believe how they fought over nothing. So, when my parents got into a free-for-all, which was pretty often, my sister and I went into our bedrooms and completely shut the fighting out. Sometimes it was difficult to escape, though, because they went on and on. We always had to move around the house like we were walking on eggs, because

84

my parents would be very uptight with us all day, and the slightest little thing would start them off."

Emotionally estranged from her mother and father, Tina turned to her older sister for direction, comfort, and help. "The only thing that got me through those family conflicts was my sister. She always told me not to worry about it. So I listened to her and didn't worry. I just could not attach myself to home because it was so filled with conflict. I knew I had to make it on my own because I couldn't rely on my parents for love. I realized that I was an individual and the source of my love and togetherness. If I wasn't together, then everything would crumble. So I developed into a self-sufficient person, to the point where I could fit into any situation. I very rarely got depressed. I know some of my friends got depressed and freaked out, but I never did. I've always had a feeling of peace inside. Very few things ever ruffled me."

Even though Tina's parents fought with each other and clashed with their children frequently, they remained adamant about Catholicism. "My parents always went to church and always said their rosary. We said grace before meals and during Lent we went to church a lot. But, they were only blindly religious. We never sat around and talked about Jesus, even though he was the basis of our religion. There wasn't even a Bible in our house until I started taking religion courses in school."

Tina attended parochial school for several years, where she developed a spiritual outlook. "The nuns always used to say the soul was eternal, that when you die, your soul continues on and, if you're good, you'll be eternally in heaven and, if you're bad, you'll be eternally in hell. The thought stuck in my mind: "Don't do anything bad because you're eternal and you'll want to be holy to get into heaven.' The nuns used to say that becoming a nun was the key into heaven. So I decided I wanted to be a nun because that way I'd be safe."

Like many young Catholic girls with aspirations to be a nun, Tina gave up the idea when she reached adolescence. Yet, her dedication to the Catholic church remained intact. "I don't know why I didn't question the validity of the church then. It had been ingrained in me that the Catholic Church was the true religion and it didn't

85

dawn on me, until I was in college, that the church was actually very sterile. When I got to college, I quit going because no one was around to tell me I had to go."

Academically and socially, Tina was successful at school. She associated with the most popular students and had many close friends. "I had always been a front-runner in school, starting back in grade school. I was a pom-pom girl and president of this and that, but it was never an egotistical thing with me, just a duty. When it became competitive in high school, it completely turned me off. Then I started turning away from rah-rah things."

Psychological Tendencies

It was not difficult to determine which among these eighteen premies had experienced severe emotional problems in their childhood (Walt and Mary Ann) and which appeared to be fairly well integrated and healthy like Tina, but those with moderate emotional problems were not easy to assess. John, for example, did suffer somewhat from feelings of inferiority, especially in the company of the opposite sex, although he was apparently not driven by his psychological problems to convert, for conversion came very slowly for him and seemed quite rational in its development. It is difficult to say whether John is typical of others of his age and class, since, according to recent opinion in psychology, our society has become increasingly neurotic. Feelings of inferiority have supposedly become quite common, while the mentally healthy person, what Abraham Maslow called the "self-actualized" person, seems as rare as good humor among cynics. Since even psychologists do not agree about what is psychologically "normal," I hesitate to use the term here.

Of the eighteen premies studied, seven could be classified, in Starbuck's terms, as converts seeking relief from their sense of sin, while the remaining eleven more closely fit his description of those who convert out of sheer attraction to the spiritual life as a new learning experience. Indeed, these are two important ways people learn: By trying to solve personal and social problems through attempts to

GROWING UP

reduce, minimize, and eliminate psychological and social conflicts, and second, by entering new experiences in order to attain new knowledge and insight. I see these as the two most important motivating forces behind the spiritual evolution of these young people.

Contrary to the popular belief that people who join movements like Divine Light Mission experience sudden conversions of a highly irrational nature, my experience of these eighteen premies suggests that people are both more rational and conservative when it comes to personal change than is normally supposed, and that radical changes of belief and behavior are rare. Mary Anne's way of changing seemed to be typical. "By the spirit, I was led to all these different gurus to listen to what they had to say,. and if I could flow into it without having to take a heavy action, then I knew it would be the right thing to do. If they demanded that I change myself drastically, too fast, then I wouldn't flow into that. I'd gotten pretty mellow by taking drugs and doing yoga, and to do anything intensely different from that wasn't in the flow for me."

Uncaring Institutions

The idealism of these premies was one of the motivating forces behind their conversion. They wanted to create a more caring world. It is true that seven were emotionally in conflict and thus susceptible to conversion, but they were also the most adversely affected by the institutions of family and school and the most anxious to change their lives and the society so that better relationships with others might be possible. Whether we recall the story of Alan, who suffered from many emotional problems, or Marc, who seemed quite well adjusted, there is a similar idealism about the future. Alan needed a more loving family and friends; Helen a more responsive and supportive school atmosphere. Matthew and Marc, both politically active before their contact with the Mission, wanted to create a more positive response from our political system, which was involved in the Vietnam war at the time.

Milton Mayeroff's little book, *On Caring*,[3] nicely expresses the

87

essence of such relationships. To care for people, he says, is to dedicate oneself to the growth and actualization of others as autonomous beings. Caring, then, is the opposite of using another person to satisfy one's own needs. Caring people, he continues, do not impose their own direction on those they are caring for but allow the direction of the other's growth to guide what they do and how they help. They appreciate the other's independence. Caring of this quality means accepting others without conditions, loving them as they are rather than trying to bend their minds and wills to satisfy one's needs for control.

The Family

Half of these eighteen premies testify to a malaise in the American family. This parallels a finding by Armand M. Nicholi II in his study of 17 college student's who converted to Christianity.[4] He found that changes within the American family during the past two decades left many of these 17 converts spiritually lost and in need of a religious outlook. The changes in the family he cited as important were: the replacement of spiritual values with materialistic ones, leaving both parents and children confused about basic priorities; the relegation of the care of children to baby-sitters, nurseries, day-care centers, camps, boarding schools, and the television set. Parents, he concluded, play an ever-decreasing role in caring for their children, and become increasingly inaccessible, both emotionally and physically, to their children.

As in many American families, it was not uncommon for the parents of premies to create ideals and expectations for their children which had little to do with their children's needs and which became a source of considerable frustration and guilt. One premie, for example, had a mother with a fixed idea of how her children should be, who worked with every manipulative device she could to mold them into that pattern. Never living up to her mother's ideal for her was one of the factors this premie identified as contributing to unhappiness in her youth. This was also a source of discontent in Walt's life, for he had to deal with the guilt stemming from his failure to meet his mother's expectations that he should become a lawyer or scientist. Mary Anne's mother related to her in a similar way, feeling that Mary Anne should accomplish in her life what she had failed to achieve in her own.

Those with the most severe problems came from families in which the parents were intent more on having their children conform to parental expectations and needs, than on meeting their children's needs for autonomy. We saw this in Alan's case, when his mother refused to let her children bring their friends home after school. She seemed to have little sensitivity to her children's need for association, or to be willing to meet those needs.

The more emotionally stable tended to come from more caring families, where the parents encouraged their child's independence. Matthew's parents gave him quite a lot of autonomy. Even when they could have pushed him to give up his political convictions, they held back. And when he decided he would rather go to jail than Vietnam, they supported him. Marc's parents also trusted him to evolve in a constructive way and gave him quite a lot of discretion in running his life.

Another premie, who was emotionally well-adjusted, an excellent student, and with many close friends also had a caring family. "My parents are both interesting and wonderful people. I really enjoyed them. I really have a lot of respect for them. My father is a pretty jolly fellow, who doesn't usually get irate about things. He's just an easy-going guy, who is interested in what he's doing and who always takes a very deep interest in his kids. He's always been concerned about me, through my adolescent trials, my drug stage, and now that I've come to Guru Maharaj Ji." The caring attitude of these parents became evident also in their effort to get their children to relate to one another in a more constructive way through professional family counseling.

Helen, too, came from a supportive family. Her emotional difficulties stemmed primarily from the sexually repressive mores of her religious training. In fact, sexual problems were fairly intense for eight premies, which lends some support to Carl W. Christensen's findings[5] that sexual conflicts often precede sudden conversions. Eastern spiritual movements might be especially attractive to such

89

people because of the norms of sexual abstinence in the ashrams and the general prohibition of promiscuous behavior.

In considering the influence of family on child, it is important not to adopt a conclusion based on what seem to be safe presumptions: for instance, that if a person comes from an unhappy home then serious psychological problems must definitely follow; or that families with a stable structure (mother as housewife and father as breadwinner), contain built-in guarantees that the child will be cared for and loved; or that a child from an uncaring home will tend to be more emotionally disturbed (Tina's case is evidence that children have enough resilience to survive a poor family situation).

Influences outside the family, such as school, church, and friendship, strongly affect the development of children, and good experiences in these areas of life can compensate for problems at home. Thus, close attention must be given to all four realms—family, church, school, and friends—for no one is significant without the broader context.

Church

The church can play a part in fostering feelings of personal inadequacy in children by indoctrinating them to think in terms of angels and devils, saints and sinners, heaven and hell. The story of the fall of Adam and Eve is a reminder that people are basically sinners in need of salvation, that they cannot be accepted for what they are. Indeed, it has long been known that attendance at revival meetings is a catalyst of conversion, for the evangelist, with his religious invective, makes the listener feel like a sinner, consequently raising the level of fear and guilt, and thus receptivity to conversion. In the fundamentalist churches it is still common for ministers to play on the themes of sin, hell, damnation, and redemption, as we saw in Alan's case. The minister who made him feel that the wrath of God would fall upon the heads of nonbelievers struck fear into his heart, as he realized his belief was shaky. He felt personally inadequate, knowing he was not as good as the minister said he should be, yet thinking he did not deserve God's wrath either.

A spiritual outlook is precisely what most of these eighteen premies had failed to develop through their religious education. Disenchantment with the church was a common reaction, for the eighteen as well as the larger group of forty-one premies. There is considerable difference, although it was not statistically significant, between the attitudes of premies and the forty nonpremie students toward their early church experiences. Premies were much more likely to be harsh in their criticisms of the church. This difference, however, might be explained by the fact that, since premies are immersed in an eastern spiritual movement, they are apt to be somewhat more critical of the conventional churches. Yet, the group of college students was also very disillusioned with the churches and had dropped out in large numbers. In fact, there is scarcely a difference between the two groups on this issue: 87 percent of the premies left the church in adolescence, in comparison to 82 percent of the college students.

The twenty-nine followers of Krishna expressed about the same level of dissatisfaction with organized religion as premies. In fact, in almost all respects, the backgrounds of both groups were similar, although the followers of Krishna were more likely to have come from broken homes and to have expressed more biting criticism of public education, including college. But their dropout rate from the mainstream churches was almost indistinguishable from the premie and college student groups, 86 percent having left the church.

The high dropout rate from the churches for all three groups should make us wonder whether there is a developing spiritual void and crisis in this country, and whether the new spiritual movements are not responses to the failure of conventional religion. From these eighteen accounts, a drab picture of our religious culture emerges— one of plentiful church buildings and congregations, but little spirituality in everyday life; of ministers who implore their congregations to believe in God, but who offer them no way to experience God. Even among those who attended church regularly, usually at the urging of their parents, there was a feeling the Sunday morning service and Sunday school were good rivals to academia as experiences in boredom.

Disillusionment with organized religion occurred while premies were in their teens, although many did not defect until they left home for college. One premie quit because the Catholic church changed its mass to English and also because her family had moved to a new parish whose priest she disliked. John simply lost interest and became bored by it all, attending only for the sake of his parents, like many others. Both of these premies quit attending church when they arrived at college, which was a safe distance from their parents. It is possible that parental control had a detrimental effect on their interest in religion, but that view is weakened by the fact that some were not forced by their parents to attend church. This latter group attended on their own initiative but withdrew after becoming disenchanted.

One of the major condemnations premies leveled against the church was that it was hypocritical, that going to church seemed to have almost no spiritual impact on people's lives and in fact, in some cases, appeared to have a harmful influence. They learned this from their own experience. Tina, for example, had to contend with the hypocrisy of her parents who had one fight after another, while both were dogmatic Catholics who attended mass every week, performed the rituals of the church, and expected Tina to do the same.

The most typical expression of discontent with the hypocrisy of the church was expressed by another premie. "My wife's parents are very religious. They go to church all the time, but they're not very spiritually realized. They have no love, no genuine feelings for others. They'd talk about brotherhood and then go home and its 'Shoot them niggers and kill them hippies.' What I experienced at church were a bunch of people who got very dolled up and were having a big social function. That's all it was. Church had no bearing on their everyday lives, no effect whatsoever. Monday through Saturday, they didn't think about religion."

It would be easy to dismiss this criticism as coming from converts to an eastern religion with a spiritual chip on their shoulders were it not for the overwhelming evidence which supports their claims and confirms their experiences with churches. In a national sample of church-goers, for instance, Milton Rokeach's findings, which were strikingly similar to a large number of other studies, showed that the religiously "devout" were on the average more bigoted, more authoritarian, more dogmatic, and more antihumanitarian than the less devout. He found that those who placed a high value on spiritual salvation tended to be more anxious to defend the status quo and less sympathetic to the plight of black people and the poor. They had reacted with fear or even glee to the news of the assassination of Martin Luther King, Jr., and resisted the church's involvement with social and political issues in our society. Yet these very people, as active Christians, claimed to believe in compassion, caring, and forgiveness, which led Rokeach to say: "If hypocrisy is a discrepancy between a person's espoused values and his conduct and his position on important contemporary issues, then these data from a representative sample of Americans strongly suggest a hypocrisy deeply embedded within many religiously oriented individuals. And by implication, the data point to a hypocrisy deeply embedded within organized religion as a social institution." [6]

It was this sense of hypocrisy which many of these young people responded to in their adolescence. They saw that church-goers who espoused the value of love had lives that were conducted in an uncaring way. Ironically, the fact that all groups—premies, college students, and the followers of Krishna—defected from the churches in droves during adolescence may have been a blessing, for the evidence reported by Victor Sanua in his review of the scientific literature on the subject points to the conclusion that "religious education as it is being taught today does not seem to ensure healthier attitudes, despite its emphasis on ethical behavior. This should raise a major point of discussion among religious leaders to determine whether possibilities exist to remedy this failure to communicate the ethical aspects of religion rather than its ritual." [7]

All major religious denominations are represented in these eighteen cases: Protestant, Catholic, and Jewish. Only the fundamentalist protestant churches seem to be underrepresented, which is perhaps not surprising when we stop to consider that there are still strong pressures within fundamentalist Christian circles to ensure the conversion of youth; whereas, the mainstream churches no longer seem to operate in a way that demands the spiritual conversion of the young. Having become both more rationalized and secularized since

93

GROWING UP

1900, there is in fact an opposing tendency which frowns on eruptions of deeply mystical feeling and thus places a taboo on the emotionally charged conversions which had been recognized at one time as a sign a person was ready to become a part of the spiritual community. Carl Christensen has come to a similar conclusion: "It is my impression that the incidence of religious conversion is decreasing. Within the framework of the large Protestant denominations increased sophistication in the urban and suburban churches is not conducive to religious experience."[8]

Even in the Catholic Pentecostal movement we see a strong prohibition against uncontrolled spiritual outbursts, due primarily to the movement's close association with the church and the clergy, both of which support a more calm and rational religious approach. Michael Harrison has mentioned this in his research on the Pentecostal movement, noting that violations of the rational norm are treated with firm but gentle control. Unlike classical Protestant Pentecostals, he says, Catholic Pentecostals learn not to shout, to gesture violently, or otherwise to display emotional extremes. Although people at meetings are intensely involved, they usually appear in full control of themselves, even when praying in tongues. On one occasion when a participant's prayer in tongues became too loud and turned into sobbing, several leaders quietly led him from the room.[9]

With the churches discouraging spiritual experiences, the awakening which Starbuck observed before conversion in adolescence failed to materialize for these eighteen young people. Instead they became bored, then disillusioned by the excessively social atmosphere and the apparent hypocrisy of the church.

School

Interestingly enough, most premies reported good experiences at school, although it was the social rather than the academic side which was the source of satisfaction. This was also the case at college. Although ten of the fifteen premies who were admitted into college dropped out before coming into contact with Divine Light Mission, they had warm feelings for their college experience on the whole. Their attitudes were not significantly different from those of

94

the nonpremie college students. Both groups were critical of the academic side of college while they praised the opportunities for personal growth outside of the classroom.

Even premies who characterized their college experience as "good" judged the academic sphere harshly. The following was typical of their feelings. "The intellectual aspects of college were very dull, but college was a meeting place for all sorts of interesting people. Such varied life experiences I had there opened me up personally to a lot of things."

Nonpremie students who considered their college experience to have been good or very good were just as likely as premies to condemn the academic atmosphere. One student commented, for instance: "I think college is absurd. It bums me out that they insist you get grades and take final exams. But still I learn for myself as much as possible. I like learning on my own, with the professors as guides."

Another was somewhat more critical. "Academically, my college career has been a farce; no special direction, doing requirements, putting in as little time as necessary into the classes I dislike, but putting in lots of time for the classes I like. Socially, I like the place. It allows me to be. It gives me the time for exploration, experimentation with people and relationships which have made me realize some things about myself."

There were also angry feelings. "Most of it's bullshit, but I will graduate because I'm not going to let this asshole institution take my money and sweat without giving me my seal of approval."

Eight of the ten premies who left college dropped out; Alan was expelled for dealing drugs, and Mary Anne flunked out after she lost interest and quit attending classes. The eight who left voluntarily may seem like a large number, but this proportion is actually not too far from the national average.

They had many different reasons for leaving. Helen could no longer tolerate the sense of social alienation she felt there. Matthew left to pursue his spiritual interests. One premie quit when she realized that, as a hippie, school should not be a part of her daily agenda, since "good" hippies were not supposed to work. Another became disgusted with his teachers, feeling they were either extremely lazy or else not interested in their students. Still, all but Mary Anne were doing well academically and most were well accepted by their peers.

Aimlessness and Alienation

Striking among these people is the fact that after high school and well into college they had no strong sense of what they wanted to do with their lives. Aimlessness was thus an experience they had in common. This confirms Nicholi's finding that 75 percent of the seventeen Christian converts he studied described a "vague restlessness" and confusion about the meaning of their college experience and what they wanted to do with their lives. It is true that Marc and Matthew had a definite purpose in mind when they first entered college, Marc to be an engineer and Matthew a physicist. Both, however, changed their majors to disciplines in which their aims were much more diffuse and less oriented to a specific career. And, of course, Matthew eventually dropped out.

Having no idea what to do with their lives, these eighteen premies were freer than their peers to enter the counterculture, for they were not restrained by career commitments.

I think we can safely say that without a strong career objective, or aim in life, there would be a crisis of meaning. While premies themselves did not generally talk about an absence of meaning, there was a strong undercurrent of meaninglessness in their social drifting, in the recurrent suicidal thoughts of the most depressed, in the ritual of counterculture life with its hedonistic practices.

While I feel uncomfortable mentioning a crisis of meaning as an influence in their spiritual development, largely because they seemed not to have talked in those terms, we should not discount this as one of the most important factors in their eventual conversion, for, as George Anderson has argued, it is the search for meaning which makes mankind religious, whether the seeker be mentally healthy or not. [10]

As a premie from the Kansas City ashram put it: "It would be

96

easy for you to think that the phenomenon of Divine Light Mission is happening because a group of people feel some psychological need and want to believe that the Knowledge will fulfill it. Actually, we do feel a need, the need of humans to know a lasting love, to feel secure, to feel that this life has some meaning. And you should seriously consider, as an alternative explanation, the theory that there is a simple, pure energy which is making this creation and, at the same time, permeates it, and that the purpose of humanity, as the crown of that creation, is to be conscious of that energy, to fulfill the scientific law that all energy returns to its source."

Social alienation is another common theme in these accounts. Not unlike Americans in general, many premies spoke of feeling estranged from others, especially those with the most severe emotional problems. Overall, half had trouble relating to others. Some tried to overcome their feelings of estrangement through drugs. Others fell into a pattern of promiscuous sexual behavior, hoping to create the bond of affection which eluded them in their ordinary associations.

Still, if we compare the group of forty-one premies with the forty college students, we find the early experiences of premies, prior to their contact with the Mission, fairly typical of young people their age. There were no statistically significant differences between their respective evaluations of family, church, and friendship patterns. Moreover, premies were no more likely to have come from broken homes than the college students. Nor were they less likely to have come from homes in which the father was the dominant authority.

Social Rescue

There is an ironic twist to the problems of personal inadequacy, aimlessness, and alienation: while they are sources of discontent, they are also mechanisms of change, for people experiencing such feelings will strive to overcome or minimize them. They will seek out those areas of life which offer opportunities to become a whole person.

The early lives of these premies uncover an interesting phenomenon which I will call "social rescue," the capacity of one positive

97

realm of social experience to compensate for another which is causing problems, where the individual is failing to be loved uncondi-
tionally or is falling short of success. A look at these accounts shows a
persistent pattern; a child from an unhappy home was often rescued
by a good school experience or one who failed to make friends was
backed up by a loving family. The need to be cared for and successful
seemed crucial.

When one sector of social experience left those needs unsatisfied
the child tended to look to another sector where the potential for grat-
ifying them seemed greater. So it is that children use school as a sub-
stitute family or channel their energies into academic pursuits when
friends are not there to fulfill them.

One premie captured the essence of social rescue when she said
of her alliance with her sister: "One person would feel bad, but two
people could just laugh about it [her mother's manipulative beha-
vior]. It was always my sister and I against my mother." Her sister
secured her from her mother's uncaring attitudes and behavior.
School was also an escape for her, for she was beyond the reach of
her nagging mother during the time she was there.

Another insight emerges from these personal histories which has
led me to reassess my own feelings about public education in this
country. For some time now I have wondered why children should
be required to attend school for such great periods of time each day. I
saw schools as institutional babysitters, relieving parents of the responsibility of caring for their children. Now I realize school may be
secure territory for children with uncaring parents. For instance, of
the eighteen, six found school a pleasant contrast to their miserable
home lives. In school, they felt safe from one or both of their
parents. In fact, Mary Anne's sole source of support was school,
where she became absorbed in her studies to such an extent that she
could temporarily forget her violent father.

What happens to children when they lack places where they are
cared for or successful? Let's reexamine Alan's history in this light.
He felt separated from his mother and siblings. The family situation
did not produce much love, which might have bound the family
members together, even in his father's absence. At school, he could

not concentrate on his studies, consequently his academic performance was only average. He was unhappy at school and tried to make friends, but failed. His early church experiences had produced little but anxiety and, in adolescence, he became totally disillusioned and quit attending. He even tried political activism, but found it difficult to get along with the people he met.

Alan was the only one among these eighteen premies who could not find love or success at home, in school, at church, or among his acquaintances. In short, he had no emotionally secure territory. Alone, he came very close to committing suicide before coming into contact with Divine Light Mission.

Social rescue points up the importance of love in human development. Without love, social alienation drives the individual into isolation. People like Alan may have been susceptible to the appeals of Guru Maharaj Ji not simply because they were running from their problems, but because he promised them a way to find love when they were looking for a community to join where people cared for each other.

It is important not to attribute a single motive to premies, as if there were a simple way to explain their eventual conversion. There were several different motivations arising from their early experiences: the need to deal with emotional problems, to work for a more caring society, to find purpose and meaning in life, to encounter love and community. Discontent by itself is not a good predictor of conversion, for there are many other ways people can respond to personal and social dissatisfaction: by excessive conformity, by turning to alcohol or drugs, by psychological repression, by entering a career of crime.

Another important factor in the early background of these young people, however, was the extent of their flexibility, their freedom to embark on a new course. That they were church dropouts, for example, freed them from established religion so they could eventually assume a new spiritual identity and commitment. That they had no strong career ambitions or aims in life made it simpler for them to leave college and join the counterculture.

99

chapter
SEVEN

Psychedelics: Blowing Open the Doors of Perception

For most of these premies, personal consciousness evolved not from the power of the pulpit, nor from the communion of saints, but from an unexpected source—psychedelics. As Walt says: "In past ages, people weren't that far from God. But now, to get back to God, you have to practically put dynamite into your consciousness and blow it apart. And that's what LSD does."

All eighteen of these young people experimented with psychedelic drugs before their spiritual conversions. Mescaline, LSD, psilocybin, and other hallucinogens were employed to alter consciousness. But contrary to the popular belief that the use of psychedelics naturally leads to the use of harder drugs, only one premie had tried heroin.

While eighteen experimented with psychedelics, the number of "trips" varied widely from person to person. Seven tripped from 4 to 15 times; four tripped between 15 and 30 times; three from 50 to 75 times; and four over 100 times, one estimating as high as 500.

Whether a person had a mystical experience on psychedelics

depended on the nature of each experience, what was revealed to the person, and whether he or she was ready to grasp the spiritual significance of it. For example, Helen's realization that "we are all one" occurred after her second psychedelic experience, while others failed to have a similar insight until they had tripped many more times. In fact, some did not have what they regarded as spiritual experiences on psychedelics at all. Instead, hallucinogenic drugs simply altered their personal and social awareness.

Apparently there is no way of knowing when spiritual understanding will unfold through hallucinogens or whether encounters with the spirit will occur at all. There is no way to predict if the person will hear or feel God, that primordial vibration premies call the "Word." *See, the whole world has been created out of vibrations, and the source, the primordial vibration, is the Word. If you clearly listen, if you can, sometimes when there is no sound at all, not any sound—and you listen very attentively to the air which is blowing, you will hear the Word. Very attentively, if you listen to the air, you will hear this Word* (Guru Maharaj Ji, 1972).[1]

Slipping into the Drug World

Smoking marijuana or hashish was the first experience with unconventional drugs for all but one of these people (Matthew tried LSD before smoking marijuana). Marijuana was known to be a mild drug, unlikely to produce a "bad trip." Thus, its gentle nature made it an easy transition into the psychedelic world. Having experienced the new ways of seeing and exploring life "stoned," the individual was more likely to try hallucinogenic drugs. That is the way it happened to most of these eighteen premies. They arrived at the point where psychedelic drugs could be seen as just another step along the path to self-awareness, not something to be feared, but something to be anticipated.

The initial step they took into the counterculture was partly the result of a social trend: the "hippies" took on a collective identity in opposition to American institutions. During the 1960s, when aware-

102

PSYCHEDELICS

ness of drugs first began on a large scale, a social myth was developing that LSD could revolutionize the culture. The social climate in some cases encouraged drug use; and the Haight-Ashbury district in San Francisco was the national trend-setter. It was a symbol of the emerging lifestyle, of drugs, love, and flower power. Joining the counterculture became the fashion, spreading from the East and West coasts into the Rocky Mountain region.

It is not surprising that almost all of these premies were introduced to drugs and led into the counterculture by a friend or relative. Social pressure to take drugs was often intense, as in the case of one premie whose friends insisted she try psychedelics after she had just begun to smoke marijuana. For others, pressure was much more subtle, expressed in the feeling that if one's friends and many other people were smoking pot and enjoying it, then why not try it?

For those who were guided into the drug world by friends and relatives, trust was a key factor convincing them that drugs were okay, as we see in Mary Anne's story. "They didn't keep me in the mental hospital very long, but during that time I smoked a lot of marijuana. One of my friends brought me a lid of grass, and I shared it with all of my friends in the hospital, and we got stoned together. Then, the next week, somebody else would get a lid, or some hash, cocaine, or just about anything imaginable. That was the first time I had experience being with someone who was tripping on a heavy psychedelic drug. This one young man took some STP when I was there. When he tripped, he always came to talk to me, and to hold my hand. We would stay up all night and just be together. I was getting pretty mellow smoking all that grass, mellow enough to where I could kind of play the game and say, 'Now I know it's cool, and I'll never do that suicide trip again.' So I got out of the hospital that way."

Upon her release, Mary Anne fell back in with her old friends, who were already using psychedelics. "I just kind of flowed right into the drug scene. I heard from my college friends that they were all taking LSD and mescaline, so I thought to myself, 'If they can do it then I can do it too.' So I started doing psychedelics. The first time I did acid I didn't hallucinate, but I just totally flowed out of my ego into a really mellow place. After that experience, I wanted to do

103

psychedelics a lot because it was so far out. It was a group consciousness thing. We'd all been together for a really long time, so we just
all flowed together into taking drugs. If one person took a particular
drug, we all figured it was cool for the rest of us to do it. It wasn't like
we had a leader or anything. It was just that we were very sensitive to
one another. We could see the effect of the drug on the other person.
If someone took acid, we could see where it was taking that person,
and we figured that since we'd like to be in the same place, we'd go
that route too. It was very much a group thing."

Tina also entered the drug scene through influence of a friend.
When she left high school, she had never even heard of marijuana or
LSD. For her first day of college she was wearing short hair, a dress,
nylons, high heels, and earrings. She was just beginning to smoke
cigarettes. Her roommate was different. "She had been one of those
girls in high school I really never associated with, who was doing a
lot of drinking, a lot of dating, a lot of smoking, shoplifting, that
whole trip."

So that year Tina began drinking beer at one of the local
hangouts, and every Friday afternoon she got drunk with her roommate and some other friends. School was becoming secondary to her
social life.

Tina met Bob during her second semester. He was already
smoking marijuana and had just begun to experiment with mescaline
and LSD. The hippie movement was getting underway and Bob was
among the first wave of young people who were "turning on." Still,
Tina's close friends were not yet taking drugs, so by the end of her
second semester she was still innocent of the drug scene. That lasted
only until she returned from summer vacation. The first day back she
and some of her friends got together and Bob was among them. He
pulled out a pipe and casually asked if they wanted to smoke some
grass. "So I smoked some and nothing happened, but the people I
was with were all stoned and having a good time, so that was the
start."

After her first experience smoking marijuana, Tina began moving slowly into the hippie counterculture. "My roommate wanted
more than anything to be a hippie. She dressed like a hippie and did

104

all the hippie things. And she was smoking dope. At that time I wasn't even wearing jeans. I thought they were silly. But somehow I started getting into that a little bit, and before I knew it, I was into the whole trip. I just slipped into being a hippie."

Tina eventually met and became close with many others who were taking drugs. "We'd get together in David's room and sit around, smoke dope, and watch 'Dark Shadows' every day. We just watched T.V. all day and all night. There was a constant flow in and out of that room all day long."

Secure in her new life-style, it was not long before Tina decided to try psychedelics. Her first experience was with her roommate and they took mescaline. "We dropped the drug and I thought, 'Oh, my God, what did I do?' We went to see the movie '2001,' and we were sitting there waiting for something to happen. We were thinking, 'What is this? We can get a lot more stoned on grass. What is the big attraction of this stuff?' About halfway through the movie, the mescaline came on and we could feel it charging up. We looked at each other and started laughing. It was so far out because we were so close, and here we were in this incredible state together. My roommate was into watching the movie, but I was just sitting back watching hallucinations, watching everything change. That first trip on mescaline really revolutionized my life because, although smoking dope was far out, it never gave you a big enough jolt to really show you beauty and freedom. Mescaline did that for me."

With her new friends, Tina began taking acid two to three times a week, while she smoked marijuana every day. According to her, it was not just her group of friends which influenced her to use drugs: the drug experience itself opened her up to new ways of seeing and knowing.

While most of these premies were led into drugs through friends and relatives, a few were given their first drug experiences by strangers. John was one. While he was listening to a Three Dog Night Concert, a joint was passed to him through the crowd and he took a drag on it. "That's how I got started. A lot of people I was hanging around with were always talking about dope. They asked me if I had smoked dope and I told them I had, but I hadn't really. I

105

didn't have anything against it, that's for sure. It was just that it was never presented to me. So the first time I tried it, I just figured I was getting into it whether I wanted to or not."

John's drag on that marijuana cigarette did not produce much of an effect, but it did help him break the ice. "It wound up that I was getting stoned practically every night. There was just the excitement of getting stoned, then tripping out on music, and just the feeling of being stoned. I remember several times I was lying down stoned and couldn't move. I couldn't feel my feet."

Not having "anything against it" is an important phrase in John's story. All of these young people reached a point where they were willing to use marijuana. In an atmosphere where their friends and relatives were using it, and people were asking them if they smoked grass, only a strong moral prohibition against drug use could have had a counterbalancing influence. Without that moral opposition, there was receptivity, a feeling of curiosity to know and to experience the altered state of consciousness others were so highly recommending.

John smoked grass steadily for two months before he experimented with LSD. "Somebody offered me some and I said, 'Sure, why not?' I'd hardly talked to anyone who had done acid, so I really didn't know what it was all about. But my first trip was really a good one. I was really mellow. I got into watching Road Runner cartoons and things like that. It was a totally different feeling in my mind. For the next two or three weekends, I dropped acid."

Having no feelings of moral opposition to drugs, John was able to slip into the world of psychedelics feeling socially accepted and free of guilt. So it was for most of these people, with the exception of Helen, who had moral misgivings about drugs but who gave way to social pressure when she first tried marijuana and LSD.

The Psychedelic Experience

Premies saw marijuana as a warm-up for the main event—tripping on psychedelics. For all but possibly Alan, psychedelics were viewed

106

PSYCHEDELICS

as an education. Those who tried acid for the first time described an excitement and beauty which made them want to take more. And there was apparently an expanded sense of freedom and openness to people and nature, sometimes accompanied by spiritual insights which opened their eyes to the perfection of everything, and to the sense of order in the universe. Also, psychedelics showed them an alternative to American materialism. As one premie said, "In tripping, you notice the intricacies of everything. You notice how each flower is so perfect, each insect is beautiful and perfect. When you're tripping, things seem like they just flow along in a series of events that are leading up to something. And everything is just like God planned. So you really have this sense of a higher order of existence. All of nature, each season, is beautiful. You see the beauty of the snowflakes in the winter, the leaves in the fall, the new bud in the spring. At other times, when you're not tripping, you just go through life and take things for granted; they're nothing. You're too busy with material things. But when you're tripping, it takes you into true things and material things don't mean a thing."

In their early lives, these people had not experienced a feeling of closeness with nature which, apparently, can be revealed through psychedelics. Some had discovered the mystery of nature, but they had never felt a sense of spiritual unity with every living thing, often referred to as "cosmic consciousness." Drugs seemed to reveal that connection, as we hear from Mary Anne. "I remember one time I was smoking a lot of hash and I was up in the mountains. I was looking at this tree and I experienced my first taste of cosmic consciousness. I became totally one with that tree. It was so beautiful. I could feel that tree. I could be it. I realized that the same essence which was in that tree was in me. I became one with that essence. I became one with the tree, one with the forest, one with the whole universe. I was outside of my ego enough to feel that essential vibration that's part of everything, that's keeping the whole universe together." *The soul is actually an energy, a part of that energy which is vibrating within, inside of us. You see, everything is a vibration. My hand is a vibration of something. Everything is a vibration. And then there is a primordial vibration, which is, of course, the highest and the most*

107

PSYCHEDELICS

beautiful vibration of all. One vibration is vibrating, that's why all the vibrations are vibrating (Guru Maharaj Ji, 1972).[2]

For Mary Anne and Walt, psychedelics were a form of therapy because they were forced to look at the negative aspects of themselves which they had been able to repress in normal consciousness. Although facing up to their personal shortcomings was emotionally painful, both came to the point where they could more easily accept their weaknesses, thereby overcoming their earlier tendencies toward self-hatred.

Psychedelics apparently helped them deal with their feelings of personal inadequacy to the point where they were able to relate more fully to others. On the other hand, LSD only aggravated Alan's feelings of estrangement and self-hatred. However, he was the exception, for most premies spoke of hallucinogenic drugs as having had a very positive effect on their personal growth, even Helen, whose experiences were full of terror.

Although Mary Anne apparently benefited a great deal from mind-altering drugs, the going was a bit rough in the beginning. "I had a lot of bad trips at first, where I'd get really depressed and cry a lot because I was having to look at ugly things inside. LSD opens up the mind so you can see things you're holding back in your unconscious and not really wanting to confront. I had maybe forty or fifty bad, crying trips before I started having all really good ones. But even when I was having bad trips, I would get so high it was worth it to go through an awful bummer to reach the higher places. During those bummer trips, a lot of self-doubt was coming out of me—kind of like hating myself in a way, because I didn't know who I was. I had identified so much with my ego that I had really bad feelings about myself. If you have really bad feelings about yourself, you can't look through that to other people. I began to get a taste of who I really was when I got high. Then I'd come down and try to identify with that high place as much as I could. And I'd look at what I'd tried to do to myself before, trying to kill myself, and going to a mental hospital. After I'd experienced that high place, I'd come down and just look at those things I'd done and feel disgusted with myself."

Mary Anne was able to suffer through the depressions and crying

108

PSYCHEDELICS

of her first fifty psychedelic trips, while John had only to face on encounter with his weaknesses to know that LSD was not for him. After that, he took no more.

Walt was the only one of the eighteen who started taking drugs in junior high school. He first tripped on LSD during the ninth grade with two of his friends. As the drug peaked, he began to see the weaknesses of his personality. Before, when he had become conscious of aspects of himself he did not care to see, he could avoid looking at them. But acid brought his repressed side to life and he hated it. "I tried to force myself to think of other things, but I couldn't do it because I just kept seeing how my whole personality was totally phony; how I was a thousand different people. The pain got so bad at times that I threw myself through hedges and chased little kids with rocks. I even tried to run into some lady's car when she stopped at a stop sign. I took money out of my pocket and threw it away, and I punched my friend in the mouth twice."

Although Walt was trying hard to escape what the LSD was forcing him to see about himself, he could not stop the drug from its guiding role. The acid revealed his hidden problems each time he tripped, until he reached the point where it became much easier to accept his weaknesses.

There was a general feeling among these young people that psychedelic drugs had modified their values, beliefs, attitudes, and perceptions of the world. According to one premie, "Drugs open up many new doors and avenues for exploration. Life becomes pliable, bendable. The realities one may have sheltered so long suddenly bend and you see the illusion of this life. All our trips don't mean a thing and one begins to realize something far beyond our limited perspectives. So you begin opening up to yourself and to others. You begin to express yourself in a different way through dress, speech, action. Once one begins to see that mankind has no true limits, only self-defined limits, then the search for reality and unity begins."

Matthew characterized his pre-drug state as one of sleep. He had been a reflective person all of his life, but had not really considered the meaning of existence or the nature of his own being, questions which he says drugs brought into focus. Other premies talked about

109

PSYCHEDELICS

how psychedelics get people back to where they were before social conditioning or how they forced them to see through their many social roles to their real identities.

Most premies spoke of social barriers being broken down while tripping, which drew people closer together. The fact that Mary Anne and Walt could be pulled out of their isolation during their LSD experiences may be testimony to the power psychedelics could yield against the shadowy fears which had kept them hiding from others.

We know that Mary Anne had been socially withdrawn in her early years. She had not been given much love as a child and was somewhat reluctant to give it. Yet psychedelics began to change that. "When I tripped, my heart just opened up and all the love poured out through me. It made me feel good and I could see that it had a really profound effect on other people. It was experiencing love while tripping that I really got into. It was so beautiful I just wanted to stay there forever. But I always had to come down, 'cause I was taking drugs to get there, and I didn't realize there was another way to do it." *Meditation is the only medium through which you can increase your love and love will again spring forth, will make you one, and finally everything will be organized* (Guru Maharaj Ji, 1975).[3]

Walt also experienced love and brotherhood while tripping. And, like Mary Anne, he had a difficult time preserving that feeling when he came down into the "straight world." On drugs, loving others seemed easy, while, in his normal state, he felt alienated.

It is important to realize that hallucinogenic drugs were regarded as the chemical agents of a new ideal for our society. One premie spoke in this vein when she said that psychedelics showed her what the world could be like if people loved one another. Especially for those who experienced love while tripping, there was a desire to recapture that feeling in normal consciousness. Even though Mary Anne and Walt could not completely carry over their drug-induced love into everyday life, they did have an experience which made them aware of a better way in which people could relate to one another. Their loving feelings in a psychedelic state became a yard-

110

stick for measuring their capacity to show affection for others on a
day-to-day basis.

Having to come down from the loving sensations of a psychedelic experience eventually came to be viewed as a limitation of
drugs. They could take you up high, but they could not keep you
high. As that fact became known by the individual and shared collec-
tively, the idea of a spiritual search became more appealing as a
means of getting and staying high, of loving others without chemical
assistance.

Shattering the Religious Frame of Reference

What was the religious viewpoint of these eighteen premies concerning God before their introduction to drugs? God was personified. He
was seen as an old man with a grey beard who could be loving or
wrathful, depending on His mood. God listened to prayers, so con-
versations were possible with Him. We were made in His image,
which is to say that He has a nose, eyes, a mouth, a body, and all the
rest. That was the standard view. *The world thinks, people think, God
is a man. People think God has ears, nose, teeth, and he rises early in
the morning, brushes His teeth, washes out His mouth, and He is an
old man, so he brushes out His beard also. But no, God is energy.
God is perfect and pure energy, and that is why scientists say that
energy cannot be destroyed and cannot be created. This is Knowledge.
This is the Word of God* (Guru Maharaj Ji, 1971).[4]

Psychedelics undermined the Judeo-Christian image of a per-
sonalized God. The drug experiences of many premies acquainted
them with a view of God which was quite compatible with eastern
spiritualism. They came to see God as the force holding the universe
together and animating all living things. How easy it was, then, to
accept the view of God conveyed by Guru Maharaj Ji, as the energy
in the universe which can neither be created nor destroyed.

Once one senses God, a commitment to start a spirtual search
may begin. This is what happened to Tina: "My roommate and I

111

PSYCHEDELICS

dropped some acid, about a half of a tab. We had heard that that night was to be the beginning of the Aquarian Age, and we wanted to see what would happen. That night I realized that the only reason I was alive was to realize God. I was going to do anything to realize God. Before I knew there was a God and I was feeling good, but it was never, 'This is what you have to do and nothing else.' The spiritual thing was kind of a very hip thing to get into. But that night it just hit me that I knew that I had to find God, that was all I was here for, and every moment from that time on, I would search for God. I said, 'Okay, God, I know I have to be one with you, and I know I have to find you, so where do I start?' "

Mary Anne had a similarly powerful spiritual awakening on drugs. "There was one LSD trip when I guess I experienced samadhi. I merged with everything. I had taken this really heavy dose of STP, LSD, and cocaine. My friend and I were going on a Greyhound bus to Chicago, and we decided to take some drugs and really make it into a trip. At one point I felt that my body blew up in the air. It was like an atomic explosion. I didn't have a body anymore. I didn't have a mind anymore. It was like being in total bliss, total light, total silence. I had no ego, no personal identification. As far as I can see, that's where I'm aimed right now. That's the highest thing I've ever experienced. That one experience was a taste. I have no idea whether it lasted two seconds or eight hours, because it was totally timeless, and completely blissful and perfect. After that experience I didn't take LSD much anymore. I felt I didn't have to. I knew if I took it again, it would never be that good, so I didn't take any for a really long time. I didn't come down from that trip totally, 'cause I really broke through something at that point."

Not all of these premies were spiritually awakened through their use of psychedelics. Walt felt drugs were taking him somewhere "far out," but not toward spirituality. John found drugs opened him up socially, but he did not experience it as a spiritual event. One premie put it in the following way: "I guess drugs started me on a search for unity, but I did not realize at the time that unity springs from God. I experienced living, not the great white flash of God. I was very heav-

112

ily into people, not spirituality. Drugs just made me want to relax and flow with life."

Thirteen premies spoke openly about drugs stimulating their spiritual curiosity and belief in God. "I've been involved with Christian things my whole life. I was active in the choir and church group. I liked it. Right before I got into drugs, I was reading the Bible and conscientiously trying to figure it out, but I couldn't relate to it. I read that all you had to do to be saved was believe in Jesus and have faith, but I couldn't really feel that faith. So I just forgot about religion until I freaked out on dope. From then on, God started becoming a reality for me, something I could really feel."

Psychedelics and Spiritual Awakening

There is little doubt that psychedelics were an aid in the spiritual awakening of these premies, for they changed their religious outlook, replacing their Judeo-Christian conception of a personal God with an organic view of God as energy. Against a background of disillusionment with the mainstream churches, this new insight produced a dramatic change because it awakened a new respect in them for the supernatural.

Furthermore, the drug-use pattern of the eighteen was very similar to that of premies from the midwest and south, suggesting that psychedelics may have been an influential factor in the spiritual awakening of a much larger number. In fact, the most striking differences between the premies and the nonpremie college students centered on drug use, according to the statistical analysis of the questionnaires. Premies were much more likely to have taken psychedelics than the college students: 95 percent of the total premie group had used them, as compared to 67 percent of the college students. More important, perhaps, is the fact that more premies (65 percent) than college students (25 percent) who used psychedelics had spiritual experiences while tripping.

Premies also used psychedelics more frequently. The average es-

113

timated number of psychedelic experiences for the premie was about 60 to the college student's 20. There was also a difference in the duration of use between the two groups. Premies had experimented with psychedelics over a two-and-one-half-year period on the average, while the average duration of use for college students was one year.

The followers of Krishna reported drug-use patterns almost identical to premies. About the same proportion had used psychedelics (89 percent), and about as many had spiritual experiences while tripping (45 percent). Furthermore, the average number of trips on psychedelics (59) and the average time span of their drug experiences (two and one-half years) were nearly identical to premies. These findings suggest that psychedelic drugs have had an impact on the development of the new spiritual movements considerably beyond that of Divine Light Mission. This view is supported in two works on the Hare Krishna movement. In separate studies, Francine Daner and J. Stillson Judah indicate that psychedelic drugs were instrumental in the spiritual awakening of the followers of Krishna, although disillusionment with drugs set in prior to their conversion.[5]

My findings are contradicted, however, by Armand Nicholi II, whose study of seventeen Christian converts was mentioned earlier. He stated: "Some investigators have implied that drug use itself has led to a preoccupation with the supernatural. My findings in this and other studies do not bear this out. Drugs do not precipitate interest in the spiritual; the opposite holds true. Students turn to drugs because of an interest in the spiritual and because of a hope that drugs will meet their spiritual needs."[6]

At most, only two premies I interviewed could be regarded as having been on a spiritual search before they tried psychedelics, a fact completely at odds with Nicholi's findings. As a rule, premies made no reference to having taken psychedelic drugs initially for spiritual reasons. Instead, they mentioned social influences and curiosity as the two main reasons they tried psychedelics for the first time. Although the vast majority did not have spiritual interests before they first took hallucinogens, thirteen said that psychedelic drugs had awakened them spiritually.

Those who received word of the magical power of psychedelics

114

PSYCHEDELICS

as an avenue into religious experience began to expand their conceptions of tripping. For example, one premie had initially begun to experiment with psychedelics as a lark. "There was no fasting the day before, no meditating, no praying to God before taking the drug. It wasn't a sacrament. It was hell-raising." Yet, after staying on the physical plane with psychedelics for some time, he heard that psilocybin could put him in contact with God. With the expectation that it was possible to enter the spiritual realm while tripping, it was not long before he had his first mystical experience.

Contact with people who had already reached spiritual awareness through drugs simply reinforced the notion that tripping should have spiritual meaning. Premies who failed to report spiritual experiences with drugs tended either to be socially isolated or living with people who had little interest in the spiritual value of drugs. Yet, for premies whose friends had discovered the mystical potential of drugs, it was only a matter of time before some spiritual awakening would draw them more fully into the group.

This turning toward spirituality can also be partially explained by the tendency to extend the imagination once the most obvious aspects of an experience have lost their novelty. Premies first explored the most immediately accessible features of psychedelic experience—the intensification of colors, hallucinations, the beauty of simple things, the feelings and sensations which they said rushed through them like waves of electrical energy. As these experiences became mundane, they began exploring more subtle levels of psychedelic reality. One reason premies may have had many more spiritual experiences on psychedelics than college students is that they explored the drugs more deeply.

115

chapter
EIGHT

Between the Sacred
and the Profane

In the mid-1960s, a few gurus from the East had come to the United States with little fanfare and even less luck attracting followers. Psychedelic drugs were still in vogue and the counterculture was pushing the belief that LSD could transform our society into a cooperative family. But as the number of "bad trips" multiplied, and the novelty of new insights wore off, that belief began to erode.

By the early 1970s, a large number had already taken their experiences with drugs about as far as they could and were ready to follow gurus. Their loyalty to drugs and counterculture life had diminished to the point where they were prepared for a new commitment. The spiritual movements were to grow out of the decaying counterculture, as it was in its final days as a lifestyle and social vision.

There was a point when at least ten premies were actively searching in both the drug and spiritual realms. Others, whose first contact with spirituality was Divine Light Mission, were still milking psychedelics for a last drop of realization, or could no longer get as high on drugs and were waiting for something new to come along.

117

BETWEEN SACRED AND PROFANE

By the beginning of the 1970s, word was slowly spreading about meditation and yoga as alternatives to drugs. Within the counterculture a new group of people emerged who identified strongly with spirituality and had given up drugs in search of the "permanent high." They became the early explorers of the spiritual world, the vanguard which would start the mass exodus out of drugs and into mysticism. People began to discard their blue jeans for yoga pants in order to find a social niche in the newly developing spiritual community. As Tina so honestly admitted, it was a "hip thing" to find a guru and to join a spiritual movement. Spiritual movements were regarded as higher, purer callings, and there was condemnation for those who were still dealing or using drugs.

Before the appearance of these spiritual movements, there were few acceptable ways out of the counterculture. Returning to standard careers was regarded as a "cop out" and thus taboo. The spiritual movements had a unique set of attributes which made them good avenues of escape from the counterculture. They were the offspring of psychedelic experience, not a trap laid by the establishment to lure people back into middle-class life. They were also being publicized as more substantial and meaningful than anything the counterculture life had to offer.

Most importantly, the bizarre features of the new spiritual movements, with their strange rituals and unorthodox beliefs, made them seem sufficiently foreign to middle-class life to be palatable to the disaffected. These movements offered the convenient possibility of rejoining society while still remaining separate from it. Thomas Robbins' study of the Mehr Baba movement offers a similar conclusion. He argues that the new spiritual cults functioned as resocialization agencies by providing continuity between counterculture and conventional values and by allowing members to express their hostility against the dominant mores while being slowly socialized to accept them. [1]

Premies who had been terrified by their drug experiences, but who had caught a glimpse of the spiritual, welcomed the shift to spiritual practices. For example, Helen stopped taking drugs soon after she was told that yoga and meditation went beyond drugs. Given the

118

frightening experiences she had had tripping, she was ready to trust those in the spiritual vanguard who were urging people to give up drugs.

Others had to experiment with spiritual practices first in order to find out for themselves whether that was the direction they wanted to take. "Drugs make one want to relax and flow with life, and lots of people told me yoga could do that without the use of drugs. So I tried it and discovered that to be true, and slowly drugs faded out for me. Drugs only point to something beyond this material world. Drugs can be the beginning, but they are far from the end." *One premie came to me and asked this question, "Why do you want us to leave these drugs?" I said, "Well, now you have to realize this Knowledge, haven't you?" And he said, "Yes." And I said, "Well, suppose you come to my home and you bring an automobile. Do you bring the automobile right to my room?" He said, "No, I leave it outside." And I said, "Same thing here. You used to take drugs, and you say apparently these drugs brought you to a point. But then you took Knowledge and that was beyond them. So now leave the drugs and proceed purely, proceed naturally"* (Guru Maharaju Ji, 1972).[2]

Religious books played a surprisingly important role in the spiritual awakening of these premies, as nearly all of them had become acquainted with spiritual literature through their friends and relatives. The appearance of spiritual books on the counterculture scene set the direction for what was to come. Timothy Leary, who had helped people to understand their psychedelic experiences, was losing popularity to his former Harvard colleague, Richard Alpert, who had pushed the potential of psychedelics to their limit, had gone to India looking for something beyond drugs, and found his guru. He returned to the United States with a glimmer in his eye and a new name, Baba Ram Dass. *Be Here Now* was the story of his transformation from drug user to devotee.

His book came at an opportune time, for disillusioned hippies were already looking for something better to do than take drugs. With such a receptive audience, his book achieved widespread popularity and had electrifying effect. Soon, Baba Ram Dass was the folk hero of the emerging spiritual community, because his experiences provided inspiration to those who had left psychedelics and were turning to a spiritual solution.

Spiritual books gave coherence to psychedelic experience, helped point to what lay beyond drugs, and offered a whole range of new ideas and spiritual practices to try. Terms like "karma," "reincarnation," "yoga," and "Godhead" were part of a new language whose power was measured by the large number of people who were soon using it. And of course there was social status for those who first spoke the new language.

Venturing into the spiritual world was partly a result of personal aspiration. As Matthew says, "My drug experiences, the books I encountered, and the innate yearning toward spiritual experience were all interwoven. But the inner drive was the crucial factor. The immense power of this yearning gave me the feeling that the results of past lives spent in spiritual pursuit were coming to bear on this life. I know that drugs themselves do not necessarily lead to spiritual aspiration. It is the inner tendency of the person taking the drugs that determines the direction drugs will take. It is the same with books. I had lived many years totally unaware of the spiritual section of bookstores, even when they were right before my eyes. It was my inner tendency that led me to notice them and grasp their meaning."

Social Influences

Social ties, even more than psychedelics, had the most compelling impact on the development of spiritual aspiration and commitment for premies. In fact, Benjamin Weininger argues that conversions are brought about through the intervention and acceptance of another person who acts as a catalyst when an individual has reached a point of great inner conflict.[3] Certainly the vast majority of premies were introduced to spiritual practices and beliefs through social influences, as we see in John's case. "I moved into a new house with some new roommates. One of them was doing hatha yoga. He was going to yoga classes every Sunday night, and I went to one of the classes with him and really got off on it. So I started getting into that. I didn't know too much then and I wasn't desperate enough to start searching on my own. I was like that up until the time I received the Knowledge. I wasn't really desperate to start a spiritual search. I was generally happy. I was getting high doing hatha yoga and was pretty contented with that."

None of the premies, except one, were attracted to Christian movements or were tempted to return to the churches of their youth. An explanation for this reluctance may be found in the fact that none were in close personal contact with a Christian during the critical period when they had developed spiritual aspiration and were looking for a spiritual direction to take. Had John moved into a house where a loving Christian lived, he might be a devout Christian today.

Putting Out Effort

Whereas John took up yoga with only very weak spiritual aspirations, Mary Anne developed a strong desire to search for God. Nothing could hold her back once she had been introduced to yoga by her close friends. "I did a lot of asanas. As far as meditating, I really didn't know what it meant. I just sat down and tried to wipe all thoughts from my mind. I learned to relax more than anything else in yoga. During that time I read *The Tibetan Book of the Dead*. It was about a year after I had had that white light trip on the bus. It told about the experience I'd had. I thought 'Wow! Somebody else knows about this too.' *The Tibetan Book of the Dead* just laid out what had happened to me, so I got a very much deeper understanding. I was even more determined to do whatever I could to get there again." *There is a glorious sun, not the sun you see in the sky but a sun which is within ourselves, which is much brighter, much, much, much brighter than the sun you see in the sky. When the sun you see in the sky comes out it only dispels the darkness, but when this sun comes out it dispels the darkness and the ignorance both. It is much brighter than the sun that shines out. It is all within us, it is just within us* (Guru Maharaj Ji, 1971).[4]

Early spiritual experiences provided Mary Anne with a taste of

121

the benefits of spiritual practice, but did not show her how to attain enlightenment. Instead, she felt overwhelmed and lost. "Asanas relaxed me, pranayama gave me a rush, and chanting got me high, but the more I did those things, the more I could see the illusion of the physical and mental planes, yet I was not able to see what was real. So they put me into a spiritual void, a state of consciousness which increased my desire to be filled up. I really prayed a lot 'cause I figured I needed a teacher to show me how to get back into the white light."

Lost Between Two Worlds

Walt experienced a great deal of frustration vacillating between drugs and spirituality. He had "burned out" on psychedelics to the point where, when he took acid, very little happened to him. His spiritual awareness had expanded as a result of his drug experiences, but the going was rough. "I spent most of one summer in the mountains in spiritual darkness. I tried to read a book about yoga, but I couldn't get into it. I was in one of the most beautiful places on the planet, but I was bummed out most of the time. I was keeping a diary then. I'd sit down and write about how I couldn't find happiness, how my mind was crazy and I couldn't find any peace. At that time I couldn't get off on psychedelic drugs any more. So I'd play my guitar and it would give me pleasure for ten minutes, then I'd get bored with it. I could read a book for thirty minutes, until I got bored with that. I just figured I was lost, because I was trying all these things to find peace and I couldn't find it. Not being able to score drugs bummed me out, so I got to the point where I could get drugs easily, and that didn't bring me peace. College bummed me out, so I quit 'cause I thought it would make me happy, but it didn't. Working a job full-time bummed me out, so I quit and did odd jobs, but I still was unhappy. I was bummed out because I wasn't living in the mountains, so I moved to the mountains and I couldn't even find peace there. I just got to the point where I couldn't fool myself into thinking that external things were causing my unhappiness and that, if I

122

changed external conditions, I would find peace. I knew that the answer lay within and that nothing on the outside would bring me happiness." *Many people think that by creating an external atmosphere, a special environment, that we will be able to get that peace. But no. External atmospheres are limited to external things, to external organs. You can get something externally, but when we want to experience that internal Knowledge, we have to create a completely peaceful atmosphere inside us* (Guru Maharaj Ji, 1972).[5]

Walt eventually returned to Boulder from his mountain retreat and found a job. Athough he was coming to the end of his interest in drugs, the spiritual path was not yet a viable one for him. "I'd come home from my job and just sit staring into space because I had nothing to do. I had no friends and I couldn't even read books. So I'd just spend my evenings walking to the store, where I'd buy a few donuts, and then I'd walk home again. I was still trying to squeeze some realization out of drugs every time I could. I'd take some psychedelic drug and then walk into the mountains and try to experience something but it just didn't happen because I was burned out on drugs. I lived for the weekend, hoping I could score some good acid and go to the mountains where I might experience a little inner peace. That's what I was living for, nothing else interested me at all." *The world has only learned one thing, how to demand and obtain gratification for its sensual desires. Everybody is blind to the important things. Everybody is concentrating on their stomachs. So how am I going to be able to give them the Truth, which is good for the heart? People are completely relying on their brains to get what they want, even if it is something beyond the brain's capacity to obtain. But the brain is not pure, and can never obtain the pure thing, the thing for which we are really searching. That is why we are so restless* (Guru Maharaj Ji, 1971).[6]

Spiritually Lost

Tina grew away from drugs into spirituality, was caught between those two worlds for a time, then, feeling lost, she came to feel a need for a teacher. She was one of the eighteen who definitely started a spiritual search as a result of hallucinogens. When she flashed on the thought that the only reason she was alive was to realize God, she did not hesitate to seek out a friend to help her get started. "I had been friends with this guy named Peter. He was a very spiritual person and he was always telling me to get my trip together and I never knew what he was talking about. The night I had that God experience, I just had to talk to someone, so I went over to Peter's house. I told him I finally knew what he had been talking about and that I wanted to know where to start on the spiritual path. He handed me *The Aquarian Gospel* and told me to read spiritual books because he didn't know much either. So, I started reading books about Buddha and Krishna because he had told me to find out how the saints lived. I really loved reading about them."

Although Tina's religious insight on drugs made her want to go higher and higher on psychedelics, she was taking acid less frequently but continued to smoke marijuana regularly. At that time, she was still tied to her close group of hippie friends, although she was no longer living with them. Her bond to them was slowly dissolving, freeing her to start a new direction. "That summer Peter and I got an apartment. It was not a sexual relationship, but a spiritual one. He was teaching me some spiritual things, and I was teaching too. I didn't spend much time with my other friends. I'd left them in the dust because they couldn't relate to what I was doing and I couldn't relate to them. We were still very close, but we weren't together much."

About that time, a spiritual fair came to town and Tina and Peter went. "Peter and I woke up really early each morning and we went to the fair and got home late and talked. I tried to understand what he was saying because he was a little bit further along on the spiritual path and could explain things to me."

When the fair was over, Tina felt herself slipping back into the mundane and routine, but her spiritual interests were getting a stronger hold on her. "I'd never been so anxious to get into a trip before, so excited to see myself grow spiritually. I read the Bible and *The Aquarian Gospel*. Most books were too heavy for me, but *The*

124

BETWEEN SACRED AND PROFANE

Aquarian Gospel explained everything so clearly I ended up reading it four times. At that point, I didn't know you were supposed to have a spiritual master. I didn't know that was a necessary thing at all. I just thought you learned about the spirit on your own. When I read *The Aquarian Gospel* for the fourth time it really hit me, that it was talking about the Word of God. It said the Word could not be spoken. Jesus kept saying this throughout the book. He healed people with the Word and He said that the Word was inside, that it could not be spoken by carnal lips. I kept wondering what the Word was. I really started wondering what Jesus meant when he said the Word could not be spoken." *At night in my room, air comes and passes sieves and it makes that noise, it tries to whistle. The primordial Word. Take a brick—a brick has this primordial vibration in it. Take air—air has this primordial vibration in it. Take sun rays—sun rays have the primordial vibration in them. And as soon as this vibration is taken out, they are done; nothing is left. The whole world is based upon this Word, because this is the first source of the world to be created. This was the fundamental basis for the whole world to be created out of—this Word. From this Word came the whole process of creation. Because of this Word, God was able to create the whole universe. If this Word was missing, God wouldn't have been able to create any of it. The Word is such a powerful thing that when a little bit of it comes into a thing, the thing becomes alive. So this Word has to be deeply realized* (Guru Maharaj Ji, 1972).[7]

Tina took acid for the last time during the summer before she received the Knowledge. "I dropped some acid, sat back, and didn't dig it. I saw how messed up I was and how my mind was really in control. My soul really wanted to come out but my mind just kept going and going, and I got to a point where I wanted my mind to shut up. I didn't want to hear it any more. I knew I had to get my mind under control. So that was my last trip. I knew drugs weren't the way any more. I knew there had to be something else." *Ignorance is only created by the mind, and the mind keeps the secret that you are something divine away from you. That is why you have to tame the mind first. The mind is a snake and the treasure is behind it. The snake lives over the treasure, so if you want that treasure, you will*

125

have to kill the snake. And killing the snake is not an easy job (Guru Maharaj Ji, 1972).[8]

Exodus From the Drug World

Among the members of Divine Light Mission it was widely believed in 1972 that those who received the Knowledge and became involved in the movement were quick to give up psychedelic and harder drugs, such as heroin. This was the case for the group of eighteen premies, for most had stopped taking drugs before they received the Knowledge. In fact, 65 percent of the larger premie group and 68 percent of the Krishna followers had quit using drugs before their entry into their respective movements. These findings, supported by other research on the Hare Krishna movement, suggest that drugs were losing their vitality before the new spiritual movements had gained much momentum.

The stories reveal no single explanation for this loss of interest in drugs, as individuals were influenced to quit using them in different ways. Some premies stopped taking them when, through a mystical experience while tripping, they realized the urgency of taking a turn toward spirituality. Others, such as Helen, were eager to quit after unhappy encounters with their unconscious. There were also a few who had "burned out" on psychedelics; the drugs had simply lost their capacity to get them high or to teach them new things about themselves and the world. Tripping, therefore, lost its sharp contrast with normal consciousness, and thus much of its appeal.

The loss of interest in drugs experienced by premies and Krishna followers was in sharp contrast to the group of nonfollower college students who had used psychedelics. While premies had given up drugs on the whole, 66 percent of the college student drug users who said they had tried psychedelics were still using them. This difference may be explained by the fact that premies tended to have many more mystical experiences on drugs, to have taken a greater quantity of them, and over a longer period of time. Through their more extensive use of psychedelics, they seem to have discovered that drugs

126

could not supply the answers to the many profound questions which had surfaced while tripping. This leads to the ironic possibility that the greater the individual's involvement with hallucinogenic drugs, the more likely he or she will abandon them entirely. Dabbling in psychedelics, as the college students were prone to do, just seemed to prolong their use.

It would be a mistake to think that the use of psychedelics is a necessary step in spiritual transformation. More important are social influences and the individual's need for meaning. In fact, what many of these premies acquired through their psychedelic experiences could have been learned directly through spiritual practices, but these people had learned earlier to mistrust religion. It took mind-altering drugs to make them aware that religion was not synonymous with "church," that there was a spiritual world waiting to be explored outside of conventional religion.

While active in the counterculture, these young people had been heavily exposed to cooperative living, so their values were changing in a direction which was compatible with eastern mysticism. Their spiritual awakening made them receptive to the values and practices advocated by the new spiritual vanguard, which they tried and found more rewarding than drugs.

It was not long before most had embraced the belief that spirituality was the key to the resolution of personal and social problems, a factor John Lofland regarded as a determinant of conversion in his work, *Doomsday Cult*.[9] Disillusioned with politics and the counterculture as vehicles for change, this belief in the potential of the inner revolution gave them hope, an ingredient quite indispensable to the individual embarking on a fundamental change of outlook. For hope encourages risk-taking, while it gives meaning to the pain and turmoil of change.

With this faith in the power of spirituality to change the world, soon they were discarding the hippie self-image for a spiritual one. This new image was bound up with a spiritual ideal, which was loftier than that of their counterculture days, although they were similar in some respects. Love was still central, but purity and service to God and humanity replaced the antiestablishment mentality of the hippies. Where, before, they had felt free to indulge their desires, now they were beginning to see desire as something they needed to control.

This new ideal created an inner conflict, for it was further removed from their personal capabilities than their hippie ideal had been. The increasing gulf between their new spiritual ideal and their abilities spawned feelings of personal inadequacy, which premies characterized as being lost. Feeling lost, they were more receptive to the idea of finding a guru.

chapter
NINE

Preparation

Most of these premies had passed through a period of reorientation and were feeling lost. Those looking for a guru were busy checking out different spiritual teachers or were wondering when a guru would find them. Others, who had not yet come to believe in the necessity of surrendering to God and a guru, continued with spiritual practices and drugs, hoping they would destroy the "veil of illusion" which prevented them from seeing ultimate reality. Some, like Alan and Walt, were just desperate for relief from their feelings of inferiority, alienation, and aimlessness.

The vast majority of these young people learned about Guru Maharaj Ji through friends, acquaintances, or strangers. In only a few cases was initial contact with the movement through a poster or some public announcement in the news media. Yet, it is unimportant how individuals learn about a movement, as long they are prepared for what the movement and leader have to offer.

When Guru Maharaj Ji first came to the United States in 1971, there was no media outcry against him and his materialistic life-style. Instead, positive word-of-mouth advertising brought hundreds of hippies to the mountains to see and hear him. Soon, the first wave of new premies were telling people around Boulder about how "blissful"

129

the Knowledge was and how being in the guru's presence (called
"darshan") would "blow them away." It was no wonder that, bombarded with so many positive communications about Guru Maharaj
Ji and the Knowledge, these eighteen young people became interested in seeing and hearing him.

Ready and Willing

Tina's first contact with Divine Light Mission was Robert. He had
been heavily involved in drugs, had been spiritually awakened, and
had gone to India in hopes of finding a guru. There, he heard about
a young saint called "Guru Maharaj Ji." He sought him out, received
the Knowledge, and returned to the United States to spread the news.
"His first night back, Robert gave us satsang, although nobody knew
it was satsang at the time. He just started rapping and everybody nodded their heads. But, for me, he might just as well have been speaking Russian. I didn't know what he was saying, but it didn't matter
because the vibration coming out of him was really strong. He was
pulling my soul out, and it felt really good." *Satsang means the company of Truth, and Truth is something you cannot see but you can realize. Satsang is also something that you cannot see but you can feel.
This feeling when it is expressed outwards is satsang* (Guru Maharaj
Ji, 1972).[1]
    Robert promised to bring Guru Maharaj Ji to the United States.
"We said 'Far out! Robert's bringing us his guru.' I had no idea that
Guru Maharaj Ji could be my guru too, because Robert was so high
and I was much too low spiritually to have that happen to me. He
had told us that Guru Maharaj Ji could open our third eye. I'd read
about the third eye, and I thought to myself, 'My God, the third eye,
that's everything. What Robert's experiencing out of his third eye
must be incredible. He must be so zapped out.' *"These dual eyes are
good for seeing the duality of the world, but to see the oneness of God,
we need the one eye of Knowledge* (Guru Maharaj Ji, 1972).[2]
    Two weeks later, Tina heard that Guru Maharaj Ji was going to
visit Colorado. Her friends had tacked up a picture of him on her

PREPARATION

door announcing the date of his arrival, which was the first picture she had seen of him. "The news hit us really hard. 'He's coming!' people were shouting, and we were running around and bumping into each other. Then we went out into the yard and said the Lord's Prayer. Afterwards we said, 'God, whatever you have in store for us, thank you. Just help us to be prepared for Guru Maharaj Ji's coming,' even though we didn't have any idea what we meant at the time."

Intent on seeing the guru, she and a few friends traveled to Colorado to become part of a small group of people who welcomed Guru Maharaj Ji to the United States. "It came time for him to come into the airport. We each held a flower. We were all filling up with an incredibly good feeling. I'd never felt that way before. I was so excited to see the boy who I'd heard so much about. We were told how to greet him and the people in charge told us to kiss his feet if we had a chance. But they warned us that he walked very fast so not to trip him. The only picture I'd seen of him was in a suit, but when he entered the airport he was wearing a sport shirt, plain pants and black patent leather boots. We put garlands of flowers on him. Then I remembered I was supposed to kiss his feet if I could. He walked by at that moment and stopped for just a second. My mind said, 'I ain't kissing anybody's patent leather boots.' But then I heard another part of me say 'Do it!' So I got down and kissed his feet and I just got filled up. I was off and flying after him. From that moment, I had no doubts he was my guru."

When Tina arrived at the Wall Street cabin where Guru Maharaj Ji was staying, her desire to receive the Knowledge was great although she felt unworthy. Word spread that the young guru had come and people from Boulder, Denver, and the surrounding area were arriving. "A lot of people came who were curiosity seekers, and they left fairly quickly. But people who were really into Guru Maharaj Ji came with their sleeping bags and stayed the entire time he was there. Satsang went on twenty-four hours a day. No matter where you were, you couldn't escape it."

Tina spent three days at the cabin before receiving the Knowledge and during that time, she saw the playful side of the guru.

131

PREPARATION

"Guru Maharaj Ji played the whole time he was there. He never got heavy. People would come to his door and he would throw cans of water and paint at them. He played with squirt guns, flashed pictures of himself for us to see, and took movies of everybody. It was just constant play the whole time he was there and he loved it. Love flowed back and forth between him and his devotees."

After watching so many others receive the Knowledge, Tina was more inclinded to think that the Knowledge was for anyone who was sincerely ready, and she knew she was. She found herself saying: "If Guru Maharaj Ji will accept me, I'll receive the Knowledge. I promise I will be devoted to him if he will just give me his Knowledge and his love." *If you come to me with a guileless heart, you will surely receive this most ancient spiritual Knowledge which, if practiced upon, will give us perfect peace of mind* (Guru Maharaj Ji, 1973).[3]

By the third day, about 300 people where gathered around the cabin talking and some were crying. "There was a lot of crying because, when you come to your spiritual master, you surrender your life to him. It takes a period of dying. Some people were crying because they were preparing to surrender. But there were tears of joy that Guru Maharaj Ji, the Lord, had come to save us. I cried every time Guru Maharaj Ji gave satsang. And some people were crying uncontrollably all the time, guys and girls. But it was such incredible crying. It was like a release from a lifetime of searching. When you find Guru Maharaj Ji, the search is over. There's nothing more you need to do. You just let go because it feels so good to be home." *If you want real satisfaction, then it is the mind that has to be conquered; it is the mind that has to be satisfied. And the means to do this is by using a special Knowledge, a special way, a special system. And this is the system that has been described by all the saints. A thousand suns may rise and there will still be darkness. Man will still be in frustration; man will still know, but when a man finds the Guru then he will have the eternal Light. Three kinds of light—sun, moon, and fire—can be seen by everybody. Pigs, dogs, donkeys, and men, they can all see these three lights, but the Divine Light is the fourth light and only human beings can see this, and only those*

132

PREPARATION

human beings who go to the Master and ask to be shown it (Guru
Maharaj Ji, 1972).[4]

After three days of waiting, Tina was finally selected to receive
the Knowledge. "My heart started beating so hard, I couldn't believe
it was about to happen. I had all these expectations of what the
Knowledge was supposed to be. But the only thing I could relate to,
from my experience, was that the guru was going to open my third
eye, and it was going to be like taking 10 million caps of acid. It was
going to lay me out flat. I remember thinking, 'Its going to be so
heavy because I'm going to see God.' I could barely breathe."

Misgivings

Martha was Walt's first contact with the Mission. He met her one
day when he was smoking marijuana and playing his guitar with a
group of people in a city park. He had been reading P. D. Ouspen-
sky's *In Search of the Miraculous,* in which the author argues that the
key to realization is "self-remembering."

Martha asked him if he had heard about Guru Maharaj Ji. He
had, but he was not looking for a guru at that time. "Gurus just
didn't interest me at all. If somebody had told me that Guru Maharaj
Ji owned a Mercedes Benz, I would have responded then the way
some people do now, 'Rip off!' "

Even though he paid little attention to Martha's satsang, he did
hear her say that Guru Maharaj Ji could show him the Word of God.
He saw a connection between what she was saying and what he had
just read about self-remembering. The thought that he might be able
to transcend his mind intrigued him, for he saw his mind (ego) as his
chief enemy. He was feeling personally desperate and ready to accept
anything which promised to end his depressions. "At that point, I was
just desperate. I was ready for anything. I really wanted something to
come along."

Martha told him about a program at the university where a
Mahatma would be giving satsang in two days. Although he had not

133

understood much of what she had said, he was interested in hearing the Mahatma. The night before the program, he wrote in his diary: "This path has been rough, but it is getting a lot clearer and I feel like I'm getting closer to something."

The following evening he went to listen to the Mahatma. "I couldn't understand a word he said. He spoke about love and peace, but I didn't know what he meant, so I left confused. I didn't comprehend what he said, but there was something about his energy which made me think the Knowledge might really be something, so I went away from that meeting very interested. I had the feeling there was something cosmic about the whole thing." In fact, that night, he told his roommate that Guru Maharaj Ji might be the new Messiah.

Although he was not deeply interested in receiving the Knowledge at that point, he decided to drop by the Divine Light Mission office to find out more about the Knowledge. He was told that the Mahatma was going to give satsang again, so he left the office with plans to attend. "I went to hear the Mahatma and there were some Krishna people there who called him a fraud. I watched their egos getting uptight, while the Mahatma stayed spiritually centered. He just kept telling them he was their brother. Something about that moved me so much I knew I had to receive the Knowledge."

Yet, he had grave doubts about his own readiness. "My mind was so crazy then I can't describe it. My whole life had been ruled by feelings of frustration and rejection, and I had been seeking some crazy thing everyone told me did not exist. I was a fraud and all my drug experiences had burned me out over and over again. A lot of people reject Guru Maharaj Ji because they cannot stand the thought of bowing down before him, but I had no trouble doing that. It was the easiest thing in the world for me because my ego was so shattered by all my tripping it wasn't together enough to protest. I just couldn't understand how I was going to receive the Knowledge 'cause I thought I was too deluded and messed up." *My knowledge is like a river. Let a lame man come, it is the same water; let a rich man come, it is the same water; let a poor man come, it is the same water; let an enemy come, it is the same water; let a friend come, it is the same water. The same water is flowing for everybody. This Knowledge is the*

PREPARATION

same for everybody. External things do not affect this Knowledge because it is internal (Guru Maharaj Ji, 1973).[5]

Like Tina, Walt's first encounter with Guru Maharaj Ji was at the Denver airport. "I saw him and I was disappointed. I thought he was just a pudgy kid. I really got depressed because I couldn't see anything special in him. I thought I was doomed to stay in darkness and loneliness." But for the next few days he stayed in the company of premies, asking them questions and listening to their satsang. A turning point came when Walt went to hear the guru. "He was so clear and perfect. He was totally beyond anything I'd ever seen before. I had no doubts in my mind about him after that."

Yet, he still had serious doubts about himself. "Up to that point, I had a super inferiority complex when relating to spiritual people. I couldn't be around them because I thought they were so high and I was so messed up. I couldn't even stand to look at them because I thought they were filled with light and truth. I was thinking of finding a monastery in India and living twenty years as a humble servant in order to prepare myself to receive the Knowledge."

Guru Maharaj Ji had urged his audience to go to the Denver ashram the next day to receive the Knowledge. Although Walt did not consider himself spiritually qualified, he interpreted the guru's statement as a command. So, the next morning he was among a large group of people waiting to receive the Knowledge, his moods vacillating wildly. One moment he was sure he wanted the Knowledge, the next, he would fall into despair at the thought he was unready.

The Mahatma eventually came downstairs and asked the people congregated there how many were prepared to receive the Knowledge. A large number started toward the room where the Knowledge session was to take place, and Walt was among them, still weighted down by his feelings. "I really felt bad, like the worst piece of shit in the world. I was so ill at ease I tried to shrink into the floor so no one would notice me."

When everyone was seated, the Mahatma asked if there was anyone who was not yet prepared to receive the Knowledge and Walt raised his hand along with five others. They were asked to leave.

135

PREPARATION

Feeling desperate by then, Walt decided to go to talk to one of Guru Maharaj Ji's closest disciples about his confusion. He was taken to one of the Mahatmas, who assured him that he should receive the Knowledge. But the Mahatma's assurances were still not enough to overcome Walt's lack of confidence, so he spent the rest of the day listening to satsang. "That night I heard a few people give satsang who were my age and had recently received the Knowledge. They were talking about the trouble they had had preparing themselves to receive the Knowledge, when suddenly I realized that they were just like me. They were not really high people but were confused like I was. At that point, I started to think that maybe I could receive the Knowledge too."

About ten o'clock that evening Walt was about to fall asleep when the Mahatma came in and asked if anyone was waiting to receive the Knowledge. Knowing that Guru Maharaj Ji and his Mahatmas were leaving the next morning, Walt decided he'd better move fast, so he and eight others went to the Knowledge room. The Mahatma began asking questions of everyone, and if they did not answer to his satisfaction, they were asked to leave. Walt's turn came. "Finally, he came to me and I thought 'Oh, no, here it comes.' But he said, 'You're definitely ready,' and he went on to someone else. That really blew my mind because I thought I was the most unready person in the whole place."

Rejected

While Tina and Walt easily gained the Mahatma's approval to receive the Knowledge, others had more difficulty. One premie, who I will call Andy, had drifted into Kundalini Yoga through the influence of his roommate, Shawn. They had heard that Guru Maharaj Ji was up on Wall Street, but neither of them were willing to take the time to go see him.

Then, one day, Andy saw a poster on the university campus announcing a program featuring the guru. His reaction to the poster reflected a genuine lack of interest in finding a spiritual teacher at

136

that time. "I wasn't sure I should tell Shawn because we had decided to have a party the same night as the program. We were going to get all of our old friends together and we'd already made some of the preparations for the party. I didn't want to tell him about the program because I thought he might want to go and he'd probably draw me along with him. And I didn't want to miss the party. But I ended up telling him anyway. As I had expected, he split and went to the program, but I stayed for the party, which turned out to be a real drag."

Shawn was excited when he returned home that evening. "He was very blown away by the experience, by the love he felt coming from the young guru. I became fairly interested because I knew my roommate very well and I realized that it must really be something to get him so excited. He was very spiritually oriented and he obviously saw a lot in the kid, so I found myself becoming interested too."

Guru Maharaj Ji and his Mahatmas left Colorado the next day. For several days afterwards, Shawn gave Andy satsang, talking about how the guru could open up his sixth chakra, the ultimate goal of Kundalini Yoga. Andy began to develop great expectations about the power of the Knowledge, as Tina had.

In a short time, a Mahatma returned to Denver and Andy eagerly went to hear him give satsang. "When I walked into the satsang room and saw the people involved in the movement, I felt a strong positive vibration coming from them. When I saw the Mahatma and heard him give satsang, I knew something very far out was going on. I was sure I wanted to receive the Knowledge. It seemed obvious to me that those people were experiencing something I hadn't, so I decided I wanted it too. I knew I was moving toward spirituality, but nothing had yet been strong enough to pull me deeply into it. It seemed to me that the Knowledge was possibly what I was looking for." *We don't claim that we are the only way, that only we can give this spiritual Knowledge. Instead, we tell you to search and find out what is the best way. But what we do say is that we have the spiritual Knowledge and we also will give it* (Guru Maharaj Ji, 1972).[6]

Andy returned to Boulder that evening filled with enthusiasm. A Knowledge session was planned for the next day and he, Shawn, and

137

PREPARATION

some friends were planning on going. The next morning, Andy was waiting to receive the Knowledge. "I remember the happy smiles of the people there, the sense of a very cosmic thing about to happen, and I wanted to be a part of it." When the Mahatma walked in, he felt awed by him, and he hoped the Mahatma would sense how much he wanted to receive the Knowledge. "The Mahatma proceeded to blow everybody away by going around the room, looking at people, and telling them how many times they had been to satsang. Everybody was saying, 'Yes, how did you know?' He picked out the people who had only been to one satsang, which included me, and asked them to leave."

Andy went outside and sat down to listen to some premies giving satsang. "Those of us who had been asked to leave talked about what we could do to make ourselves ready to receive the Knowledge. That included creating a stronger desire for it, a stronger need for it. I imagine each of us realized that, even though we wanted the Knowledge, we could have had a much stronger desire for it. We finished talking and went away intending to hear a lot more satsang, because we couldn't think of anything more important to do at that moment."

He listened to satsang that afternoon and evening. At the evening program, it was announced that a Knowledge session was going to take place the next day. So, Andy and two friends rose early the next morning and made their way to the Knowledge session. "We were sitting in the back of the room and the Mahatma came in and began to ask people questions. He was feeling out their thoughts and desires to see if they were really ready for the Knowledge. Finally, he asked if anyone had had other spiritual masters. For some reason, I told him I had been doing some Kundalini Yoga through the teachings of Yogi Bnajan. Well, he told me to go away and listen to more satsang."

There were tears in Andy's eyes as he left the room, for he was disappointed and bewildered about what to do next. Having nowhere to go, he decided to return home. On his way to the bus depot, he received some inspiration from an unlikely source. "This drunk started walking along with me, asking me for a quarter every now and then for bus fare. He told me he was a poet and he asked me if I

138

wanted to hear some of his poetry. I said 'Yes,' so he started reciting a poem. It said something like, 'Old man wandering in the darkness, looking for the eternal answer, but not knowing where to go.' I heard that and thought to myself that it was pure satsang. It was Guru Maharaj Ji saying those words to me through that poor drunken slob."

Andy listened to satsang regularly for the next few days. Then he went to receive the Knowledge again, only to be turned away once more. He had had a relatively strong desire for the Knowledge in the beginning, but having been rejected by the Mahatma so many times, his desire was growing. He was more determined than ever and the next morning he was back again trying to get into the Knowledge session. This time, however, the Mahatma allowed him to stay. "I was feeling very meek and I was trembling with tears in my eyes, because I was about to come into such close contact with my life. My heart was opening up where, before, it had been closed."

Curious

Whereas Andy had a strong desire for the Knowledge, but had to overcome obstacles, John had very little desire and faced no obstacles at all. He was curious because he had heard many things about the Knowledge although he had very little idea about what it was. He had quit taking drugs and was not actively looking for a guru.

He and his girlfriend had heard about Guru Maharaj Ji and were intrigued by the guru's age. So, they decided to check out the movement by attending satsang. He had no intention of receiving the Knowledge at that point, yet he left satsang feeling quite positive about what he had experienced there.

A short time later, he and his girlfriend split up, so he was forced to find a new place to live. As fate would have it, one of his new roommates was a devotee of the guru. John had taken up Hatha Yoga through the influence of a previous roommate, as you will remember, and now he was getting ready to enter Divine Light Mission in the same way. "I went to satsang with this girl, my roommate,

139

because she was going and I didn't have anything else to do. I really got high on it because there was a lot of good energy there. I'd never confronted anything like it before. The energy I'd experienced through Hatha Yoga was pretty mellow compared to the energy at satsang. It was something very intense and unique which I'd never encountered before."

John was happy to attend satsang because of the "positive energy" he felt there. But he was unwilling to accept the belief that Guru Maharaj Ji was the Lord. "There were people at satsang who talked about Guru Maharaj Ji as the Lord of the Universe, but I couldn't get off on that at the time. That kind of talk brought me down on satsang. I could never conceive of God coming down to earth in human form. That's why I could never get into Jesus." *How are you going to see who is the real Lord? It's simple! First of all, you are going to receive his Knowledge—what he gives you, and then you are going to see. If it is true, you are going to go ahead and bow down to Him and say, right you are my Lord, and if it is false, throw it away. I don't claim myself to be God. I don't claim myself to be any prophet, any Messiah, anything. I just claim myself to be the humble servant of God, and I have brought this message for you–I have brought this Knowledge for you. That's for you, not for me. I have realized it. It's okay with me now. It's for you, and you should receive it. If you don't believe me, okay, many people don't believe me. Maybe they think, "He is a child; he is kidding." But it is before you, and you can test it, you can see. If I am kidding, it's before you, and five million people have received it all around the world. How to receive it? Go to a source, I say I have it. You want? By all means you can take it. What you need is love. And not that love you give externally, but I seek a part of that love you give to God—Pure Love, that's all I seek* (Guru Maharaj Ji, 1972).[7]

A turning point came for John when he went to hear Guru Maharaj Ji. "Going to that program was the most incredible thing I'd ever run into. I wasn't affected as much by seeing the young guru as I was by the energy there. It was very intense and it built higher and higher. I still had doubts about God coming down to earth in human form, but listening to Guru Maharaj Ji's satsang, I openly received

140

his vibrations and they just emptied my mind. The words he said didn't strike me that much. All he said was, 'You can search for peace in this world, and if you can't find it, come to me and I will show you how to find it.' My conception of a guru at that time was an old man with a white beard and hair speaking words of wisdom. Yet, Guru Maharaj Ji's satsang wasn't wisdom so much as it was just very light and flowing. When he spoke I could sense something totally different about him. I guess it was his vibration. It just really hit me hard."

During the program, he learned there was going to be a Knowledge session the next day at the Denver ashram. He decided to go if he could get a ride. "If I hadn't gotten a ride, I don't know if I would have made any great effort to go. I did have a slight desire to receive the Knowledge, although I guess I was mainly curious to find out what it was."

Most of that day he listened to satsang. "I got so much satsang my mind was really gone, although not in a positive sense. I just got to the point where I couldn't really grasp what was going on. Finally, the Mahatma began to ask questions like, 'Are you willing to dedicate your life to this Knowledge? Are you willing to cut off your head for it?' I was saying 'No' to a lot of things. The Mahatma had said that people who could not answer 'Yes' to his questions should leave and go hear more satsang. At one point, I did feel like getting up and leaving, but I didn't. I probably didn't want to go because people would have looked at me. Also, I was thinking, 'If this experience will truly show me God, then this is where I should be.' The Mahatma was directing questions to different people, but he never turned to me. If he'd asked me a question, I would probably have said 'No' and left. During that time, I was hoping he wouldn't come around to me with a question. I sort of wanted to stay because I'd come so far."

The chance omission of John from direct questioning was a key factor in his eventual conversion, for he was allowed to receive the Knowledge, having only a faint desire for it, and even less preparation.

141

PREPARATION

Attraction to the Movement

Most of these premies had already broken away from the counterculture and were identified with the emerging spiritual community.
Why they were attracted to Divine Light Mission rather than some
other spiritual movement was partly situational: they came into contact with premies and Guru Maharaj Ji when they were between
commitments and thus were free to begin a new one.

Many were attracted to the movement when they learned that a
friend, relative, or acquaintance was interested or involved. As we
saw, Tina was drawn to the movement through her contact with
Robert, Andy through the influence of Shawn, and John through his
fateful encounter with his premie roommate. However, there were a
few, like Walt and Alan, who had no friends, relatives, or acquaintances in the movement. Their feeling of attraction stemmed largely
from the positive impressions they had of premies and Mahatmas.

"Picking up on the positive vibrations" and "feeling the intense
energy" are common phrases in all eighteen stories, as these young
people recalled their first experiences of the movement. Even Alan,
who had fallen into a deep depression, reported feeling some relief
during his first encounter with premies, an experience which made
him think they had something he needed. Feeling "blissful" while
experiencing the "positive energy" of satsang was a critical part of
their preparation, for it was interpreted by these young people as
proof of the Knowledge's power to elevate the human race into a
higher state of consciousness. Having experienced this potential
themselves, they were more eager to talk to premies, which convinced them all the more that they should receive the Knowledge.

These young people found the beliefs of the Mission generally
compatible with their own orientations, a fact which made the movement all the more attractive to them. Only Alan seemed completely
unprepared by his earlier experiences for the movement's appeal, but
he was feeling so desperate he was ready to grab at anything which
promised to give his life meaning and direction.

One of the appeals of the Mission was the boldness of its claim
that Guru Maharaj Ji, through his Mahatmas, could give initiates a

142

PREPARATION

direct experience of God. This promise might have been shrugged off as an exaggeration were it not for the fact that new premies were enthusiastically passing the word that they had encountered God during the Knowledge session and had been "blissed out" by the experience.

With its claim that the guru could reveal God, the movement created a mystery which was accessible only to those who were allowed into the Knowledge session. Since premies vow to keep the proceedings of the session secret, there was no way these young people could have learned about the Knowledge. When they asked about it, they were told they had to receive the Knowledge to find out. Shrouded in mystery, the Knowledge became all the more attractive to them, which, in turn, increased their desire to be initiated.

chapter
TEN

Encounters with God

Feelings of anticipation were running high once these young people had secured a place for themselves in the Knowledge session. Six were expecting to have a powerful spiritual experience, thinking that the Mahatma was going to open their "third eye" and that they would be enlightened. A larger number were hopeful of some startling spiritual insights, but were not anticipating a dramatic change. Some, like John, were just curious to find out what the Knowledge was, since they had heard so much about its power to transform people, or had witnessed its influence in the generous actions of premies and Mahatmas. And a few, like Walt, were ready to be saved from their personal problems.

Just as there were different expectations about the Knowledge session, there were varying reactions. There were those who were "blissed out" by the Knowledge, who were completely satisfied it was the Truth they had been seeking; those who were disappointed for various reasons, feeling, for example, that they had experienced much of it before; and those who came away confused, not fully understanding what had happened.

Twelve of these premies were "blissed out" in varying degrees, while six left the Knowledge session disappointed or confused. The

145

negative reaction of the six was not strong enough to extinguish their interest in joining the premie community, however, because all six eventually became devotees. After the Knowledge session, some overcame their disappointment or confusion in the process of discovering what the techniques of meditation could do or by remaining linked to others who were heavily involved in the movement.

The expression "receiving the Knowledge" conveys the somewhat misleading impression that the Mahatma, who is now called "Initiator," presents the Knowledge as if it could be wrapped and offered as a gift. It is true that the Mahatma (Initiator) gives instruction in the techniques of meditation; those techniques, however, are not the Knowledge, but rather are the means by which the initiate is put in touch with the Knowledge, the inner light which Guru Maharaj Ji has called the power of God. *This is the mystery of nature, that there is a hidden Light in everything, and you have to realize what that hidden Light is, what that hidden thing is, what that hidden current is in you that is constant and can never die. These are the teachings of all the saints on record. That thing that is making things alive is the most constant thing in the world because it is the power of God, and this is making everything alive* (Guru Maharaj Ji, 1971).[1]

The claim that the guru could reveal God was affirmed through the experience of those who were "blissed out." As one premie said: "We grow up thinking that we are doing our own breathing, yet we cannot stop our breath by holding it, for at some point we will have to gasp for air and go on living. The techniques of meditation used in Divine Light Mission reveal how the Knowledge is breathing us."

Meditation on the inner light is one of ways premies are taught to contact their life force. Several premies had experienced the light in childhood while holding their eyes closed tightly. Others were caught completely off guard. Marc was one. "After concentrating on the third eye for so long, my first experience of divine light was beyond words. I got the feeling that this 14-year-old boy who could show me that simple means of seeing the light must really have something. It's such a subtle way of experiencing the light, which is in all of us, you don't have to use a mantra or anything else because it's always right there inside of you. You get the feeling that it is

146

ENCOUNTERS WITH GOD

something real being shown to you, that it's the Truth and is beyond words. At the moment you concentrate on the light you have no thoughts and you realize that, if you could be in that light all of the time, it would solve all of your problems." *There is a musk deer which has musk hidden in its belly button, always giving off a scent, and this scent intoxicates the deer. He is naturally attracted to it, yet does not know where it comes from. So he looks everywhere for the source and in the end in crazy frustration he jumps off from the mountain and falls and dies. You are just like this musk deer. You run around searching for the light, the source of your life, the abode of peace and understanding, and all the time it is inside you. But you don't know it.* (Guru Maharaj Ji, 1971).[2]

Listening to the celestial music, the musical sounds each meditator experiences differently inside the inner ear, is another way premies learn to experience their life force. A premie put it in the following way: "We're constantly in this world of sounds, with loud voices and cars rushing by, every kind of sound you can imagine. But there is one sound from which all sounds come and that is the celestial music, the music of life which is in all of us." *Today, the guitar is played. We love it. Today, rock and roll music is played. We love it. Today, jazz music is played. We love it. Classical music is played. We love it. But there is a music going on inside of yourselves also, and God plays that music* (Guru Maharaj Ji, 1971).[3]

Premies believe that by concentrating on what one might call the inward flow of the body's moisture in the mouth and throat, one can experience the "river of life" within. This is meditation on the "nectar." "In this world of exterior taste," a premie said, "you can taste everything imaginable. But there is an inward taste also. To turn the taste inward is to discover a river of nectar flowing within. It is the river from which all tastes stem. It is the river of life that Jesus spoke of. Upon drinking from this river, there is complete satisfaction."

Finally, by focusing on the rhythm of their breathing, premies were taught to become aware of the Word in each breath as the basis for meditation and action. " 'In the beginning was the Word and the Word was with God and the Word was God.' The Word is an un-

147

speakable vibration that's keeping us alive." *This Word is hidden, and then it is just shown to you. You understand it, you catch it, and then you receive the satisfaction of mind, because to our mind this Word is a church* (Guru Maharaj Ji, 1971).[4]

By trying to focus on their breathing during the day, premies seek contact with the Word, the spiritual source of their lives, which reminds them of what is common between themselves and others. Concentrating their attention on the inner light, celestial music, nectar or the Word during meditation, premies reported a general quieting of their mental activity. With calmer minds, they said they were better able to experience the Knowledge. Therefore, they regarded meditating in a disciplined way over time as an essential step in the development of a more meaningful, less tense and more fulfilling way of life. *What is meditation? Perfect concentration upon a perfect thing is called meditation. Just remember that. For then you are making your soul and God into one, at that time you are receiving perfect communion with God. Because you have put all your mind into the Knowledge, into that peace which is God. Do you see? So you are doing everything at that time. You are worshipping, you are talking, you are seeing, you are listening, you are experiencing, you are touching, you are feeling, you are everything* (Guru Maharaj Ji, 1971).[5]

The "Blissed Out"

Tina's encounter with the Knowledge was fairly typical of the most "blissed out." "The Knowledge was more than I'd ever comprehended. What happened to me was so beautiful, subtle, and simple. It was absolutely perfect. And the Knowledge session was so full of love. The Mahatma just gave and gave, wanting us all to understand and to be really devoted to Guru Maharaj Ji. My Knowledge session lasted eight hours, but it didn't seem that long. My mind didn't think about anything during that time. And my soul was soaking up everything. It was just digging so much of what the Mahatma was saying, for he was answering everything I'd ever asked. It was so perfect and beautiful that I came out of the Knowledge session raised up.

148

Others experienced a childlike ecstasy. "After the Knowledge session, I ran outside. All day long I ate ice cream cones, swung on swings, ran around. I felt like it was my spiritual birthday. I was a child of God. Once you receive the experience of God in the Knowledge session, you can carry that over into all facets of your life, so that all the things that used to bother you are not so heavy or confusing. You can see the light; you can find the lesson in every action."

There was a deep feeling of thanks for Guru Maharaj Ji, because he had shown them God and set them on a new and more meaningful course. Feelings of enthusiasm gave rise to the conviction that Guru Maharaj Ji and Divine Light Mission were "the way." Not only were most of the "blissed out" ready and willing to surrender, they were eager to spread the Knowledge in order to realize their vision of a world at peace.

The Disappointed

The six premies who were disappointed and confused were less well prepared for conversion and commitment than the "blissed out." For example, five of the six had no friends, relatives, or close acquaintances in the movement before their initial contact. Three held views in conflict with the Mission's beliefs. Five had had little to do with premies before receiving the Knowledge.

John walked out of the Knowledge session disappointed. He had had high expectations that it would be a "cosmic experience," but in fact it was much less than a dramatic event for him. "When I saw the light it didn't strike me as anything new because I'd seen it several times before. I remember experiencing the light when I was about seven years old. I used to sit in church and close my eyes real tight and I'd see it. The same was true with the music technique. I remember sitting on top of a mountain watching the sunrise and hearing the same sound, although I didn't know what it was at that time. The Knowledge is like that; it really isn't anything new. The Knowledge session reveals what's there and that it's always going on."

John's heart warmed toward the movement when the Mahatma

149

showed him how to experience the Word of God. "The Word meditation surprised me the most because it was so simple. Premies were always talking about the Word, so I expected that when I came in contact with it my mind would be blown away, and it was. I had not anticipated that the Word would be something so close to me, something which keeps me going all the time." *From where is your breath coming? Who is making your breath alive there? Just observe it. You weren't breathing at night, were you? You never thought to take a breath at night. You never said, "Well, I am going to sleep, but yet I will be taking a breath." You just went to sleep. And still your breath was going on, the Word was helping this breath to go on ahead. If we realize that Word, it will be quite clear before us what is making us alive every moment. And what is making leaves alive. What is making birds alive. What is making animals alive. What is making the whole world alive* (Guru Maharaj Ji, 1971).[6]

Even though John was surprised at the simplicity of the Word meditation, he was not moved to put the techniques into use. "After the Knowledge session, I didn't meditate that much because the Knowledge seemed too simple. In fact, I probably would have fallen away from the Knowledge afterward if it hadn't been for my roommate. She was going to satsang a lot and I just went along with her."

Another premie recalled: "When I came out of the Knowledge session, I was sort of disappointed because nothing really happened. I'd expected all kinds of things. Other people were coming out of there laughing and hugging each other. 'Boy, what phonies,' I thought. The next day I was wandering around wondering what trip I was going to get into next."

This premie was in spiritual limbo, knowing he was developing strong spiritual aspirations, while doubting that the Knowledge had the power to change his life radically. The next day he found a job, just to occupy his time, and that evening he halfheartedly decided to try the Word meditation. "I was sitting there doing the Word technique sort of half-assed, hardly putting any effort into it, when I found myself getting drawn deeper and deeper into it. I started getting rushes of pleasure up and down my body. From that experience I knew there was something powerful happening. So I got into meditating on a regular basis."

150

1. Guru Maharaj Ji at the age of eight meditating in an Indian ashram in front of a picture of his father, Shri Hans Ji Maharaj Ji.

2. Thirteen-year-old Guru Maharaj Ji speaking on Wall Street in 1971, an area in the mountains near Boulder, Colorado, where he launched the American phase of his mission.

3. A view of the stage area and a part of a gathering of about 6,000 at the "Guru Puja Festival" in Montrose, Colorado, in 1972.

4. Guru Maharaj Ji at the age of 15 speaking informally to premies in London during one of his unscheduled appearances outside of a Mission ashram. He had started the movement there just before coming to the United States in 1971.

5. The Millennium Festival, held at the Houston Astrodome in November 1973, caused widespread disappointment among premies and created a burdensome debt for the Mission.

6. Guru Maharaj Ji speaking at the Millennium Festival in Houston, Texas, on November 10, 1973.

7. During 1974, the Mission embarked on an extensive social service program, although its efforts were eventually pared back. Here, premies visit with disabled children.

8. Guru Maharaj Ji walking near his California residence on his birthday, December 10, 1976. His wife, the former Marolyn Johnson, is on his left carrying their son, while a premie to the Guru's right holds their eldest daughter. They now have a second daughter.

ENCOUNTERS WITH GOD

Both of these premies remained in touch with the Mission through fateful circumstances; one through his living arrangement with another premie, the other after the surprising sensations of his first meditation. Although both were free to join a spiritual group, it is questionable whether either of them would have become involved had it not been for these fortuitous events.

The Confused

Walt left the Knowledge session confused, for his experience had been both incomprehensible and bland. "The Mahatma went around the room revealing the light technique to everyone. I heard people go 'Wow!' But when he got to me and showed me how to see the light, I hardly saw anything. Then he revealed the nectar, music, and Holy Word. I was very tired, so I didn't experience very much. When the session was over the Mahatma told us to meditate and then go to sleep. I tried to meditate, but I was feeling so depressed I didn't have much success."

Having decided not to see Guru Maharaj Ji off at the airport the next morning, Walt returned to Boulder, still feeling depressed and wondering whether he would ever be able to meditate or be devoted. "I went back to my apartment in a very confused state of mind. But I did put up a picture of Guru Maharaj Ji on my wall. That night I went to see a friend and he and some of his friends were drunk. As I looked at them, I realized that something had happened to me because I felt so far removed from the game of getting drunk and stoned. I suddenly saw that I was no longer interested in doing that. My friend asked me if I'd received the Knowledge and I told him I had. He immediately started making sarcastic jokes about how I was a saint, and how he couldn't measure up to me. He was only joking, but it made me feel bad. Yet, when I left, I was feeling high about receiving the Knowledge, as if I'd been liberated a little bit. I went home and was taking a shower when, all of a sudden, I felt the presence of Guru Maharaj Ji very intensely. I bowed down right there in the shower, close to crying. I just felt his grace so much. It was like he was telling me, 'You're okay, for you're under my shelter now.' "

151

Another premie, who also had been poorly prepared to receive the Knowledge, was confused even by some elementary terms. "After the Knowledge session, I went outside and cried, for I had no idea what the Knowledge was. I even said to a friend, 'Incidentally, what's a guru? The Mahatma kept talking about guru; what's that?' I didn't even know what the importance of the guru was." *Guru has got more significance than God. Why? There's a very logical explanation to it—how actually Guru is bigger than God. See, let me explain it from my way. When I was born, God existed, but I never saw God. I never knew Him. Either He was ashamed to turn up out of a hole, you know, or so on; I just never knew Him, until Guru Maharaj Ji came into my life, till Guru Maharaj Ji came in my way, and showed me and revealed me that secret. And the day he did that, there it was, I knew God. So to whom should I give significance? This is something that you can decide, to whom should I give significance? God was there, I was there, I was alive, God was alive, and God was right in my heart. I just never knew Him. To whom should I give significance at this moment? My guru, because he is the one who revealed me that, he is the one who told me. I never knew if God existed. My guru is the one who revealed God to me* (Guru Maharaj Ji, 1972).[7]

This premie might have walked away from the movement at that point, had it not been for the vow she took during the Knowledge session. "I was crying because I knew I'd gotten myself into something I wasn't sure about. I'd committed myself, for I'd made promises in the Knowledge session I knew I had to keep. I'm the kind of person who values promises. Whatever I say, I'll do. Every night for the next week I sat around with some other girls who had received the Knowledge and we wondered what it was. We also weren't sure we could get up at 4:30 in the morning to meditate or to meditate on the Word all the time. We weren't particularly glad we'd gotten into it."

Conversion

"To be converted, to be regenerated, to receive grace, to experience religion, to gain an assurance, are so many phrases which denote the process, gradual or sudden, by which a self hitherto divided, consciously wrong, inferior and unhappy, becomes unified and consciously right, superior and happy, in consequence of its firmer hold upon religious realities."[8] Although written primarily about Christian conversions, this comment by William James could easily have been made about premies, furnishing support for the idea that conversion is governed by a common set of principles and dynamics.

In psychology, we learn from E. T. Clark's *The Psychology of Religious Awakening* that individuals who experience dramatic conversions tend to be guilt-ridden; from Joel Allison's research that they are better able to employ the services of the unconscious in the ego's development; from Leon Salzman's work that repressed anger plays a key role; from William Sargant's *Battle for the Mind* that they tend to be simple but stable introverts; from Theodore Levin and Leonard Zegans that a dramatic conversion may help to break down developmental impasses; and from Carl Christensen that sexual conflicts may precipitate sudden conversions.[9]

Christensen's enumeration of the stages of the conversion experience offers a good overview of the thinking in the field.

1. There are the predisposing factors of a specific unconscious conflict, religious belief, and adolescence.
2. There is a conscious conflict which is related to the unconscious conflict producing guilt, anxiety, and depression (anger).
3. An acute reaction is precipitated by intensification of the above through participation in a religious meeting.
4. There is withdrawal from others with a sense of estrangement and often a feeling of unreality.
5. This is followed by a feeling of submission—of giving up or giving into.
6. There is a sense of sudden understanding accompanied by a feeling of elation and by an auditory and sometimes visual hallucination. (a) There is a feeling of change within the self or in relation to someone outside the self. (b) The change is experienced as happening to one, not by one, and is associated with a sense of presence. (c) The change modifies one's subsequent behavior.[10]

However dramatic conversion may seem, it is but one stage of a larger process of change. We will see, especially in the experiences of the "blissed out," how one step leads to another until the person has

153

ENCOUNTERS WITH GOD

become eager for and receptive to a real transformation. Some of these steps have already been discussed, so I will only briefly mention them here; others will be explored in somewhat greater detail.

By the time they had been admitted into the Knowledge session, most premies had already been well-prepared for conversion. *Discontented, they had found conventional means of change ineffective.* This made them wonder what other measures could be taken to rectify their problems and to straighten out the world. Through their psychedelic experience and contact with spiritual people, *spirituality became the answer they were seeking.* Naturally, there was a tendency during this time to experiment with various forms of spiritual practice, such as meditation and yoga. *The positive experiences gained from their first journey into the spiritual world made them more determined to take a spiritual direction.*

Drawn more deeply into spirituality, *they developed lofty spiritual ideals.* They wanted to become loving, peaceful, and happy; ideals which demanded more than cosmetic changes. This was a time of great inner conflict because these ideals were well beyond the reach of their abilities.

Eager to pursue their spiritual interests, *they struggled to change on their own, only to watch their efforts fall short.* This was a low point in their development because whatever they tried seemed to have little effect. Many eventually tired of the struggle. As fatigue set in, *feelings of futility, of being lost and incapable, partially immobilized them.* No longer believing in the value of their individual efforts, they began to think they needed the outside intervention of a spiritual authority. So they started looking for a guru to follow. They were hoping for a breakthrough of some kind, thinking that possibly a guru's grace might provide the necessary impetus to get them through their impass.

"Blissed out" premies like Tina arrived at the point where they were ready to surrender. They had come to realize that, not only were their individual efforts hopelessly inadequate, but they were also self-defeating. For, if their individual attempts to change succeeded, it would only serve to strengthen their egos, while they had come to see the individual ego as an obstacle to spiritual progress. This put them

154

in the state described by Christensen "of giving up or giving into." In terms of their ultimate conversion, this was the first of several important changes.

Mistrusting the individual will, *they became more receptive to spiritual experience.* This was a critical development because, being more receptive, they were less apt to sit in judgment of the Knowledge experience, which was the tendency of the "disappointed" and "confused." Not judging their experience, the "blissed out" were more deeply affected and moved by it.

Experience of the universal spirit (Knowledge) was the dramatic turning point. As each meditation technique revealed their inner spiritual essence to them, they saw the simple but incredible wonder of life. This had the effect of changing their perceptions of themselves and the world. Everything was seen in a new light, as they recognized manifestations of the universal spirit everywhere. Even people with divergent beliefs were seen as sharing a common spiritual source. This understanding helped them overcome their alienation while it gave them a basis for believing that a world community was possible, if people would only recognize that they were one in spirit.

Premies who had an intense experience of their spiritual essence were likely to abandon the old way of seeing themselves and to identify with the universal spirit. This fundamental shift of their identity meant they were no longer tied emotionally to their personalities as the core of their being. Instead, they were seeing themselves as individual manifestations of the unifying energy—God. This was expressed by the premie who said that her experience of the spirit made her feel like a child of God. Having experienced the underlying spiritual unity of life, these premies were awed by it. They were seeing themselves as spiritual expressions and servants of God.

Unable to relate directly to an abstract God, premies came into a devotional relationship to Guru Maharaj Ji. He became the tangible expression of the Infinite, which explains why premies tend to see him as the Lord. Seen as a living manifestation of the universal spirit, premies could express their love and devotion to God through their connection to the guru.

Identifying with the spirit and seeing themselves as lovers and

155

servants of God and guru, premies tapped a hidden reservoir of potential within them for experiencing more love, peace, and happiness in their lives. This renewed their confidence, gave them a more positive view of themselves, and removed many of their doubts about what to do with their lives.

Premies who identified with the universal spirit in this way became detached from their personalities to such an extent that they were much less affected by their personal quirks and problems. Seeing their personalities as a result of social conditioning and not of any "real substance," they could step back and examine their behavior as one might thumb through a book, with a certain degree of aloofness. No longer identifying with their old problems, they could laugh at things they felt and did which, in the past, might have led them into a depression. Detachment from their personalities essentially freed them from emotional blocks which had prevented their further development. Alan received relief from his suffering in this way. After receiving the Knowledge, he was amused by his emotional upsets because he knew that his personality was only a product of socialization and nothing to really worry about. This attitude immediately improved his ability to relate to others.

Aside from all the psychological and social explanations one could offer to explain their conversions, the fact is that, during the Knowledge session or afterward in meditation, these young people had a spiritual experience which deeply affected them and changed the course of their lives. It was an experience which moved many to tears and joy, for they had found the answer they had been seeking. It was an experience which gave their lives more positive direction, meaning, and purpose. It was an experience which brought them into a new relationship to life and removed many blocks to growth. It was an experience—which sages have spoken about throughout history—of the oneness of life.

156

chapter
ELEVEN

Metamorphosis

Generally, premie conversions were followed by a period of enthusiasm, during which time many felt as if their lives had taken a radically positive turn. For the most "blissed out," it was almost a euphoric state, as their experience of the spirit, identification with it, and emotional detachment from their personalities produced feelings of joy. This experience sometimes lasted only a few hours, although there were some premies who remained in this state for several days. During this period of elation they had little choice but to share what they had experienced with anyone who would listen: "I gave satsang to everybody I saw," said one premie, "because I was really happy to be on the road to the realization of my soul."

Following the enthusiasm phase life began to return to normal, as premies were rudely awakened to the fact that their negative feelings and desires, the sources of personal turmoil before their initiation, remained to haunt and tease. Another danger was that premies might forget the uniqueness of the Knowledge experience, diminishing it to the point where they would lose interest. As I was told: "After awhile, as the new experiences became 'normal,' or integrated into our lives, it was easy to lose consciousness of the richness and

157

METAMORPHOSIS

depth of the Knowledge experience, making satsang, meditation, darshan, and attendance at programs essential as a reminder."

Normalization was a potential threat to the deepening of spiritual commitment, for after the great anticipation and excitement of the conversion experience, disillusionment could set in, which could lead to withdrawal. Probably at no other time was interaction with other premies more important, for as enthusiasm waned and the Knowledge experience lost some of its novelty doubts began to develop in somewhat greater abundance. Those who were more securely established within the premie community could shed their doubts because they were encouraged to express them openly. This was a counteractive force to disenchantment.

What took place next was called "purification," which premies described as the struggle between their "higher" and "lower" selves. The conflict between these two inner tendencies was one of the chief sources of personal growth for all premies as they attempted to find a resolution. They realized fairly quickly that, instead of a brief skirmish, a drawn-out battle between the sacred and profane would be necessary to finish the process of liberating the spirit. "When I first received the Knowledge, I thought in six weeks I would reach the point of spiritual enlightenment. But I soon discovered that it's a slow process because I had desires and attachments to contend with." Realizing the inevitability of a protracted spiritual struggle, this premie became more convinced than ever that she needed Guru Maharaj Ji's help.

The Way of Surrender

Driven by a strong desire for change, the "blissed out" had cut themselves off from competing commitments, had become partially absorbed into the premie subculture, and were determined to surrender. There was a sense of inevitability as they accepted the next step in their commitment. "It was time to end what I'd been doing," recalled Tina, "and to follow Guru Maharaj Ji. That's all there was for me to do."

158

METAMORPHOSIS

Typical of the group of premies who surrendered, Tina did not question whether she should be active or not, for she was ready to respond to Guru Maharaj Ji's call for help. *As you know, many countries are fighting or trying to fight just because they think that they are enemies and that they must destroy. The idea should be brought out that people are not enemies, but are children of God. All have been made by God, and it's not good if a brother fights with a brother. You see, what I want to accomplish, or what I want to bring down onto the earth, is peace. That's my point, to give this Knowledge, this Word, this Light, which has been revealed by all saints* (Guru Maharaj Ji, 1972).[1]

Tina received word about the trip to India and, of course, she was eager to go. With fourteen other premies, she put on a rummage sale, collected coke bottles, and raised $3,000. Although she and the others worked very hard, she attributed their success to Guru Maharaj Ji's grace. "There was no way we should have been able to raise that much money on the junk we sold. That was pure grace. Guru Maharaj Ji always says that if you put forth the effort, he will grace you. And we had put forth the supreme effort." *Guru always has to give His blessings to you, you need that, then you'll roll right on* (Guru Maharaj Ji, 1972).[2]

Tina did not receive any money herself from the rummage sale, but three days before the mass exodus of premies to India, a friend gave her $200 so she could make the trip. Having greater contact with Guru Maharaj Ji in India, she was able to identify with him more fully and to learn more about her own shortcomings. "Being in such close contact with purity makes you see all the garbage and dirt you have inside, and you know that you have to get rid of it. That's what it's like when you're with Guru Maharaj Ji. You see perfection manifested in him, and you realize that is how you're supposed to be, so you start cleaning up. Cleaning up is sometimes difficult because it means that part of you has to die, your lower self has to die in order for your real self to emerge. So that's the way India was for me, extremely high but difficult because I was cleaning out. I got rid of more personal garbage in India than at any other time in my life."

Facing the emotional crisis of undoing personalities conditioned

159

METAMORPHOSIS

by years of socialization, the "blissed out" turned to Guru Maharaj Ji for direction. They needed to believe that he knew who they were and that he was in control of their spiritual evolution, since they had already given up the idea they were in control. To secure themselves during this period of confusion and turmoil, they had to believe in his omniscience. Some premies even began to desire a personal relationship with him, in order to reassure themselves, in much the same way devout Christians speak of needing a personal relationship with Jesus.

Tina was one who longed for a personal relationship of this kind. "It is a beautiful thing when a premie develops a personal relationship with Guru Maharaj Ji. If you develop a personal relationship with him, you begin to really feel close to him. Otherwise, you may feel he doesn't even know who you are, but he does. I know he does without a doubt. Just before I came back from India, I went to see him for the last time. I had to see him. I ran into the ashram, and there were people all around his door. I got down on my knees and prayed. 'Guru Maharaj Ji, I'm leaving and I need to see you for just one minute more.' Before I knew it, the door flew open and he came walking out. Other people were around, but he looked at me and I was drawn to him. I looked right at his feet, and he said, 'Yes, you're leaving,' and I said 'Yes.' He said, 'Where are you going?' and I said 'Ohio.' And he said, 'That's very good.' I kissed his feet and he walked in and closed the door. Well, that was worth three days of crying for me. I always had this little question in my mind: Does Guru Maharaj Ji really know what we are thinking? Does he really know everything? Does he know me? That experience showed me he really does. I felt so close to him then. When you have an experience like that it makes you want to know the Guru Maharaj Ji inside even more, because when you really get to know him and realize that the Knowledge will make you like him, you just try all the harder to become what the Knowledge is."

Another way premies developed a personal connection to the guru was purely spiritual. "Its inevitable," said Tina, "that we're going to love Guru Maharaj Ji. When you meditate, you start realizing what the true self is, and love naturally grows because that's what

160

spirit is, love. Then you begin to recognize that true spirit is now manifested in a body, and that's why we love Guru Maharaj Ji. We don't love him for his physical appearance; we love him because he is showing us the spirit within us. So, if you are doing what Guru Maharaj Ji says, then you naturally begin to surrender to him. If you don't, there's a very good chance you will never get into the Knowledge, for we don't know how to love God because God is a very abstract thing. But there's a bridge that comes between us and God, and that's satguru. So if you start loving satguru, who is infinite and finite at the same time, you start learning how to love that infinite thing, God. Guru Maharaj Ji doesn't want us to blindly worship his physical form. He wants us to experience what is true. Suddenly, God is not an abstract thing anymore, but everything else in this world becomes abstract and God becomes very real. Before I received the Knowledge, it was the other way around; the world was real and God was some abstract thing." *All the saints have been trying to give something to people so that they might be in perfect union with God. Jesus came and He gave something. He gave the lesson of love, but He didn't speak only of love, He gave something that put people into love. I am doing the same thing now, giving something to people so that they might be in complete love, so that they might be in the true love which flows towards God rather than the love which flows towards materialism. Suppose I love this fan and this fan comes to an end. If it breaks, then my love will break. But God is something that can't break. Love towards God is very pure, and such love will increase and spread* (Guru Maharaj Ji, 1972).[3]

Seeing Through Projections

John had walked out of the Knowledge session disappointed. Had it not been for the fact that he was living with a committed premie, there is a good chance he would have eventually dropped out of the movement. He was neither determined to become a devotee nor was he very much interested in becoming deeply involved in the movement.

When John first heard about the trip to India, he had still not

161

METAMORPHOSIS

begun to meditate and was not interested in going. However, he changed his mind when he heard that there were going to be 2,000 Mahatmas there. Intrigued by the thought of being around so many "evolved souls," he even resisted attempts by his father to suppress his interest. Unhappy that John was turning away from the Catholic Church, his father had warned him that breaking away from the church could mean hell for eternity. That John was at least attracted to the movement at that point was clear from his insistence that he was going to India anyway.

Initially, John had been unable to accept the belief that Guru Maharaji Ji was the Lord. In fact, it bothered him when other premies referred to the guru in that way. He regarded the guru as a spiritual guide to emulate, but he did not feel the intensity of love which normally accompanies surrender. "I knew I had the capacity to feel a lot more for him. Sure, I prostrated to him, but I wasn't doing it from the heart. I knew he was someone special, but I didn't have the feeling of love for him that much."

Resisting surrender, John was neither as willing to conform nor as uncritical as the "blissed out." In India, some people protested the rules laid down by the Mission's leadership and others were packing up and leaving. John was among those who criticized the rules. "At that time, I figured the leaders were trying to take something from me. I felt they were demanding too much."

By the time of Guru Maharaj Ji's birthday party, John's disillusionment with the Mission had reached a critical point. He wanted to leave India and return to the United States, but was unable to because of an agreement he had with his airline which required that he stay in India for a specified period of time. From the beginning, he had felt both attracted to and repelled by the movement and Guru Maharaj Ji. A part of him wanted to jump headlong into commitment while an inner voice kept telling him to stay back. He was confused as a result of this conflict, which made him receptive to a breakthrough. "A lot of realizations came to me during the birthday party. I'd seen people bowing down to Guru Maharaj Ji, and something would sort of turn off in my mind. It was like I really didn't

162

METAMORPHOSIS

have too much of a feeling for him, or very much love either. My mind kept telling me that the people prostrating before him were only doing it because everyone else was. As I was observing the party, something clicked inside my mind, and I realized it was only my mind thinking those things about people, that their bowing down was real. I thought to myself that maybe they really loved Guru Maharaj Ji. I began to think there might be something real going on. I realized that my mind had been judging others from my own prejudices. After that realization, I started meditating seriously and then things began to happen. That was the turning point for me. There was something I saw that made me decide to dedicate my life to this thing." *If you don't meditate, you won't realize. And I must tell you one thing, and that is that you don't meditate for me. You meditate for yourself. You should get high. I am high enough; you should get high. You need this meditation because you need to get high. You must get to that point where you can also reach the infinite state. I have given you this Knowledge, therefore it is your duty to meditate upon it* (Guru Maharaj Ji, 1972).[4]

Having realized he was projecting his own skepticism and hypocrisy onto other premies, John was able to see more clearly the meaning of the Mission and the purpose of devotion. That he was preparing to surrender seemed fairly evident, since he was looking for supporting evidence in his dreams. He awoke from one dream he could not remember, but with a strong feeling that he had to dedicate his life to Guru Maharaj Ji. In another he connected the experiences of premies to those of the early Christians, feeling that premies were going through changes equally compelling and beautiful. Where initially his disillusionment had driven him into the role of the observer, he began to feel more at home in the premie community as a participant.

Upon his return to the United States, he was determined to be a devotee. He was meditating regularly and was trying to be obedient, unquestioning, loving, and in service to God and guru. Yet, his commitment was still quite delicate, for he began slipping back into old habits and ways of thinking when he visited his parents and fam-

163

ily on his way back to Colorado. Without other premies close by to reinforce the new pattern of behavior, John was soon back into the old role which had secured him a social niche in his family.

When he arrived back in Colorado his understanding of the guru-devotee relationship became clearer. "It says in several scriptures that the quality of a guru is in what he reveals. He shows you who you really are, but it turns out you are really him. If he can truly show you your true self, then he must also be a part of you. The guru is only a mirror reflecting back who you really are. He is totally unified with what I've been meditating on and he can teach people how to get there. And that's what Guru Maharaj Ji really does. He teaches us how to get to that one point inside. Slowly I realized that he is the embodiment of that thing which is inside of us all." *Knowledge is within, inside of us, but we have to understand the way to realize it. Our face is right with us, but we cannot see it until and unless we have a mirror in front of us. That's the thing. We have to have a mirror. The mirror is the Perfect Master. Like water, he is also known by different names* (Guru Maharaj Ji, 1973).[5]

Having seen Guru Maharaj Ji in this light, John was ready to accept the belief he was the Lord. Where once his feelings toward the guru had been lukewarm, his next encounters with him touched him deeply. "Seeing Guru Maharaj Ji was really far out for me after that. I had no choice but to prostrate before him. It wasn't like I decided to do it beforehand. I'd just see him and automatically hit the floor. The feeling I had for him was just so incredible."

Conflicts of Half-Devotion

Walt had left the Knowledge session not fully understanding what had gone on there. His experience is particularly interesting because, although he was quite determined to become a devotee, his feelings of inferiority and paranoia prevented his complete surrender. He had only a glimmer of hope that, by himself, he would be able to find his way through the maze of changes he knew would be necessary to reach his spiritual destination. Feeling so completely inadequate, he

METAMORPHOSIS

needed to be assured of the spiritual protection and guidance of the guru.

In the two months following the Knowledge session, Walt was far from "blissed out." "When I came to Guru Maharaj Ji's Knowledge, it wasn't followed by a burst of happiness. I just knew it was the Truth and that I'd better try to realize it. For some people, coming to Guru Maharaj Ji is the most blissful experience, but, for me, it was pure misery."

Being among premies should have raised his spirits somewhat, and it did at times, but often it simply reminded him of how emotionally troubled he was feeling. "When I listened to satsang back then, I was very paranoid. I couldn't say anything and I'd try to avoid looking into people's eyes because it was so painful. After satsang was over, I'd leave as quickly as I could so I didn't have to talk to anyone afterwards. They all seemed so joyful and happy, and I was feeling completely messed up."

Somewhat overwhelmed by his feelings of inadequacy, Walt was still determined to realize the Knowledge in hopes that it might eventually free him from his persistent depressions. "I'd get up at 5:30 in the morning and try to meditate, but it was really hard because my mind was always speeding so fast. I couldn't concentrate on the techniques for more than thirty seconds. During that time, I'd have two thousand different thoughts. I was totally lost. But I did learn that I was not my mind, where before I thought I was. I started to realize that my mind was my worst enemy, so I put a sign up on my wall which said: 'Mind is the Enemy. Fight!' "

As if it were not enough to be restrained by inner forces, Walt also had to contend with the opposition of his best friend, who was hostile toward the movement. "My friend's mind was really dark then concerning Divine Light Mission and Guru Maharaj Ji. He was really down on me, as almost hateful vibrations came from him. We were so close, yet at times we were like enemies. We could hardly talk at all during those first few weeks after I'd received the Knowledge."

Caught in the crossfire of his friend's antagonism and his own spiritual inclination, Walt chose to move out. This, of course, made

165

METAMORPHOSIS

him freer to enlarge his commitment to the movement and to Guru Maharaj Ji. Even more so because two of his new roommates were premies. Having cut himself off from a source of conflict, he achieved a greater sense of social solidarity with premies and became more fully enclosed in the premie community.

When the time came for the trip to India, Walt decided to go. Still confused, he went to London first, where he walked around propagating the Knowledge. His mind was still racing and his meditations were not improving much. In India, it was the same. "The whole time in India, I was confused about God. All of Guru Maharaj Ji's devotees would be singing and I'd have to force myself to sing. People would be prostrating to him, and I'd have to force myself to prostrate. People would go on a morning procession and I'd have to force myself to go. I was forcing myself to do everything."

Although there were many opportunities for Walt to develop close bonds with other premies, he chose to remain aloof, wandering around by himself feeling lonely and lost. When the time came for Guru Maharaj Ji's birthday party, premies were busy making costumes, but he did nothing and finally attended the party in his Indian whites, which was the standard form of dress. Yet, there were signs he was beginning to feel more like a part of the community, since he and a few other premies had formed a band for the occasion.

Walt felt so far from his spiritual goals, he was afraid. This sense of dread was nourished by Guru Maharaj Ji's satsang during the party. "I got really bummed out on his satsang. The only thing I heard him say was 'Those people who do not realize this Knowledge will go to hell and never return.' That's the only phrase I remember and I was going 'Oh, no! I'm going to hell because I'm not realizing his Knowledge."

This fear made it all the more urgent for Walt to change, which only increased his feeling of hopelessness. When he returned to the United States he was quite depressed about his prospects, although when he stopped for a visit with his family he was encouraged by a number of subtle changes. "The first night back home, one of my friends came over and suggested we smoke some dope. We did, but I didn't get off on it at all. Then this girl I knew called me and invited

166

me over to spend the night with her and I told her no. I just realized I was totally detached from those things." The effect of these changes in attitude was to increase his feeling of self-confidence, which made him somewhat more determined to change.

By the time he returned to Colorado, he was more determined than ever to "quit fooling around" and take devotion seriously. "The time had come for me to become a devotee. I couldn't be a spaced out, confused kid anymore. Then, it was like Guru Maharaj Ji started gracing me with good meditations. I'd get up in the morning and meditate and really feel good, just filled with joy. I was in a period of grace. It was like Guru Maharaj Ji lifted me out of my mind for that period. It was a blissful and happy time."

Walt was only temporarily in this state, however, for soon he was depressed again. Desperate for a breakthrough of some kind, he found himself wanting to take psychedelics again, so he tripped with a friend. During his psychedelic experience, he came to a number of insights which reflected his own state of confusion and his desire to be saved. "It really became clear to me how everyone is crazy. I saw that it was Guru Maharaj Ji's will to let the world go crazy, and then he was going to come at the last moment and rescue us all. I was looking at one of Guru Maharaj Ji's pictures. Focusing on his smile, I really knew what that smile meant. It wasn't the smile of a kid who was really high, but the smile of the same being who died on the cross. He was the supreme being of the universe."

Having come to the point of believing in the guru's spiritual powers, he was able to accept his own suffering as part of the guru's plan to save the world. He realized that, if he could be brave and bear his pain, he would eventually be transformed. He also began to feel a much deeper sense of love for the guru. "I saw Guru Maharaj Ji in New York. Up to the point when he walked in, I was dulled out. But when he came in I fell to the floor and started crying a little bit. Something deep inside of me started welling up. I was very blown away."

In a positive state of mind as a result of his contact with Guru Maharaj Ji, Walt decided to return home for a short visit. Like John, being outside of the premie community made him vulnerable to old

167

habits, feelings, and desires. "I started getting a great deal of sexual desire for the girl I had turned down before, which completely brought me down. It just blew my mind back into a crazy, confused state. I lost my whole sense of peace. Knowing I had to get out of there, I finally managed to get a ride back to Colorado."

Still spiritually and emotionally unsteady, he turned to psychedelics once again. "There's a part in *The Aquarian Gospel* where Jesus goes into some crypts to face many tests of character. During that psychedelic trip, Guru Maharaj Ji put me through every test in the book. After I went through those tests, I rose above my mind and convinced myself I was a Mahatma. I was into an illusion that all the Jesus Freaks in town were going to be at the bottom of the mountain when I went down. I thought everything was blissful and would eventually come together. I actually believed I was at the end of my spiritual search. Well, when I got to the bottom of the mountain, there were no Jesus Freaks there to greet me, so I walked along the road giving leaflets to people."

Looking at this psychedelic experience, there is a definite change in the way Walt was beginning to see himself. Although certainly exaggerated, viewing himself as a Mahatma was in striking contrast to his earlier identity as a "spaced out, confused kid." Conversion requires a degree of self-confidence of this kind. At the very least, there must be some sense that one is able to change for the better. Combined with this sense of positive potential was a deepening desire to submit to the guru, as we see in the following encounter with Mata Ji, the guru's mother. "I told her I really wanted to be devoted and I really wanted to love Guru Maharaj Ji, and to please show me how. She told me that any pain I was feeling was blessed pain, that I was feeling it because Guru Maharaj Ji had not revealed something to me, that he knew about everything happening to me and that it was happening for a reason. She told me to keep meditating and to remember the Holy Word. I really felt good after that."

Assured that Guru Maharaj Ji was in control of his life, Walt entered a period of spiritual elevation again. For some time afterwards, he worked joyfully at the ashram preparing for the Guru Puja festival which was to be held in Montrose, Colorado, that summer. But at the festival he went into a depression once again.

168

METAMORPHOSIS

When he returned to Boulder, he was still longing to be a devotee, but had begun to tire of the struggle. He was impatient being in a state of half-devotion and was looking for an end to his conflicts. His breakthrough came in an unusual place. "I was sitting in satsang with my former roommate, who had received the Knowledge by then, and I asked him if he wanted to go outside and talk. We went out to the parking lot. We turned around and there was a big, shiny car right next to me. I looked in the back seat, and there was Guru Maharaj Ji. He rolled down the window and looked at me. I fell to the ground and prostrated to him. I got up and I never felt so close to him as I was then. There he was just looking at me and he wasn't talking to a thousand people. He was relating to me on a one-to-one basis. He asked me how many people were at satsang, and why I wasn't there. He was just speaking idle conversation, but actually what he was doing was looking at me and saying, 'Yes, I'm your Guru, I'm your Lord.' At one point, I asked him if I could make a request, and he said that was fine. I said, 'Will you please let me realize a bond of love with you? I cannot stand living in a half-devoted way. I really want to be devoted. I really want to love you." He grinned and told me that love was good, but it wasn't everything, and that I should keep meditating and everything would be fine."

Walt's encounter with Guru Maharaj Ji in the parking lot was a definite turning point in his conversion and commitment, for it gave him the security he needed. "It was almost like he came to Boulder that night just to give me assurance. He came so he could roll down the window, look at me, and say 'Yes.' And ever since that point my faith has been like a rock. There's no doubt now that Guru Maharaj Ji is really taking care of me."

Commitment

Now let us consider briefly some of the commitment mechanisms which typically exist in movements like Divine Light Mission, where individuals are encouraged to invest and sacrifice, to renounce competing commitments and share in various forms of social communion, to humble themselves, and to surrender.

169

METAMORPHOSIS

Investment and Sacrifices

There is substantial agreement among those who have studied the subject that commitments develop strength, not in spite of investments and sacrifices, but because of them. Rosabeth Moss Kanter's view reflects recent thinking on the issue. "Investment is a process whereby the individual gains a stake in the organization, commits current and future profits to it so that he must continue to participate if he is going to realize them. Investment generally involves the tying of a person's present and potential resources to the organization, future gain to be received from present behavior." On the other hand, "Sacrifice operates on the basis of a simple principle from cognitive consistency theories: the more it 'costs' a person to do something, the more 'valuable' he will have to consider it, in order to justify the psychic 'expense' and remain internally consistent." [6]

Even before their initiation, these people were encouraged to invest and sacrifice. They were expected to attend satsang, to do service in the ashram as a sign of sincerity, and to give in any way they could. During the Knowledge session, it was common in 1971–72 for Mahatmas to encourage personal offerings, by way of donations of money and valuables, and gifts for Guru Maharaj Ji were quite common since expressions of thanks to him, as guru, were backed by years of eastern tradition. After their entry into the movement, premies were expected to contribute as much of their time, energy, and resources as possible. Total commitment and surrender were strongly encouraged from several quarters, mainly from the Mahatmas, Guru Maharaj Ji's mother (who had been one of his most ardent supporters before their feud), and other devotees.

The trip to India made additional demands. Most premies had to either sell their personal possessions or borrow money to finance the trip. Living in India taxed them further, for they had to live in cramped quarters, eat strange and sometimes unpalatable foods, and listen to satsang for hours in a language they did not even understand. Many also fell ill from the typical travelers' diseases.

For those like John who were not yet ready to make a strong commitment, the heavy sacrifices expected of them in India were almost too much. In fact, according to reliable reports, many premies

170

who were in John's position withdrew from the movement rather than pay what they regarded as a heavy price for membership. Hesitating to develop strong commitments, they were willing to give moderately and no more. Had the Mission demanded less of them, perhaps their doubts and other obstacles may have been overcome by gradually investing and sacrificing, to the point where they might have been willing to give more.

Social Enclosure

Social enclosure is the process by which the member's activities come to be centered in the movement. The effect is to deepen commitments by encouraging the termination of competing obligations outside of the community and by increasing social communion with members, which makes the member more dependent on the community for the satisfaction of needs and more reliant on its beliefs for comprehending the world. Actually, there is a tendency for new members of a movement to alter their social lives by spending more time with other members and less with old friends, especially if they are critical of the direction being taken. A typical case was that of a premie who, after receiving the Knowledge, noticed an immediate change in her social network. She stopped seeing old friends and formed new friendships with premies or others who had begun a spiritual search similar to her own. She characterized that period of her life as a "scary time," for she experienced emotional conflicts having to break up the order of her social life.

By renouncing the outside world and increasing contact with members, the individual's commitment to the community is secured. Eventually the movement's ideology is taken on, which draws the person closer to other members as a result of their shared beliefs. When everything can be understood and explained by reference to ideology, the member is armed with a new power to deal with life and a way to combat conflicting views of reality. An ideological perspective provides a sense of order, security, predictability, and meaning, as well as assurances about the fulfillment of prophecy.

Within the Mission, social enclosure took its characteristic form. We have seen that during the screening procedures before the

171

METAMORPHOSIS

Knowledge session those who were following another guru were asked to leave. The belief was that, once the individual had received the Knowledge, there was no need to be committed to any other teacher or method, since the Mission was considered by many as the "ultimate path." The consequence was to diminish the strength of competing obligations so the initiate's life could be focused more completely on the Mission's goals and activities. It is true that some premies were involved in The Church of World Messianity, but that was frowned upon by the Mission's leadership. Eventually, the leaders became openly opposed to this dual membership and urged premies to quit The Church of World Messianity so they could invest more of their energies and resources in the Mission. This pressure came primarily from Mahatmas and organizational leaders, and its effect was to deepen the involvement of some premies, while others defected (as we will discover later in Joan's case).

While the leaders were encouraging the renunciation of competing commitments, social communion between premies was being fostered by their frequent attendance at satsang, their interaction with other premies during the performance of various services, their sharing of common meals and living arrangements, and by periodic programs during which masses of premies came together for several days to praise Guru Maharaj Ji and the Knowledge. In fact, the most powerful sources of social communion among premies were their mutual respect and love for the guru and their recognition that they were united in the spirit. This gave them a group identity and distinguished them from the outside world.

Mortification

"Mortification helps destroy the old self, prideful and oriented to the standards and status of the outside. It paves the way for the person to gain a sense of self and a new source of status and self-esteem. . . . At the same time, through mortification, the new self is oriented around devotion, loyalty, and obedience to the movement."[7] A guru may self-consciously set out to diminish the hold of the follower's ego by mortifying it through a series of humbling experiences, believing it is when the ego has lost its self-importance in relation to God's

172

METAMORPHOSIS

greatness that an inner revolution is possible. Thus, mortification may be regarded as a necessary and positive step by both the guru and his devotees.

From 1971 to 1973, but less so today, mortification was prevalent in the Mission. This had the effect of destroying the widespread hippie identity, along with its costume and lifestyle. As Tina said: "My identity as an American, dropout bum with middle-class upbringing and Catholic background began to fade away. Guru Maharaj Ji just showed me my true identity. And there I was with nothing to attach myself to. I couldn't do the same old things. There was now a deeper meaning to my life."

New premies were encouraged to change the way they looked and behaved. "In 1972, our ashram was a loose, hippie-type place, but Guru Maharaj Ji put a stop to that. First of all, the guys were told to get haircuts and shave off their beards. Some people really freaked out about that because they hadn't realized that whole game was over." As late as 1976, there was a move underway within the Mission to extinguish the remnants of the hippie language from premie communications, to remove such expressions as "freaked out," "far out," "right on," and "spaced out." It was this assault on the hippie identity which helped to prepare the way for a new self-image.

Even before these young people had joined the movement in 1972, they were expected, as part of the eastern tradition, to humble themselves before God, Guru Maharaj Ji, his Mahatmas, and his family. Seeking entry to the Knowledge session was itself a reminder of their inferior position, as they submitted to the authority of the Mahatmas, hoping they would get in.

In 1973, I attended a screening session where the Mahatma had to decide which of about thirty people would be admitted into the Knowledge session. When he entered the room there was a noticable change in people's behavior as they began to relate to him as if he were a highly evolved spiritual being. Several people prostrated to him, their bodies and faces flat against the floor. The Mahatma asked everyone in the room a question to determine the extent of their sincerity, and from time to time he selected someone whom he thought was ready to receive the Knowledge. When he had finished

173

METAMORPHOSIS

choosing people, a half dozen of the rejected rushed up to him, prostrated at his feet, and begged him to let them into the session, which, I discovered later, was standard practice.

The humble position of premies was also emphasized by the great social distance between them and Guru Maharaj Ji. This distance was inspired by the presence of the guru's bodyguard, whose appearance served to create an aura of power around him, by special rooms set aside only for his use, by pictures of him surrounded by flowers, and by the use of platforms which elevated him above his followers. There were also times when premies had to wait as much as two hours for him to arrive at a program. To an outside observer, such behavior would probably be viewed as arrogant and inconsiderate, but to premies it was a lesson, in that it challenged their egos.

Even when the guru seemed to consciously humble them, they could find a lesson in it, as we see in the following account. One morning I was in Denver outside of the ashram waiting for Guru Maharaj Ji to come out, and there were quite a few other people hanging around too. Somebody came down and told us to get in line, that he was going to give us darshan, to be with us in person. Then somebody else came down in a while and told us he was watching television and he wouldn't be down for an hour. We stayed around for that hour and then somebody else came down and told us it would be even later. So we sat around some more. Then someone else told us to stand in line again for darshan, so we got in line again. This went on and on. It was driving me crazy. Then we were told to go into the ashram and prenam, you know, to prostrate, in front of his picture. I was thinking, 'What is this bullshit? He's upstairs watching the tube. This is ridiculous!" So I went in, and as soon as I prenamed, it felt really good. I found myself thinking, 'It's pretty nice down here. I could just stay here forever.' But one of the Mahatmas was there and poking people to move on. So I got up really feeling lightheaded. He'd done something to me! It was a perfect lesson. He was trying to tell us that darshan is not his physical body. If you get greedy and dive for his feet as soon as he walks by, that's not going to do it because he controls it. He can give you darshan at any time right where you are. He doesn't have to be there personally. That was a good lesson and I was so happy afterwards."

174

METAMORPHOSIS

Regimentation is another way an old identity is undermined. This was especially common after the Guru Puja festival in 1972, when an exhaustive set of rules governing life in the ashrams was laid down. Premies who wished to live there were required to sign oaths of poverty, chastity, and obedience and to follow the ashram routine religiously. This meant rising in the morning at 4:30 A.M., singing Arti, a devotional song, and sitting in meditation for an hour. Breakfast followed, then service: tasks assigned by ashram officials who were considered channels for the expression of the guru's will. Therefore, obedience to organizational leaders was regarded as obedience to Guru Maharaj Ji. This resulted in a fairly disciplined atmosphere, which tended to homogenize premie behavior.

As was the case for all meals, lunch was vegetarian and lasted about an hour. In the afternoon, service was continued, although premies could not leave the ashram without signing out and then only after permission had been granted. Only those on official business were allowed to leave. Visiting friends or just strolling around the city were unacceptable uses of time, for all of their effort was supposed to be concentrated on the achievement of the Mission's goals.

Dinner was normally served at 5:30, followed by satsang, which lasted about two hours. After satsang, they meditated one hour, then retired for the night. Each day the same general routine was followed, although I observed quite a lot of flexibility as individuals were given considerable freedom to act contrary to the rules.

Although life was quite regimented in the ashrams in 1972, there were other living arrangements outside of the ashrams which were more open and flexible. For a while, there were Premie Centers around the country where fewer rules and restrictions existed. Premie houses developed very early as loosely structured cooperatives, where there was, and continues to be, almost no regimentation at all. As a result, premies have always had some discretion about the type of involvement and living arrangements they want.

Surrender

While mortification tended to undermine a premie's old identity, surrender to Guru Maharaj Ji supplied a new one, as each premie

175

identified with, idealized, obeyed, and lost the capacity to criticize him.

Premies developed an emotional tie to the guru through identification, for he was regarded as the perfect manifestation of the universal spirit and of the changes they wanted for themselves. Strongly identifying with him and the spirit, they began to internalize new values through his example. They tried the best they could to measure up to him or to the standards established for them as devotees.

While identification with Guru Maharaj Ji was encouraged within the premie community, the belief he was the Lord set him at a great psychological and social distance from his followers. Premies were able to accept the notion that he represented the ideal state of being they should strive to achieve, but they could not quite entertain the possibility of reaching it. This created some confusion, as we see in the following comment: "Guru Maharaj Ji is so awesome I really don't identify with him, although that is where I hope to be sooner or later."

Idealizing the guru by alluding to his extraordinary spiritual powers aided the premies' identification with him, encouraged their surrender to the inner spirit, and gave them assurances about change. Having seen the futility of their own efforts, they seemed to project superhuman powers onto him so that their transformation and their hopes for a peaceful and loving world could be guaranteed. The tendency to idealize him was so great among some premies that they actually believed that, had he willed it, he could have single-handedly changed the world.

Believing the guru to be a saint, premies were ready to conform to his wishes (as well as they could), while many lost the capacity to criticize him. Even during the height of the public scandals which hit the Mission in its formative period, I did not hear premies express even one critical comment about the guru. Given their view of him as the Lord, it was as clearly outside the realm of possibility for them to oppose or criticize him in any way as for Moses to have told God that he wanted to edit the Ten Commandments.

Devotion to Guru Maharaj Ji seems similar to the type of unquestioning affection children feel for their parents during the time

176

before adolescence when they are emotionally merged with them. This is one of the reasons that, once formed, a follower's strong emotional bond with a leader is so hard to break, especially when the leader is viewed as divine. This dependence may be a positive experience for the follower, however, in the sense that it creates both security and trust, which pave the way for a change of identity and values. Erik Erikson has called this stage of development the "psychosocial moratorium." It is the time when the child's high regard for and trust of the parents provides the basis for an identity and an accompanying set of values. The security of this trusting and affectionate relationship, he argues, takes the pressure off of the child and therefore nurtures the formation of the child's identity.[8] Applying Erikson's approach to the case of Malcolm X, who had developed a devotional relationship to Elijah Muhammad, I have proposed the possibility that a follower's emotional attachment to a leader may culminate in a new identity and may lead, as it did in Malcolm X's case, to independence.[9] There is no assurance that autonomy will develop, however, and this is a pitfall premies should be aware of. I believe there is a time when the devotee's autonomy from a guru, like independence from one's parents, should be achieved, otherwise surrender remains only an instrument of social control to serve the guru's ends, rather than a means of bringing the person into an individual relationship to God and the world.

The emotional disengagement of children from their parents seems to take a natural course, but for adults who have emotionally merged with a guru becoming more independent must be more conscious and deliberate. A danger is that, by idealizing the guru, the devotee preserves the distance between them so it always appears as if more needs to be done. This of course provides the devotee with the rationale for the continuation of dependence on him. Some followers may be able to face the trauma of separation, while others may have to be pushed away when the time is right.

If both guru and devotee are psychologically or socially dependent on the relationship, then neither are likely to initiate a rift and the devotee may become permanently fixed in that regressive state, never to go beyond the role of obedient child. This stunts the devotee's personal development by keeping him or her trapped in the collective, so what is uniquely individual is never brought to the foreground and nurtured. It seems to me that a good guru, like a good parent, would encourage his followers to discover their uniqueness, so they might exist in the world with full command of their potential.

Some people oppose the guru-devotee relationship because they feel it represses the individuality and sense of personal responsibility of the follower. They warn against the dangers of surrender, while they praise individualism, feeling that each person possesses sufficient resources to reach enlightenment without having to give up autonomy.

Such people would not be surprised to hear that mortification played a role in the Mission in 1972, for they would regard that as confirmation of their suspicions about gurus and what they see as the dubious ends they serve. From a western perspective, this position is understandable. Yet, to be objective, we need to understand mortification and surrender as they are viewed in the eastern spiritual tradition. Perhaps we will be able to put what Guru Maharaj Ji says and does into a broader context by examining the eastern view of the guru's role in general.

The Revolutionary Role of Gurus

Seen from the eastern perspective, the guru's role is revolutionary, not in the sense of overthrowing a political order, but in overturning his or her followers' perception of the world. In this sense, the guru is regarded as the destroyer of socially conditioned patterns and the creator of a new way of being in the world. As Krishnamurti has said: "Real revolt, true revolution is to break away from the pattern and to inquire outside of it." [10]

Therefore, shattering his followers' world view is one of the most pressing tasks of the guru, a view expressed by Don Juan, Carlos Castaneda's guru in *Tales of Power*. "The first act of the teacher is to introduce the idea that the world we think we see is only a view, a description of the world. Every effort of the teacher is geared to prove

178

this point to his apprentice. But accepting it seems to be one of the hardest things one can do; we are complacently caught in our particular view of the world. A teacher, from the very first act he performs, aims at stopping that view. Sorcerers call it stopping the internal dialogue, and they are convinced that it is the single most important technique that an apprentice can learn." [11]

With this goal in mind, gurus encourage their followers to question their own beliefs and concepts as a way of preparing them to see a new world. This has been an overriding appeal in Guru Maharaj Ji's satsang, for starting in 1971 he has urged premies to see through and become detached from concepts. "If you want to stay in the world," he has said, "be like a lotus flower which stays in the dirty water. You can live in the world of concepts, but live in such a way so that they don't affect you." [12]

Gurus also speak frequently of the need to quiet the mind so that the spirit can be experienced more directly and fully. In fact, this is one of the chief purposes of meditation as a spiritual practice. Like most gurus, Guru Maharaj Ji speaks often about the need to quiet the inner dialogue, recommending meditation as a way to silence the personality's various voices which incessantly jabber within and prevent a direct experience of the spirit. His position is similar to Krishnamurti's, who has said: "When the mind is swept clean of image, of ritual, of belief, of symbol, of all words, mantrams, and repetitions, and of all fear, then what you see will be the real, the timeless, the everlasting, which may be called God; but this requires enormous insight, understanding, patience, and it is only for those who really inquire into what is religion and pursue it day after day to the end." [13]

To approach a guru seeking enlightenment, supposedly one must be eager and willing to change, entering the relationship as Tina did, wanting to be reborn. Then there is a feeling of trust and receptivity which makes the follower ready to give up old patterns for new ones. Guru Maharaj Ji often spoke in this vein in 1972, when he told people to come to him with a childlike heart, empty and ready to be filled up. Bubba Free John, an acclaimed perfect master living with a group of his followers north of San Francisco, is even

179

more straightforward: "You should not approach me if you are not willing to be undone. The Guru does not come to satisfy devotees or disciples. A satisfied disciple is still the one he was. The Guru is only interested in the utter, radical dissolution of that whole limitation that appears as his disciple." [14]

A guru who has realized God is thought to have seen the basic equality of everything at the level of "pure being." It is assumed that his goal is to bring followers to the same level of understanding, so they too may live in harmony with God. Many gurus who demand obedience from their followers are said to utilize the followers' dependence to make them equal eventually, although this is clearer in some spiritual traditions than others. For example, in Zen Buddhism, the Zen Master urges his students to reach enlightenment so they may leave him and go into the world. Shunryu Suzuki has expressed this equality between student and master in many different ways. The following is one: "When everything exists within your big mind, all dualistic relationships drop away. There is no distinction between heaven and earth, man and woman, teacher and disciple. Sometimes a man bows to a woman; sometimes a woman bows to a man. Sometimes the disciple bows to the master; sometimes the master bows to the disciple. A master who cannot bow to his disciple cannot bow to Buddha. Sometimes the master and the disciple bow together to Buddha. Sometimes we may bow to cats and dogs." [15]

It is unclear even today whether Guru Maharaj Ji sees his followers as his spiritual equals, who need only reach his level of enlightenment, for he has made contradictory statements on the issue. On the one hand, he has said that when his followers reach the point where they have learned A, B, and C, then he will already have gone to a new level of perfection of D, E, and F. [16] This puts him forever beyond the reach of his followers, possibly prolonging their dependence on him for guidance and discouraging their ultimate autonomy.

On the other hand, he has also repeatedly emphasized the spiritual equality of everyone, arguing that ego and individuality are the chief obstacles in the way of realizing oneness. For example, a premie asked him in 1971 whether he thought the ego was an illusion

METAMORPHOSIS

which had to be overcome and he answered by saying: "That is 'I,' that is ego, and that has to be overcome. Ego come, delusion come, black light come. Opposite projection. Mind always brings duality, and what is the other word we use for duality? Individual? This is my individual property, that means this is mine, that is yours. Mind brings duality, soul brings reality. That's why there is delusion. Really there is no individuality. When everybody is one, there should be no individuality. Everything should be one. But ego carries the word 'I' with it. 'I' is the individuality, the mind." [17]

While we in the west value individualism, it is seen as an obstacle to happiness and peace in many forms of eastern spirituality, Divine Light Mission being just one case. Humility, seeing one's smallness in the larger picture of life, is regarded as an essential step in the follower's transformation and the world's salvation. This is thought to produce a change of heart in the follower, from wanting power, position, and material goods to loving God and serving humanity. As service to God and humanity supersede personal greed, a new chance for human harmony and peace is believed possible. Seen in this light, mortification and surrender are a revolutionary strategy, the means by which gurus attempt to fundamentally shake the foundations of culture. In this respect, we could say that gurus want to reach deeper than the surface changes which we see so often these days.

Giving Thanks to the Guru

Devotees shower a great deal of affection on their gurus, through smiles and loving glances, by lying prostrate at their feet, and in the offering of flowers and gifts. Giving tokens of appreciation to the guru is, I have been told, a traditionally accepted and expected way for devotees to express their gratitude.

The guru himself may encourage the giving of gifts, both to allow devotees to express their growing feelings of love and to counteract selfishness and dependence on material objects. By expressing love toward the guru (which is also to say the universal spirit), devotees are learning to love others in a new way. Guru Maharaj Ji has said: "You think that your wife, your husband, your children will

181

METAMORPHOSIS

give you love? No. It is the love of selfishness. Baby loves mother because mother gives him milk, but not because they have a connection. No, just because of selfish love. In the same way, you love everything because of selfishness. But you love guru without selfishness. It is pure and perfect love; it is that love which cannot be disturbed by mind at all." [18]

In the eastern spiritual tradition, giving thanks to a guru is not only a tribute to the guru but to the spirit as well. It is an expression of thanksgiving for God's grace and a recognition on the part of devotees that nothing really belongs to them and what is given to them is theirs only to use for a time. By giving, devotees believe they are returning to God what they have received through His grace.

Giving gifts to the guru is also considered a way of learning how to become free of attachments to the material world. Whether it is a memento or a large sum of money, those who give in order to break their dependence on materialism are thought to experience a new sense of freedom. Yet, as one premie told me, breaking such dependence does not mean devotees will denounce material comforts, but only that they will no longer rely on material goods for their happiness and peace.

The Lifestyles of Gurus

Many of the luxuries surrounding America's new gurus are gifts from their followers. Guru Maharaj Ji is not alone among the new gurus who are surrounded by material comforts. A casual glance at the lifestyles of other gurus in America does not turn up any signs of poverty. This raises an obvious question: Why is it gurus insist on their followers becoming detached from the material world, while they seem to be completely immersed in it?

Detachment means losing dependence to students of eastern thought. A guru may be surrounded with material luxuries, they believe, and not depend on them in the least for his peace and happiness. Trungpa, Rinpoche, a Tibetan Buddhist teacher, has expressed this idea: "Then, of course, the next step is giving away one's possessions. But this is not necessarily connected to austerity. It does not mean that you should not own anything at all or that you should give

182

away what you have immediately. You could have a great wealth and many possessions and you could even enjoy them and like having them and probably you have a personal interest in them—like a child's toy, or adult's toy for that matter. It isn't a question of not seeing the value of possessions, the point is that it should be equally easy to give them away."[19]

The western mind tends to see this as a rationalization of self-indulgent behavior. Yet, while many people feel gurus have accumulated more than their share of wealth, their followers believe they are getting no more than what they deserve. From the premie point of view, for instance, Guru Maharaj Ji's opulent lifestyle seems in harmony with their view of him as the Lord. They want him to live like the king that they feel he is. Idealizing him as they do, they are more than happy to supply him with luxuries.

From this perspective, Guru Maharaj Ji's opulence can be understood as a natural outgrowth of his followers' need to idealize him and to set him at a sufficiently great distance so that beliefs in his extraordinary powers are preserved. In short, premies have a stake in maintaining his luxurious way of living. The fact is that followers, not leaders, are the chief obstacles to equality, for followers need to elevate the leader so they have an ideal to strive toward. This point of view may seem strange, yet, if we look at other spiritual movements across the country, we find other followers elevating their gurus to a high spiritual status and surrounding them with material goods.

While we can partially explain Guru Maharaj Ji's lifestyle in terms of collective dynamics, another point of view would question why he has accepted the luxuries premies have gladly given him. Several explanations could be offered: that he is following tradition; that he recognizes his followers' need to elevate him to a point where he becomes the ideal to emulate; that he sees no conflict between his lifestyle and his spiritual mission; and that he is not attached to the comforts surrounding him. Of course, there is also the possibility that he is ambitious and materialistic, as so many people believe.

It is difficult to understand the motives behind Guru Maharaj Ji's lifestyle, just as it is impossible to know whether he is, as premies believe, an authentic saint. I have thought about this issue a great

METAMORPHOSIS

deal and have come to the conclusion that there is no way of knowing, by objective measures, whether the guru is authentic or not. That can only be determined subjectively, for, as one premie told me, "You can only see Guru Maharaj Ji with your heart." Instead of considering the guru's motives and authenticity, perhaps it would be more constructive to ask whether his followers have benefited from their relationship to him and what impact his efforts are having on our society.

chapter
TWELVE
Changes

In 1972, many of these premies spoke with conviction about their *"rebirth,"* as if some miraculous transformation had taken place. Looking back later, in 1976, they were more apt to describe their conversion as a gradual change, which, through their everyday experience of the Knowledge, had deepened their appreciation of life and expanded their ability to love and live in harmony with others. Most agreed with the premie who said, "I wouldn't call my conversion a 'rebirth,' rather it was and continues to be an unfolding process."

I waited five years to complete this study in order to observe the changes in the movement and in the lives of premies. I fully expected that some would become disillusioned and leave, giving me the opportunity to examine how people defect from movements. Of the eighteen premies interviewed in 1972, three did leave the Mission, all before Millennium 1973.

I will turn to the three defectors in the following chapter. Here, I want to explore some of the changes which have taken place in the movement and in the thinking of the premies who remain active. In 1976, an extensive questionnaire was mailed to the fifteen who were still committed, covering a wide variety of topics. Thirteen of the fif-

185

CHANGES

teen responded, many in great detail. From other sources, I know
that the two who failed to reply are still active in the movement and
show no signs of leaving. In addition, a detailed evaluation of
changes in the organization and in premie beliefs and attitudes was
secured through a premie whose intimate Knowledge of the Mission
is impressive. She has had close contact with the national headquarters in Denvèr and with local premie communities. Together,
these two sources of information offer an illuminating picture of the
changes which took place prior to the close of 1976, and of the dramatic shift in the movement's direction in 1977 as a charismatic revival was begun which elevated Guru Maharaj Ji once again to the
status of Lord.

As 1976 drew to an end, the Mission had been shaken by a
number of changes which had relegated Guru Maharaj Ji to the
status of "humanitarian leader" and had stimulated more independence on the part of premies. Bureaucratic or corporate principles
had replaced the mass movement character of the Mission. Devotion
and surrender to Guru Maharaj Ji were being played down by the bureaucratic leadership. As a result of encouragement from the guru,
premies were leaving the ashrams in rising numbers. Contributions
were falling off, due in part to the decentralization of the organization. And many premies were becoming almost as interested in their
personal careers as in the future of the Mission.

Essentially, the movement was in a state of crisis: If the trend
continued moving in the direction of bureaucratic domination and
excessive individualism, then there was a chance the Mission might
lose its mass character and degenerate into a cult, leaving Guru
Maharaj Ji's goal of world peace to die for lack of interest, enthusiasm, and manpower. Reacting to this situation, the guru took the initiative halfway through 1976 by asking two members of the Board of
Directors, including the President, to step down from their posts and
to assume a different form of service within the movement.

Later that year, he met with premies for a program in Atlantic
City. I do not believe this was a calculated attempt on his part to extend his authority, for as early as January he had mentioned the need
for more programs: "As you know, when premies receive Knowledge,
I become more involved with them, and every year it's been more

186

and more. As a matter of fact, we've been thinking about putting in a few more programs. Why limit it to the dates of Guru Puja? We want to have them so that more premies can come and we can get more involved and that love can evolve around us more and more."[1]

During the Atlantic City program, a spontaneous feeling of devotion and surrender to the guru occurred, reviving the millennial atmosphere reminiscent of 1971–72, and including the beliefs surrounding his widely acclaimed divinity. Against a background of increasing secularization and bureaucratization, premies were ready for a charismatic renewal.

This is the classic struggle between the bureaucratic and charismatic forces in history, which Max Weber considered the dynamic of social change. As a type of authority, bureaucracy leans toward order and efficiency, while charisma introduces creative disorder through heroic leaders who demand the personal loyalty of their followers in order to expand their potential to change the world. It was this conflict between the tendencies of order and disorder which Weber saw as the source of fundamental change in society.[2]

Premies have responded enthusiastically to the call of Initiators (formerly "Mahatmas") for personal rededication to Guru Maharaj Ji. Affected by a growing sense of confusion and despair about the Mission's future by the end of 1976 and by increasingly secular interests, they were ready for a change in their commitment.

Curious to discover how these fifteen premies reacted to this situation, I sent a short questionnaire to them in March 1977. Their responses offer a dramatic and fascinating contrast to their attitudes toward Guru Maharaj Ji just a few months earlier, which is testimony to the power of charisma as a catalyst of social change. Yet to fully understand how this charismatic revival came about, we need to look at the changes in the movement which prepared the way for countless premies to surrender once again.

Changes in the Movement

By 1973, the Mission had been pretty well decimated by the press, as one scandal after another reached public attention. First, there was

187

the claim by the Indian government that Guru Maharaj Ji and his family had smuggled jewels and large sums of money into the country, a charge which was eventually dropped with apologies from the government. Later, a member of the press who had thrown a pie into Guru Maharaj Ji's face as a prank was beaten into unconsciousness by one of the movement's most noted Mahatmas and at least two other premies. Then, of course, there were numerous newspaper accounts of the guru's life-style, which pictured him as more interested in accumulating wealth and power than in changing the world.

That premies had lost their capacity for criticism was fairly clear to me, for not once in all my many references to these scandals or charges did they criticize Guru Maharaj Ji. Many rationalized the scandals and his life-style as a part of his plan. Others argued that even bad publicity about the Mission was good, because it at least made people aware of the guru and the movement. Some blamed those around the guru. At that time, premies were thinking that Guru Maharaj Ji was so spiritually perfect and powerful he could do no wrong and that no obstacle was big enough to stop him from reaching his goal of ushering in the new age of peace.

These beliefs spawned serious hopes that during the Millennium festival in 1973 a new age would dawn in Houston. Manifestations of this hope were to be found in the many speculations and prophesies about what would happen under the Astrodome. Premies expected thousands to descend on the festival itself, and many millions watching the proceedings on television to see for the first time how spiritually pure their guru was and how compelling his message.

Fed by rumors before the festival that something earth-shattering might happen there, premies lost no time imagining that the teenage guru was going to let out all the stops and turn the earth on its axis. Then there were the sometimes frivolous but often serious predictions that beings from outer space would descend on the Astrodome. As one premie close to the Denver organization told me later, even premies who were normally quite realistic in their views were taken in by these collective fantasies.

As the festival approached, all attention within the premie community turned toward Houston. Expectations were running high that something very cosmic was about to happen there. Curious to experience it firsthand, I flew to Houston and made my way to the festival. Fighting through pickets from the local fundamentalist Christian community who were freely expressing their hatred toward the "false Messiah," I made my way into the Astrodome. Contrary to the predictions I had heard, it was nowhere near filled to capacity.

As I discovered later, the turnout had been very disappointing to many premies. Also disappointing to many was the response of the press corps, which had been amassed there as part of the Mission's effort to publicize the movement. They had hoped the festival would trigger a change in the attitudes of newspaper and television newsmen and newswomen, but just the opposite occurred. Representatives from the media became quite hostile toward the guru in his first press conference, charging that his answers to their questions were flippant and arrogant.

With the crowd smaller than expected and an alienated press corps, premies waited for something miraculous to happen. Yet, by the end of the festival, even that expectation was unfulfilled. No beings from outer space had come and no dramatic display of cosmic energy had lit up the Astrodome. Although premies tried hard to find good things to say about the festival, it seemed to me that ruined dreams were hidden under their exuberance.

Before the festival, the Mission's goals and activities had been quite extravagant, reflecting the community's confidence that the movement would succeed. Afterwards, the organization was left with a $600,000 debt, and worse, the loss of its millennial dream of world peace. Immediately, the production and distribution of its publications were curtailed to meet financial obligations. Programs were cut back as the premie community began to realize that the mass of humanity was not going to flock to Guru Maharaj Ji to receive the Knowledge, as they had so fervently believed. Their enthusiasm for propagating the Knowledge collapsed under the weight of reality. "When I received the Knowledge in 1971, the general feeling was that soon the whole world would have peace, so to hold onto anything, like money, job, education, or family, was a sign of a weak level of devotion. After Millennium, there was a lot of disappoint-

189

CHANGES

ment and change. People couldn't believe that we would have to go on living in the same old world. I had to really examine what I wanted to do, since the excitement was over. As I didn't have an official position within the organization at that point, I decided I would just get a job and lead a calm life. I just couldn't get into leafleting or the usual Mission trips."

Faced with a diminished interest in saving the world, the movement turned back upon itself while premies paused to question and evaluate their commitments. Soon, simplicity in practicing the Knowledge had replaced the complex web of activities which had developed during the expansion phase of the movement. Premie Centers were closed down. Plans for hospitals and schools were set aside, although the school in Denver and a few clinics are still operating today.

For several months after Millennium, the Mission's leadership was preoccupied with internal issues, especially its debt and the problems of commitment. Forces were being regrouped and a great deal of discussion was taking place at all levels about the future of the Mission and what premies could do to get people interested in Guru Maharaj Ji and the Knowledge.

This was also a time for organizational change. Needing a focus for their energies, the leadership quite naturally began to reevaluate the structure of the Mission and to propose different ways of realigning its various departments and their functions. In response to the letdown of the festival, many premies were just content to withdraw temporarily into silence and isolation, happy to let the leadership play with their organizational charts and fantasies. This was a time when they were asking themselves why and when: why were they committed and when, if ever, would the goals of the Mission be reached.

The first rumbling of the family feud between Guru Maharaj Ji and his mother began to be heard in 1974 and was soon picked up by the press corps and publicized as still another sign of the decadence of the Mission. The beginning of this feud dated back to the time when Guru Maharaj Ji first came to the United States against his mother's wishes. In India, his mother, Mata Ji, and eldest brother,

CHANGES

Bal Bhagwan Ji, had exercised a great deal of control over the Mission due to the guru's age. That influence was still quite evident by 1973, for I was told by an official of the Mission that it was they, not Guru Maharaj Ji, who were the main instigators of the Millennium festival. Bal Bhagwan Ji was in charge of the festival and, according to Sophia Collier's account in *Soul Rush*, he was also the source of many outlandish rumors; that the stock market would dive, that 400,000 would turn up at the festival, and that natural and political disasters would be augmented by the appearance of extraterrestrial phenomena.[3]

After the festival, there was a decided change in the guru's attitude about his role in the Mission. Nearly sixteen, he was ready to assume a more active part in deciding what direction the movement should take. This of course meant that he had to encroach on his mother's territory and, given the fact that she was accustomed to having control, a fight was inevitable.

The end of 1973 saw Guru Maharaj Ji breaking away from his mother and his Indian past. He declared himself the sole source of spiritual authority in the Mission. And, unlike some gurus who have come to this country and have easternized their followers, he became more fully westernized, which premies interpreted as an attempt to integrate his spiritual teachings into our culture.

The conflict with his mother became more intense when his brother, Raja Ji, married Claudia Littman, a German citizen living in the United States. No longer wishing to be bound by the Indian tradition of marrying within one's own caste, Guru Maharaj Ji approved his brother's marriage, to the very great displeasure of his mother, who was still strongly tied to Indian customs. When Guru Maharaj Ji himself decided to marry outside of his caste, his mother became upset because she had not been asked to approve the marriage and, when it occurred, she was not invited to attend because communication between them had already broken down.

My own impressions of the situation fit the official interpretation of what happened next. "In an attempt to maintain control of the Indian Mission and the assets in that country, Mata Ji and Bal Bhagwan Ji returned to India. When they learned of Maharaj Ji's plan to

191

return there for a visit, they mounted a campaign to defame him and to interfere with his expected arrival. Mata Ji said that she was removing Maharaj Ji as Perfect Master because of his 'unspiritual' life-style and his lack of respect for her wishes."[4]

During a press conference in Lucknow, India, Guru Maharaj Ji responded to his mother's action by explaining that she had no authority to depose him because a Perfect Master is "self-existent" and no one can appoint or remove him. He felt his mother's and brother's misunderstanding stemmed from the fact that neither had recognized what the role of the Perfect Master is, even during his father's reign as satguru. He said: "They never really understood that the power of the Perfect Master is not a worldly power of dominion over people, but simply the power to bring peace and fulfillment to people's lives."[5]

Actually, the split with his mother seemed to solidify the loyalty of many premies to him, for Mata Ji's attack on his spiritual authority brought them to his defense. Perhaps an even more important factor was his marriage to Marolyn Johnson of San Diego, for she had been a "typical premie" and her marriage to Guru Maharaj Ji somehow symbolized to other premies a deepening of their own relationship to him.

After the family feud, the movement in the United States became even more fully bureaucratized and westernized. Gradually, many of the movement's Indian traditions and rituals were eliminated, even though the Indian overtones of 1971–72 had added an element of mystery which helped to strengthen commitments.

As we know, Mahatmas were demystified. By the end of 1974 they were called "Initiators" and were no longer viewed as "great souls." Many of the Indian Mahatmas who had inspired such awe had either left the movement or had been demoted from their positions as Initiators. Today, American premies become Initiators through application and personal selection by Guru Maharaj Ji. Unlike Mahatmas, who wore the distinctive orange saffron robes, Initiators now wear no special costumes to distinguish themselves from other premies.

Changes in terminology were made in an attempt to divorce the

192

CHANGES

Mission from its Indian trappings. "Festivals" became "regional conferences." "Holy Company," a term used to describe the state of being in the presence of other premies, fell from use, as did the customary Indian greeting.

With this weakening of eastern influences, premies began to change their attitudes toward Guru Maharaj Ji. Since the Mission was moving in a more secular direction, it was understandable that premies would begin to view the guru in a less cosmic way. Thus, by 1975 the official line was that Guru Maharaj Ji was to be regarded as "humanitarian leader," rather than Lord of the Universe. The word circulated that Guru Maharaj Ji himself had initiated this change, although apparently that was not the case. For whatever reason, by 1976 it was customary for premies to view him in human rather than divine terms. This change was reflected in the fact that pronouns referring to him were no longer capitalized. His demystification followed the march toward fuller secularization of the movement, which reached such an extreme there were rumors that the movement's name might even be changed to something "less cosmic."

During 1975, premies were turning to encounter group methods within the Mission as a way of extending their own growth and augmenting their sense of community. In December of that year, Guru Maharaj Ji gave the opening satsang at a conference of 250 premies working in the Denver headquarters. During the sessions which followed, various workshop and group dynamics techniques were employed by the Mission's executive leadership. Since the guru had given satsang there, premies assumed he had given his blessings to the use of these psychological processes. This stimulated widespread use of these and similar techniques across the country.

Actually, Guru Maharaj Ji had not liked the idea of the workshops and had not supported them. This came out later when he said he felt the workshops were not of any real benefit to a person seeking an experience of the Truth, then reaffirmed the necessity of satsang for that purpose. In fact, he had been saying that premies should be seeking "real understanding" of their experience and that satsang was the key. "So there's a common understanding that every one of us has to have with each other, and that relationship can only be formed

193

when we have more satsang. Because what am I doing right now? I'm explaining something to you and I'm putting an idea into you, into your brain: 'What is this?' . . . I am giving you satsang. There is the Truth behind it, and I am trying to bring you into the company of Truth more and more and more and more. I am trying to bring you to real satsang so we can *really* understand."[6]

So, as Guru Maharaj Ji's position on the encounter groups became clearer even that direction for premies collapsed, causing more confusion about the form their commitments should take. In 1971, premies had their commitments strengthened by surrender, with its underlying mechanisms of identification and conformity. By 1976, the Mission's leadership was apparently discouraging blind surrender. Where, in 1971, premies needed only to conform and obey their "Lord," by 1976 they were being asked to take responsibility to interpret, initiate, and act. Once highly regulated by a set of well-defined expectations, the behavior of premies could take many forms, a change which led to even greater ambiguity.

As surrender and devotion were discarded, reliance shifted to the tangible benefits of practicing the Knowledge, of living within the premie community, and of participating more fully within the local areas. This new emphasis on more democratic participation was being well received among premies in 1976, as we hear from one who applauded the idea of dispersing power from the top to the grass roots. "The movement is changing all the time. More and more responsibility is being placed with premies in the local communities for planning and initiating activities. The 'big government' of earlier years is ending and control is being placed at the grass roots level. If I want to get something done I have more freedom to get together with other premies and just do it, rather than waiting to see if its all right. People like to see results, whether it is child care, a satsang program, or a fund-raiser. Results can come from individual communities and can fit premie needs."

After shuffling the top leadership of the Mission, Guru Maharaj Ji began to decentralize organizational initiative and power by turning some of the decision-making over to local premie communities, while he maintained his status as the ultimate authority over spiritual and secular matters. This move stimulated another change in the movement by encouraging independent action on the part of premies. For example, the guru had inspired greater autonomy by saying in January 1976: "Don't expect that all these premies who are in the ashram right now are going to *stay* in the ashram. I *hope* they don't."[7] This comment had the effect of producing a widespread exodus from the ashrams that year, which gave rise to an individualistic attitude. This was reflected in Alan's outlook at the close of 1976. "Everyone is beginning to see that Divine Light Mission is just a bunch of people trying to meditate and love each other. All the holier-than-thou bullshit is crumbling. I don't have to wait for Guru Maharaj Ji to communicate through all the layers of leadership to me in order to learn what I need to know. Just a few months ago, I was still looking to Denver for guidance, but that is changing."

Alan felt this change in attitude was actually initiated at every level of the organization, but mostly with premies who were sincere about what they were doing and no longer needed a Board of Directors to tell them what to do, and how and when to do it. The tendency was to minimize the emphasis on converting the masses, which was a sign premies were becoming more committed to their individual paths than to the collective undertaking they had begun together. Alan expressed this general lack of commitment to maintain and expand the movement. "Only the necessities, such as taking care of Guru Maharaj Ji, arranging tours, etc., will be taken care of by the central organization of the Mission. Everything else will be taken care of by the local premie communities. The current growth is not in numbers but in spirit. I don't have any save-the-world delusions anymore. Perhaps soon we will be ready to actively spread the Knowledge again. Meanwhile, I'm going to relax and enjoy myself. I'm not worried about the fate of the Mission. I don't feel compelled to try to convert people just to expand our membership. I also don't feel compelled to restrain people who choose to leave the ashram or the Mission."

The sense of independence expressed by Alan was the trend by the close of 1976. It was a contributing factor, I feel, in the exodus of premies from the ashrams, the emphasis on the development of careers outside the Mission, the group dynamics phase, and the general lack of interest in propagation. "A quick look at Divine Light Mission today might lead one to believe that it is falling to pieces," Alan said that year. "In fact, Divine Light Mission, as we know it, may not exist too much longer. Premies are now leaving the ashrams in droves—officially, at the rate of 2 to 3 per day. That may not seem like much, but, at that rate all the ashrams will be empty by the end of the year. The staff in Denver was 250 just a couple of months ago. Now it is 80. Donations have dropped in half. Nobody knows for sure what is happening, why it is happening, or if we will weather the crisis."

Confused, premies were ready for a change which would stabilize the situation and provide some coherence to their place in the Mission and the Mission's place in the world. Trying to escape this unstable balance, they were beginning to return to the ashrams on their own in the fall of 1976. During the Atlantic City program, they were ready for a charismatic revival, for it promised to create order from the chaos. (In early 1976 I had written that the Mission seemed to be showing signs of increasing social disorganization as a result of the individualistic trend premies were following. At the time, I wondered if the Mission's days as a mass movement were over.)

Since the charismatic resurgence of 1977, there have been few indications the movement is returning to the form of bureaucratic domination which characterized its operations from 1974 to 1976. Today, the guru appears to be organizing the Mission around meditation rather than management principles. In November 1976, he referred to changes toward a more managerial mentality in the Mission as "only cosmetic and totally unnecessary. It's like trying to take a cow and put lipstick on it. You can do it, but its unnecessary in practical terms and in terms of any practical purpose. . . . Already these changes have severely affected the premies in America and these changes have also brought about questions that were put to me. . . . The changes were intended to make the organization more efficient. . . . I feel that the kind of approach that was taken was wrong, that it didn't bring efficiency. Actually, it brought deficiency into the system."[8]

196

CHANGES

He went on to discuss a more effective basis for the organization. "There's a much better chance of efficiency in our kind of organization because we understand one basic thing. We understand one fundamental thing and that is Knowledge. . . . Divine Light Mission not only has its purpose but you have to imagine that without Guru Maharaj Ji, all of those purposes are totally useless. . . . If you ask the question, what came first, Guru Maharaj Ji or the Mission, the answer is clear as possible that Guru Maharaj Ji came and made the Mission. So whose Mission is this? It is Guru Maharaj Ji's Mission."[9]

It would be easy to construe this statement as an affirmation of his own authority were it not for the fact that he often uses the name "Guru Maharaj Ji" in a much broader sense. At a conference in January 1976, a premie asked him what he meant when he used the term "Guru Maharaj Ji." Question: "It confuses me when you speak of Guru Maharaj Ji and yourself as different—that Maharaj Ji has taught you or Maharaj Ji teaches or leads you—when you're Maharaj Ji." Answer: "Guru Maharaj Ji that gave me this Knowledge is my guru and that's whom I am referring to. Of course it's not physical. What I am actually referring to is that omnipotent power." Question: "You mean God?" Answer: "Well, we can't really harness Him down into words. It would be kind of hard."[10]

Thus, we need to be reminded that the connection to Guru Maharaj Ji which premies feel is not simply to the guru as teacher, but to the inner Guru Maharaj Ji, or Knowledge, which we could call "God." What was going wrong in 1976, according to one member, was that premies had quit meditating attentively, because the knowledge experience had lost some of its novelty, as a result of familiarity, and thus some of its deeper significance. What the charismatic revival promised, then, was a deeper experience of God.

Signs of rededication both to Guru Maharaj Ji and the inner guru became quite apparent. Most of the premies who left the ashrams in the summer of 1976 began to return in 1977, when more than 600 signed up to enter the ashrams in just a few month's time. According to recent reports, ashram life is going to take a different form, with less involvement directly in the organizational work of the

197

CHANGES

Mission and less control from the top. Instead, it will be more locally based, supported, and controlled. The plans call for an Initiator to live in each ashram to make the Knowledge experience more accessible to people. The ashram may also function, at least in some places, as a short-term retreat from the world for nonashram premies.

Today, in 1979, there is more talk about propagation, although the emphasis is different. Leafleting and direct recruiting on the street are being played down. Instead, premies are being asked to express their understanding of the Knowledge in their daily interactions so others might see the benefits of the Knowledge as it applies to the practical issues of living.

Changing Attitudes Toward Guru Maharaj Ji

The most striking changes in the attitudes of premies up to the end of 1976 revolved around their views of Guru Maharaj Ji. While they still strongly identified with him as a spiritually evolved person and someone to emulate, they had abandoned the messianic beliefs which had elevated him to the status of Avatar, Divine Incarnation, Lord of the Universe, Great King, and Messiah. Beliefs in his omniscience had definitely fallen away, as premies no longer described every event in their lives as a manifestation of his power, grace, or will.

Although there were still residues of belief in his divinity in 1976, the vast majority viewed the guru primarily as their spiritual teacher, guide, and inspiration. John's view was a typical expression of the new attitude. "Basically, I see Guru Maharaj Ji as my teacher. He is the revealer of an experience we call 'Knowledge.' He's not the distant type of teacher, who doesn't know his students. He's a sensitive and careful person who knows human tendencies and problems better than anyone I've seen. The only thing he really wants to see is people living happily and harmoniously together. I'm often struck by how much he deals with the details of life, and how simple his solutions are. At the moment, I relate to him as a humanitarian leader. However, right after my initiation into the movement, I accepted the belief that he was omnipresent and all-powerful. In other words, I

198

believed he was Lord, God Almighty. Gradually, over the last five years, he has become a real human being in my eyes. I no longer put him up on a pedestal to worship as a God. Yet I love and deeply respect him for what he is doing."

Having quit imputing great powers to Guru Maharaj Ji by the end of 1976, premies assumed much more responsibility for their own spiritual growth. No longer did they fall back on the belief that they were being guided or protected by the guru's grace. Nor did they feel as bound to conform to the old ideas of devotion, with their ritualism and conformity.

There was much greater flexibility in the way they were able to apply their understanding of. the Knowledge. The change in Alan's orientation was typical. "When I received the Knowledge, I took on a whole set of religious beliefs and concepts. I thought Guru Maharaj Ji was the Lord, and his mother and brothers were divine beings. I took on a new life-style, became a vegetarian, followed a daily ritual, cut my hair, did service, donated money, sang Arti, prostrated to pictures of Guru Maharaj Ji, and told everyone about him and the Knowledge. Now I know that Guru Maharaj Ji is not the Lord, but a man who happens to know about a beautiful meditation which can help people become happier and more aware of their inner life. I don't care to bow or sing to his pictures anymore and I no longer have an altar in my room. I don't try to force my guru trip on people anymore. I am still a vegetarian and I still try to follow a daily schedule somewhat, but I'm letting my hair grow longer again. I'm not trying to be a saint anymore—that was a real joke. I'm just an ordinary person, not one of the chosen ones. In short, I'm trying to live a simple, unpretentious life."

From the beginning, Guru Maharaj Ji appealed to premies to give up their beliefs and concepts so that they might experience the Knowledge, or life force, more fully. This, as I have said, is one of the chief goals of gurus, to transform their followers' perceptions of the world through deconditioning. Yet Guru Maharaj Ji's emphasis on giving up beliefs and concepts did not prevent premies from adopting a fairly rigid set of ideas about his divinity and the coming of a new age.

During 1971, there were social forces encouraging the develop-

199

ment of millenarian beliefs within the Mission. They were developed in part by the carryover of millennial thinking from the counterculture; by the psychological trappings of surrender and idealization; by the guru's mother, whose satsang was full of references to his divine nature; and partly by the guru, himself, for letting others cast him in the role of the Lord. Given the social pressures within the premie community which reinforced these beliefs, there was little hope premies would be able to relax the hold that their beliefs and concepts had over them.

Only after 1973, when the millenarian beliefs began to wane, were premies ready for an assault on their ideology. There were two sets of beliefs and concepts they had to change: those from their earlier socialization, before receiving the Knowledge, and those they picked up from within the premie community itself.

In a sense, their withdrawal from the counterculture was probably made easier by the rigid beliefs and concepts which were in vogue in 1971–72, for they offered a concrete, alternative way of making sense of the world. Adherence to those beliefs probably contributed to the destruction of what remained of their counterculture ideology. From this point of view, the millenarian beliefs and the Indian customs they followed could be regarded as important for their evolution, since both divorced them from their counterculture life-style and beliefs. Having fully accepted an alternative reality, they were then in a position to question that too. "The flexibility of adapting to the continual changes of belief in the premie subculture comes from practising the Knowledge, which is the one common thread running through all the changes that have taken place. Experience of the Knowledge has been the constant thing, while beliefs have changed. Momentary flashes of insight during meditation, satsang, or darshan are experiences which make it easier to abandon certain beliefs and to adopt new ones. The way I see it, Knowledge is independent of any particular beliefs. The longer one practices the Knowledge, the less one can believe in anything for long."

By 1976, the community had altered its ideology to a more flexible form on the assumption that beliefs, concepts, judgments, and distinctions are obstacles in the way of a deeper experience of life. As a consequence of this increasing flexibility, premies reported a fuller

awareness of their spiritual essence. A greater joy of life, more tolera-
tion of others, an enlarged capacity to accept themselves—these, they
said, were the rewards of breaking through the artificiality of their
beliefs and conceptions of the world. "Just in the last six months, I
have begun to feel connected in a spiritual way to Guru Maharaj Ji. I
came to the point in my life where I had to make a decision. I was
not understanding Divine Light Mission and Guru Maharaj Ji. But
something beautiful has occurred as I've realized that I wasn't fully
getting the benefits of the Knowledge. I rejected much of the facade
surrounding the Mission. Well, to my surprise, I've seen beyond
those facades, to some real truths. It took a long time to let go of my
own concepts, believing they were of some value. Those concepts
held me back from the experience of the Knowledge. I guess Guru
Maharaj Ji didn't fit the image I had wanted him to. Yet, when I really experienced the peace and strength meditation allows me to feel,
my doubts and mistrust of Guru Maharaj Ji have slowly turned into
acceptance. And now I know the importance of meditation. Now I
see that it is the way in which I, the real I, can come through in my
everyday life. I have begun to experience a stronger, more loving and
secure being inside of me. That sounds funny, but when I'm really
into meditation I am clearly seeing myself and that self I see is
beyond all the conditions and limitations that exist in the ego. I am
freer to love and to experience life around me."

In 1976, all outward appearances were that premies had gone
through a major change in personal outlook since 1972, for they
seemed to have evolved from dependence to the point where they
were willing to take personal responsibility. It is true the movement
was beginning to shake somewhat from the reverberations of individualism, but premies seemed generally pleased with the way things
were going; at least, that was the surface impression.

To the surprise of everyone who had come to the Atlantic City
program at the close of 1976, Guru Maharaj Ji appeared in his
Krishna costume, a majestic looking robe and crown he had not
worn since 1975. The sight of him in his ceremonial best brought
premies to their feet singing, as nostalgia for the early days caught
them up in feelings of devotion once more.

Two more programs followed in Portland and Denver within

201

four weeks of each other, to which thousands of premies came from all parts of the country. Again, the guru appeared in his Krishna costume and, again, the old devotional songs were sung. The atmosphere was reminiscent of 1972, as Initiators began to spread the word that the time had come for a renewal of dedication and devotion to "their Lord." Acting as the vanguard for the charismatic revival, they were the first to speak again of the guru as "Messiah," a statement premies apparently wanted to hear, for since then one of the key messages at satsang has been that the guru is indeed the Lord, for premies believe he is capable of transmitting his inner light with such power as to awaken the spirit lying dormant in others.

On the whole, these premies have responded warmly to the resurrection of surrender and devotion. Alan, for example, had reached the point in 1976 where he was sure he no longer wanted to put Guru Maharaj Ji on a pedestal. Yet he has been swept back into surrender by the rising devotional sentiment in the Mission today. "We are seeing once again that the most important thing on the path of Knowledge is Guru Maharaj Ji. I know he gave me the Knowledge and that he is constantly helping me on the path, directly through his darshan and satsang, and indirectly in so many other ways. He gives me the opportunity to live in his ashram, to have satsang with his premies, to do service, and meditate. I am grateful to Guru Maharaj Ji for giving me the chance to have peace of mind and to help others. I am seeing that I am totally incapable of running my life without his guidance. I came to Guru Maharaj Ji in the first place because I was unhappy and needed help. He helped by showing me the source of peace within. I have to devote my life to him because he knows what is best for me. I would rather surrender my life to him than to anyone or anything else. I can't say who or what Guru Maharaj Ji is to anyone else, but what is important to me is that I am once again seeing that he is *my* Lord."

Premies like Alan who had given up their beliefs in Guru Maharaj Ji's messianic role have probably been the most dramatically affected by this charismatic revival, for they have had to radically shift the direction of their feelings. Others, as we see in the case of the following premie, have just found the current change a refreshing op-

202

CHANGES

portunity to reveal what they have long known but were afraid to express because of the climate of group opinion. "For me, Guru Maharaj Ji has always been the Lord, but there were times during the Mission's development when it was not 'cool' to express that idea in public. Recently, it is not so much a belief that Guru Maharaj Ji is the Lord which has come to me, but an understanding that his grace can help me develop a deeper experience of the Knowledge. When we had Knowledge reviews with the Initiators recently, who had had Knowledge reviews themselves directly from Guru Maharaj Ji, it was apparent from what they conveyed that Guru Maharaj Ji thoroughly understands the Knowledge and can lead his devotees to the point of realization. It is for this reason that we develop a desire to surrender to him. He is very precious to his devotees for he gives us the inspiration to keep going on this path."

Not all premies are following in step with the new trend. For instance, John had had a difficult time initially accepting the notion that Guru Maharaj Ji was the Lord. While the movement was operating under the idea that the guru was a humanitarian leader, he was with the majority and feeling comfortable there. Now he seems more removed, still under the influence of his old belief that God is unlikely to visit the earth in human form. "Personally, I don't feel affected by the current resurgence of devotion and surrender. To me, Guru Maharaj Ji is the one who showed me how to meditate, and my experience of meditation has not directed me, so far, towards devotion or surrender to him. My experience has not led me to believe that he is anything except a human being who can show people a way to meditate. It has never been proven to me that he is the Lord, or Messiah, so I do not think of him in that way."

With so many premies coming out in support of devotion, there has been a shift away from secular tendencies back to ritual and messianic beliefs and practices. There is more bowing, more pictures of the guru everywhere, more devotional singing, and Indian terms and expressions are making their way back into the language of premies. Encouraged by Guru Maharaj Ji, there is apparently less insistence on blind conformity to the crowd mentality. More tolerance is being shown as premies admit that individual experiences may differ and

203

each should be respected. For example, the devotional song, Arti, is being sung again, but Guru Maharaj Ji is urging those who are not moved to sing it from the heart to simply remain silent. Speaking to a conference of coordinators in Portland in 1977, he said: "This is really beautiful, you know, that everything is starting to happen over again, that premies are really understanding. But one of the things that we have to be sure about is that when premies do Arti, they understand what they're saying and that they mean it. Because there's no point to just sit there and blab about it and not even mean it. You have to really mean it. You have to really understand it. Because its a prayer. And the same thing with really listening to satsang."

At the moment, premies are being given some discretion about whether they want to participate in the resurrected ritual life. "I tend not to follow all the swings in attitudes that premies seem to manifest as a group," a premie commented. "I do think, however, that the Divine Light Mission leadership forgot an essential aspect of the whole organization; namely, that Guru Maharaj Ji is the reason we all follow the path. As for all the hoopla, chants, and singing, I don't feel comfortable with it. Guru Maharaj Ji said that premies should sing Arti only if they really feel it. I don't, so I don't participate."

At the present time, there is an attempt to find a better balance between independent and dependent forms of action, a move which is likely to prevent the replay of the disorganizing influences of 1976, at least for a time. On the one hand, premies are definitely being encouraged to surrender and to participate fully in the charismatic renewal. On the other hand, those who wish to hold back are being allowed to behave in a way which suits them. Organizationally, the balance is being struck between greater personal commitment to the guru and greater control of local affairs by premies.

Possibly it is the character of the transition the movement is in now, but there are signs of a less rigid orientation toward surrender than in 1971–72. Having had a taste of independence in 1976, perhaps premies are not anxious to swing back into the past too far, as we heard from a premie: "Maybe Guru Maharaj Ji is being seen as the Lord again, but in a less conceptually rigid way. Maybe there is the belief again that he will soon begin to bring peace to the planet as

204

the new Messiah, but the belief is more open. There are few cosmic notions involving extraterrestial beings, magic, and all of that. It seems that premies are now saying the same things about Guru Maharaj Ji's omniscience and power as they did in the beginning, but with a less defensive and insistent tone, for they have gone through quite a few personal changes since 1971. They're more relaxed about it, more sure of it somehow. In other words, the old beliefs are being reasserted but with a different tone; there's a twinkle in the eye, a positive and open attitude which seems to suggest a greater sense of personal confidence and strength. So its less narrow-minded than in 1971, based more on feelings of security than insecurity."

Generally, premies are elevating the guru to a much greater place in their practice of the Knowledge. Now the word is circulating that it is undesirable to try to practice the Knowledge without first submitting to him as the Perfect Master. Premies who are finding this change difficult to accept are moving toward the outer circles of the Mission at the moment. Some premies have even left the movement rather than watch from the sidelines. But the largest number seem to have surrendered to the guru, ready to rededicate themselves to the Knowledge.

Changing Attitudes Toward the Knowledge

Whereas the attitudes of premies toward Guru Maharaj Ji have taken a dramatic turn, their views of the Knowledge seem to have remained fairly constant from 1976 through the present charismatic revival. The following attitude toward the Knowledge in 1976 continues to be the most prevalent today. "I used to value the Knowledge lightly, not really understanding the strength it had. Now I see more clearly the benefits, not only in meditation but also in satsang and service. These aspects of the Knowledge made it complete; they are ways in which we can focus on our love center. To me, love is acceptance of myself and, in achieving that, I am better able to accept everything around me. I mean there is something beyond all the physical and mental material, something that keeps everything together. I feel this

CHANGES

thing is the Knowledge, the core of everything. If we can cut through all the beliefs and concepts which surround it we would experience the deepest peace. I guess what I'm saying is that when I am in that center of love I feel better than I ever did before. And its a natural feeling. Its not always natural or easy to get there, but when I do I know the purpose of my life and that's to be experiencing the Knowledge always, because my life will be real when I do."

In 1971–72, the Knowledge was viewed in very cosmic terms. Premies felt if they meditated regularly, attended satsang, and did service they would ultimately be joined with God. Living a pure life within the confines of surrender, they were usually holding out for more than they were getting. As I have argued, by trying to be saints they created much of their own suffering. By 1976, these attitudes toward the Knowledge had been largely discarded, as we hear from Alan. "When I received the Knowledge, there were so many trips tied to it. I thought I had to become one with God. I thought I had to renounce the world and become a celibate monk the rest of my life. I thought I had to be a Mahatma! I was often frustrated because I couldn't live up to my own loftly standards. I often felt guilty because I didn't feel an overwhelming love for Guru Maharaj Ji, and I really didn't care that much if I was around him. Now, I'm just trying to relax. Knowledge is not a certain life-style, nor is it a complicated trip. It is just that very simple energy I experience in meditation."

As premies have realized that the Knowledge is everywhere in whatever experience they are having, they have quit longing so much for the cosmic experience which was in demand after psychedelics and have come to accept more of what is happening to them at each moment, whether good or bad. Walt expressed that change in outlook. "I feel more like the experience and practice of Knowledge are a natural part of my life and not so much an imposed discipline I have to practice. Knowledge seems more expansive to me now, as I realize that others, besides premies, are in on it. I am more satisfied with whatever experience I'm having, rather than looking for something supposedly higher."

CHANGES

Personal Changes

Looking back over their lives since receiving the Knowledge, most premies found it easy in 1976 to think in terms of an "old self" falling from grace and a "new self" emerging from the experience of the Knowledge. The differences are striking, as we hear from a premie who was guilt-ridden and frequently depressed before her initiation. "Neurotic would be the best term I could use to describe my 'old self.' All of the world was a potential stimulus to gratify my ego or to be down on myself. There were never any shades of grey, just up and down. Basically, I was very negative about my life. I can remember experiencing a lot of pain and frustration and when things didn't go my way I would get upset. I can remember questioning if love even existed, and if it did, was it worth anything. One principle I lived by then was that the more complicated you could make your trip, the 'groovier' you were. Being heavy was 'far out,' so naturally I tried to be heavy and complex. My 'new self,' on the other hand, can experience the flow of life without breaking it down through categorization and analysis. My peace of mind is not as dependent on events and people as it used to be. There is a new acceptance of myself, that I am fine the way I am, that I don't need to be like some other person or to do a particular trip to be okay. Also, I really am experiencing what love is, that deep personal experience which cannot be described, but only felt. Simplicity is beautiful now and I would never have imagined that keeping things simple would help to keep my peace of mind and to keep my awareness focused on the positive and beautiful side of life."

It would be an overstatement to say that the premie's "old self" has disappeared entirely and the "new self" has taken complete dominion. As I suggested earlier, we should only expect a shift of control within the individual, as the spiritual, loving side assumes a more commanding role in the regulation of the ego, especially its negative feelings and desires. The "old self" is likely to remain for some time, although in a less prominent position. As one premie put it: "Through meditation you come to distinguish thoughts from the experience of the void beyond thoughts. You gradually begin to pay less heed to your thoughts, and to realize that your 'old self' is simply a result of socialization. When you experience a deep meditation, you see that the 'old self' is not there, so it becomes less real to you. Thus, you're less bound to be it. Also, because you see it as less real, you feel less upset by it and that makes you less eager to reject it."

Before he received the Knowledge Alan was very introverted and paranoid. You will remember he had a hard time relating to people, especially females. He used drugs and drank beer and wine to escape from his miseries. He was eventually arrested for dealing drugs and was expelled from college. He spent a lot of time wondering how he had become the person he was. "My 'old self,' " he said, "was often sad and lonely. I felt I was tolerated, sometimes liked, but never loved. The 'old self' is still around, but to a lesser degree. My 'new self' still has problems, but doesn't worry about them so much. He still has the idea sometimes that people don't like him, but often ignores that idea and reaches out to them anyway. He is mellower, as the emotional intensity has worn down a lot. He is more open to other people and to new experiences. He doesn't use drugs, alcohol, or get arrested anymore."

Helen described herself as "very old, tired, and lost" before she received the Knowledge. "My 'old self' was sort of blindly stumbling along wondering if there was any real meaning to life—or desperately seeking it—unaware that there was any experience beyond this physical world. Today, I have a conscious awareness of a higher purpose to my life and a higher consciousness which is attainable. The changes I've gone through since receiving the Knowledge have given my life a strong, constructive direction. Having more love inside me has helped me develop more loving relationships with others. Its helped me focus on the beauty of life rather than so much on my own suffering and the suffering of the world."

Before his initiation into the Mission, Marc felt generally happy, but "not complete, not a whole person." "Today, I'm still generally happy, but feel more completed. I view all situations as opportunities to learn. Even 'negative' experiences seem to have their positive side and are a lesson to learn from. Above all, I'm learning to *be con-*

scious. I'm also finding it easier to be honest with myself and to trust the rate of my personal growth."

It is interesting to view the transformation of these premies in light of the "human potential movement" which is going on in so many different forms in American society. Part of bringing the "old self" under control is accepting it, then the individual becomes more willing to communicate and express the "weaknesses" which had been carefully concealed from others. Indeed, in the human potential movement, acceptance of oneself at this level is regarded as one of the keys to personal growth. This has apparently been important in the development of these premies as well. No longer identifying so strongly with their personalities, they show signs of accepting themselves more fully and seem freer to express what they feel. John's experience reflects this basic change. "It wasn't until recently that I began to feel I really have nothing to fear about letting my personality hang out. I feel my uniqueness as an individual is something that shouldn't remain hidden, because, to me, its beautiful, even the 'negative' aspects of it."

With greater acceptance of themselves and what is happening each moment of their lives, these premies find life less of a struggle. Striving for sainthood, for the cosmic connection, for enlightenment are still important. But they will continue to be less prominent, unless the charismatic revival renews the hope for a mystical breakthrough. In 1976, premies were more inclined to just enjoy life and the experience of peace for what they were. Helen's words capture the feeling. "Experiencing the Knowledge has affected my life in a subtle, but basic way. It has brought more calm, more love, into my life and has strengthened my connection to my life force, or God."

Underlying the increasing ease of living which all of these premies reported in 1976 was a basic recognition of spiritual unity, as identification with the life force, or Knowledge, affirmed their equality with others. That experience effectively counteracted their sense of alienation from others and from society, especially among those like Alan who were the most emotionally troubled before their initia-

209

tion. The change in Alan's ability to relate socially is an indication of the power of this spiritual experience. "I used to feel so inferior to others," he said, "but now I can see that, basically, we're the same. That makes it much easier for me to relate to others, so now my social life is a little better. Sometimes I even feel a lot of love and bliss inside and that is great. Sometimes I'm able to help others a little bit."

The aimlessness and lack of meaning which prevailed in their early lives has all but disappeared, for their involvement in the Mission has given their lives a definite direction and purpose. At one level, meaning developed as a consequence of their spiritual experience; at another, it emerged through the discovery of a social niche in the premie community. "I now know who I am, where I'm going, and why. Eliminating those confusions has made my life very easy."

There is little doubt in my mind that these premies have changed in a positive way. Today, they seem less alienated, aimless, worried, afraid, and more peaceful, loving, confident, and appreciative of life. We could attribute these changes to surrender, devotion, and their involvement in the premie community. Each of these undoubtedly had a positive impact, but, if we accept what premies say, none were as critical as their experience of the universal spirit. Meditating on the life-energy for five years, they report having more positive attitudes about themselves. Perhaps Walt captures the feeling best: "Today, I'm less paranoid, fearful, unhappy, hung up, and selfish. I'm still basically the same person, but now I'm more positive, confident, understanding of others, stronger as a person, and happier."

chapter
THIRTEEN

Defection

Scholars have been fascinated with the question of how commitments form, but have shown scarcely any interest in how they dissolve. One exception to this trend is Armand L. Mauss. In his essay, "Dimensions of Religious Defection," he developed a useful way of looking at the intellectual, social, and emotional features of defection from the church.[1]

Intellectual defection occurs when the individual begins to doubt the central tenets of the church's faith. Social defection results from a weakening of bonds with the members of the church, the accumulation of dissatisfying social experiences there, or the development of strong ties on the outside. Emotional defection grows from deep-seated emotional reactions to the church, as we might find in adolescent rebellion. The first two of these forms of defection—the intellectual and social—seem quite applicable to Divine Light Mission, as we will see in the accounts of three defectors.

Mary Anne

Although Mary Anne was deeply moved by her experiences during the Knowledge session, she resisted commitment to the Mission's organization. Her loyalty was chiefly to Guru Maharaj Ji, although that relationship became tenuous in late 1971 when she rejected her belief in his messianic status. "I've come to realize that Guru Maharaj Ji is not particularly to be put up on a throne to be worshipped as the Lord of the Universe. He is Lord of the Universe, but so am I, and so is everybody else. I think he's come to show us we're all equal. He's come to bring us together. We should all humble ourselves to each other and to the God within us. The true guru is inside and Guru Maharaj Ji is just an outward manifestation of that perfect guru within. I really love Guru Maharaj Ji, but I can't relate to the trip of worshipping him, because I don't think he really wants that. I think he wants people to worship the God inside."

In 1972, Mary Anne was living outside of Boulder on a spiritual commune with a group of other premies who were critical of the movement, while her contact with devout premies was minimal. She did occasionally visit the ashram to attend satsang or to perform some special service, but only when she felt moved to or when the premie community called for her help to meet a deadline.

Although she was fond of other premies, she had a strong aversion for the organization. "I've been living with a group of premies who are not totally connected to Divine Light Mission. We're all connected to Guru Maharaj Ji in our hearts, but we don't feel that the Mission is the freest expression of that. I really love all the people in the Mission and feel they're doing a good thing, but I don't think that Guru Maharaj Ji has come to build a church. Each person has to be free to be a walking temple of God; whereas organization restrains and binds."

Fairly well disenchanted with the movement's beliefs and organization, Mary Anne quite naturally showed little interest in the Mission's rituals. She did meditate on a regular basis, but she felt almost no obligation to attend satsang, to do service at the ashram, to sing devotional songs, or to pass out leaflets on the street, even though such behavior was expected.

Weakly committed, her connection to the movement was extremely delicate midway through 1972. While living in Boulder, her involvement had at least been great enough to maintain her identity as a premie. But when she left for the east coast to join a spiritual commune, her remaining ties to the Mission were severed.

Located in the countryside, the spiritual community she joined made it difficult for her to communicate with premies. Therefore, what little feeling she had for the Mission diminished quite rapidly. Living in the midst of people who were unsympathetic to the Mission, it was not long before her relationship to Guru Maharaj Ji began to deteriorate as well.

Having reached the point of feeling completely removed from the Mission, she began to think of herself as a "former" premie. Outside, she was free to take a new direction. "In the autumn of 1972, I was given the opportunity to go to India for a while, where I spent a couple of months traveling, and another seven months in the ashram of a holy man in South India. I had already fallen away from any active relationship with Guru Maharaj Ji and his organization. What I found with my guru in India was a higher teaching, one that is more open and accepting of everything, rather than one which says, 'This is the only way.' I plan to return to India this fall to live for an extended period of time. The most profound thing I learned from my experience with Guru Maharaj Ji was the transient nature of life. Everything eventually must drop away until only one's true self remains. Even one's relationship with God or devotion to a guru must drop away because even those things serve to perpetuate the illusion of duality in the long run. All experiences are steps up the path to oneness. But I am grateful to Guru Maharaj Ji for what he showed me. There is no doubt that he is a very powerful man and that he is doing his best to improve the world."

Joan

Joan was initially confused by the Knowledge session, for she could neither grasp its meaning nor understand her relationship to the Mission. That confusion did not clear up until several weeks later when she met some premies who lived up to her expectations of what a premie should be—open and loving. At that point, she made a decision to become involved; soon she was giving satsang, doing service, and singing the praises of Guru Maharaj Ji.

Prior to the Guru Puja festival in 1972, her commitment to the movement seemed to be strong, for she had accepted Guru Maharaj Ji as the Lord and had moved into the ashram. A new set of regulations governing the ashrams was announced at the festival, which significantly increased the sacrifices required of premies living there—poverty, chastity, and obedience were to be enforced. The women were told that, if they had any intention of marrying, they should leave the ashram. Since Joan did, she decided to move out and take up housekeeping with some other premies.

On the surface, there appeared to be little change in her commitment. She held tight to the Mission's beliefs and traditions while she religiously attended satsang and did service each day at the ashram. Yet there was a subtle change, for her withdrawal from ashram life gave her more time and greater freedom to participate in another movement, The Church of World Messianity. She had been initiated into the church before coming to Colorado and had befriended premies who were active in both movements.

Before embarking on the trip to India, she seemed secure and happy with the way she had been able to combine devotion to Guru Maharaj Ji and channeling light, a spiritual healing practice in The Church of World Messianity. In India, however, the Mission's leaders were impatient with her divided loyalty. "Before I went to India, I was sort of gung-ho about Guru Maharaj Ji and optimistic about the trip. I had a lot of confidence in the path I was on. But in India I experienced the organizational part of the Mission and the power it was holding over people. A lot of people were sick, so I was spending a lot of time channeling light. I couldn't believe it when people within the Mission's organization became hostile toward what I was doing. Some of the Mahatmas even said that channeling light was the work of the devil. When I first entered the Mission, the path was pretty mellow. People were saying that Guru Maharaj Ji was a Perfect Master and a high spiritual being, but they were willing to accept other directions too. To me, the freedom to choose different spiritual paths was important. So, when the leaders told me to drop my beliefs in The Church of World Messianity, to stop channeling light and just follow their path, I knew there was going to be a confrontation."

Even against the orders of the Mission's leaders, she continued channeling light to the sick, although she did so outside of the hospital and out of public view. This decision to deviate from the Mission's position reflected her growing alienation from the organization. She felt distressed and angry that such strong measures would be employed to stop her from performing a service she regarded as completely in harmony with the Knowledge.

She had not consciously decided to leave the Mission when she returned to Colorado, but there were signs she was beginning to defect. On the pretense she had heard too much satsang in India, for example, she decided not to attend evening satsang when she returned. She also quit making her daily trips to the ashram to do service. Yet she felt a close relationship to Guru Maharaj Ji and persisted with her meditations.

Her skeptical attitude about the organization began to erode her ties to the premie community. Soon she was associating more with the members of The Church of World Messianity than with premies. Pressures to quit the Mission were beginning to accumulate, especially from among her close friends who had already defected.

Drifting out before even fully aware of it, she began to criticize the Mission's beliefs, particularly those tenets which imputed supernatural powers to the guru. "I finally got fed up with their narrow approach to God, their thinking that everything that happens to you is the will of God, that either God or Guru Maharaj Ji caused it. I couldn't buy the view that if you tripped and fell that God or Guru Maharaj Ji caused it. I believe that people have their own free will, that we choose our life, that we choose things to happen. It's not God or Guru Maharaj Ji doing everything."

Joan's emotional bond to Guru Maharaj Ji began to dissolve. She ceased looking up to him as the Lord, then stopped looking up to him at all. Where she had felt a deep love for him, only a shadow of respect remained.

Having essentially abandoned the Mission, Joan completed her

215

departure when she gave up its meditation techniques for praying in the tradition of The Church of World Messianity. This change completed her retreat. She was free to enter a life of service by channeling light. Recently, however, she has deserted that calling too and is now involved in still another eastern movement.

Matthew

Matthew had been a political and spiritual loner before his contact with the Mission. Confused by the Knowledge session, he might never have become involved had he not been appointed to an official position within the ashram in order to keep it operating while the bulk of the premie community went off to India. He had lightly volunteered to donate money toward the purchase of an ashram building and was recruited on the spot, somewhat against his own inclinations. Caught quite by accident in this new position, his commitment to the organization began to develop until, within a relatively short time, he had become a devotee. His dedication to the Mission seemed quite intense in 1972. He had moved into the ashram and spoke with conviction about the Mission's great potential and Guru Maharaj Ji's plan to change the world.

The first noticeable change in his commitment occurred during his trip to India in 1972. He had been immersed in the premie community up to that point, while being bound by the requirements of his position as an ashram official. However, before his departure, he was relieved of his office, which removed him somewhat from the social influences of the organization. Even in New York City, while waiting for his flight to India, he was beginning to feel vaguely removed from the community. "I began looking at the people who were active in the Mission and feeling I was not like them. I didn't think I was an ashram type. In fact, I was feeling detached from the whole ashram scene."

In India, he was more an observer than a participant. His criticisms were nourished by a growing sense of estrangement. "There were a lot of Mahatmas there and premies were really playing up to

216

them, like touching their feet. It seemed so phony and ridiculous to me. I also felt that some of the Indian traditions which the Mission had taken up were unnecessary. For example, there's a belief in celibacy. I heard Mata Ji tell a group of mothers, 'Well, now that you've made your mistake, you'll have to live with it.' To say that having children was a mistake was a position I just couldn't accept. I began to think those traditional values were not of any use to a western person."

Although his experiences in India had weakened his ties to the Mission, Matthew had no plans of leaving the movement when he returned. For two weeks he recuperated from an illness contracted in India. After his recovery, there was little for him to do, since he no longer had an official position within the ashram. "I didn't really have a role I could sink into. In fact, there didn't seem to be any roles which were really right for me."

Eventually, he did assume responsibility for opening a Mission-operated secondhand store, but by that time he was already beginning to feel a strong desire to leave the ashram. "Finally, I just said to myself, 'Okay, I'm going to move out.' The morning I left I went to the person in charge and told her I was leaving. I tried to tell her why in order to make her understand, but I was very defensive because I really didn't know what I was doing. I was just trusting an urge in me which was telling me to get out. I didn't want to face any other people in the ashram. In fact, I just packed my stuff and snuck out the door when no one was looking."

Matthew had no intention of leaving the movement at that point, for he still considered himself a premie and intended to remain active. He kept up his attendance at satsang and continued doing service in order to maintain his contact with the Mission. Yet he was entering a critical stage, for he was starting to seriously question the movement's beliefs, its view of service, and its apparent intolerance of spiritual directions other than its own. Alongside of this questioning attitude were pressures from his best friend, a former premie, who was apparently encouraging him to defect.

Matthew could not have been much better prepared for a final break. "They had a big reshuffling of the organization after I left the

217

DEFECTION

ashram. It was going to be split up in order to create a place where premies could do the service that felt right for them. People were talking about creating a more loving and free situation, where premies could perform the type of service they wanted. That really sounded good to me. Then one day I stopped by the Mission's secondhand store and there were some people there from Denver, who were higher up in the organization. They needed some people to hand out leaflets and they asked me if I wanted to go. I told them I didn't. But they told me I did and they continued telling me that. That really upset me, especially after I'd heard about the changes in organization which were going to take place. So, I just walked away from them. I never went back to that store or to the ashram again."

Once he had left the ashram, it was a relatively easy step for Matthew to leave the movement. "The situation at the store that day was the breaking point for me, as I definitely began to lose my feelings for the Mission. In fact, I found myself wanting to avoid it entirely because I didn't want to be drawn back into its frame of reference or language. I didn't want that to happen, so I avoided any contact with premies."

Outside of the Mission, Matthew returned to his solitary spiritual search. He continued to meditate, using techniques similar to the Mission's, and took up the study of western psychology and eastern religion. After two years of study on his own, he joined another eastern spiritual community, where he is currently following its guru.

Taking Leave

Departure from a social movement is achieved in an incremental fashion it seems. Social bonds are gradually broken with the members, while new ones are formed in the outside world, until the individual has attained complete separation. There appear to be layers of disenchantment quite similar to those described by Mauss in his discussion of defection from the church. Certainly Mary Anne, Joan, and Matthew became disillusioned with the Mission's organization, doubted some of the main tenets of its ideology, and questioned its

218

authority. Questioning the Mission at that level, they reduced the number of social contacts with premies while they increased their interactions with people on the outside, many of whom possessed a strong aversion for the movement. Contact with the Mission's critics reinforced their own misgivings, which, in turn, deepened their own feelings of disenchantment, drawing them further outside of the movement's worldview and sphere of influence. Thus they felt freer to deviate from the expectations which had shaped their identities as devotees. Daily rituals changed. It became more and more uncomfortable being around premies. They found more to be critical about. Feeling an aversion for the premie community and finding themselves agreeing with the community of dissenters, their emotional attachment to Guru Maharaj Ji began to weaken, then break. At what point they abandoned their identity as a premie is unclear, but the realization that they were no longer followers of the guru must have been a critical moment, for their bond to him had been their strongest link to the Mission. Having come to admit that they were no longer premies, they eventually discarded or modified the Mission's meditation practices, a symbolic gesture of their independence from the movement.

Their unconscious effort to minimize conflict during the period of withdrawal was one of the interesting undercurrents of their defection. For they took the path of least resistance whenever possible. To avoid social conflicts, for example, Joan stopped her daily visits to the ashram. Matthew escaped conflict with his premie friends by sneaking out of the ashram and by consciously avoiding contact with them once he had left the movement.

Self-deception was one of the creative ways they managed their inner conflicts, believing they were still committed even while they were slipping out of the movement. Joan did not realize she was breaking her ties to the movement when she decided not to attend satsang, on the pretext that she had heard too much satsang in India. Matthew found it much easier to leave the ashram after he had convinced himself he was not leaving the movement, even though there were signs of disillusionment with the organization, its beliefs, and its traditions. By viewing himself as a premie-at-large, he avoided having

219

DEFECTION

to face the more difficult choice of departing from the movement directly out of the ashram. Self-deception helped these premies stay clear of conflict with their friends in the movement while it allowed them to withdraw their commitments with a minimum of anxiety and guilt.

chapter
FOURTEEN

Why Have the New Religions Lost Their Momentum?

As in the heyday of the counterculture, hopes were high in the early 1970s for a spiritual revolution realizing the dreams of rebellious youth—of a world of peace where people cared for each other. With the rapid expansion of the various spiritual movements which had sprung up across the country, there were visible and dramatic signs that what the counterculture had failed to achieve the new spiritual revolution had well in hand. Now these movements are coming into leaner years, as the number of people interested in joining their ranks has fallen off sharply. Even Transcendental Meditation, which probably demanded the least from its thousands of initiates, has shown a decline in the number of new meditators. More bizarre ideas, like levitation, are being advanced in somewhat desperate attempts to attract public attention and new members.

Divine Light Mission was affected by the decline in public interest as early as 1974, when the number of people asking to receive the Knowledge was but a fraction of the crowds which had packed the Knowledge sessions in 1971–72. The charismatic revival of 1977

221

helped renew premies' hopes for expansion, but given the general apathy of the American public, I doubt if it will live up to their expectations.

What changes since 1971 lead me to this pessimistic assessment of the future growth of Divine Light Mission and the broader spiritual revolution in the United States? To answer this question we need to understand what was behind the phenomenonal successes of the early years, when young people were filled with enthusiasm for their gurus and for God. Drawing on the earlier analysis, perhaps we will see why the spiritual revolution took the dramatic form it did and why, today, it seems to be losing its mass character.

In 1971, a large number of young people were available for a spiritual solution that involved obedience to a guru. They had been well prepared by their psychedelic and counterculture experiences to adopt the view that many problems could be solved through spirituality, and they had been spiritually awakened either through drugs or as a result of the social climate.

Many had actively pursued other ways of achieving happiness and fulfillment, only to find them inadequate. Politics had failed. Therapy had not freed the more emotionally disturbed from their personal problems. Drugs and the counterculture had reached the limits of their potential. With commitment to the counterculture coming to an end and with few meaningful career opportunities, these young people were ready for a turn toward spirituality.

It is understandable why they became interested in eastern mysticism. Through their psychedelic experiences, many had come to a view of God which was more compatible with the eastern than the western perspective. Involvement in an eastern religion was also sufficiently counter to mainstream American life that they could leave the counterculture while preserving their symbolic opposition to society and the life-styles of parents.

Watching the exodus of so many hippies from the drug scene into eastern spirituality, many other young people were curious to find out something about Hinduism, Buddhism, Taoism, and the various saints and gurus whose names they could hardly pronounce, but who were attracting so much attention. Many read spiritual literature, which recommended having a guru in an atmosphere where an increasing number of hippies were looking for gurus to follow, so they wondered if they needed one too.

When various eastern gurus arrived in this country at the start of the 1970s, hippies left the counterculture by the thousands to follow them. The phenomenon produced a dramatic effect and there was much speculation about a spiritual revolution sweeping the country and the world. However, the large reservoir of young people who were available for conversion was fairly well dried up by the close of 1973. With the end of the counterculture and the diminishing use of psychedelic drugs among young people, there was no longer a means of replenishing the number of potential converts. Full of millennial zeal, however, these young people believed that conventional people of all ages and classes were destined to join them in their world-changing efforts. What they did not understand was that the vast majority of people in this country are unwilling to develop a consuming spiritual commitment, while an even larger number would be unsympathetic and even hostile toward eastern movements which encourage surrender.

When we stop to consider that the vast majority of people are not free to become spiritually converted and committed, the future of the new spiritual revolution looks bleak indeed. First, we would have to eliminate from consideration those who are entrenched in conventional careers. Their resources are already heavily invested and, if successful, they would be unlikely to turn to religion as an alternative. Then, we could omit the mass of people who are already active church members because they would resist taking a different spiritual course. The elderly can be excluded as potential converts on the grounds that, as various studies have shown, they tend to be more cautious about innovation and thus less receptive to change. And the bulk of the poor are bound to be somewhat unsympathetic to the idea that a spiritual rather than a political or economic solution would give them relief from their problems. After all, the poor are still trying to get what affluent, white, middle-class youth who joined the spiritual revolution have largely rebuked.

Beyond the general aversion of the American public to spirituality as a solution to problems and as a way of life, there is a strong cultural bias against eastern movements. There is a general suspicion of anything as "foreign" as eastern spiritual practice, as well as a persistent appreciation for what is genuinely American. There are also habitual feelings of loyalty to the Protestant, Catholic, and Jewish faiths. Many premies discovered from the hostile reactions of their parents that these religious preferences are as deeply rooted as political party affiliations, even among those who seldom attend church. Finally, with the idea of individualism so prevalent in our culture, the thought of anyone giving up personal autonomy to a guru offends many people. In fact, the generally unfriendly attitude of the news media toward the eastern movements may have largely reflected the attitude of the public, although I am sure it played a part in shaping it as well. It was no surprise that Transcendental Meditation fared better with the media and the public, for it self-consciously eliminated religious overtones from its approach, Americanized its appeal, and played down surrender.

If most Americans are opposed to movements which encourage the abandonment of individuality, then who is left for Divine Light Mission and the other eastern movements to recruit? There seem to be three major sources at the moment, one being the group of youth who are disillusioned with conventional religion. It may not be easy, however, to convince them that there is more to religion than what they found in church on Sunday. For the experiences of these premies revealed that, after their disenchantment with the church, it took a heavy dose of psychedelic drugs to counteract their mistrust of religion and to awaken them to the importance of spirituality. Potential converts might also be found among college students, for they are traditionally more willing to explore the esoteric and novel, but even in that group the appeal might be limited to those who are strongly discontented and are not opposed to surrender. The third source of possible converts is to be found among those who are disenchanted with other eastern movements. The fact is that some of the growth of various movements in the last few years has come about by the defections of people moving from one spiritual community to another, as

THE NEW RELIGIONS

we saw in the accounts of the three who left Divine Light Mission to join other spiritual groups.

Unless a major catastrophe occurs in our society to increase the level and scope of public discontent, or psychedelics again capture the interest of our youth and turn them in a spiritual direction, there is little hope that the new religions will reexperience the success of their early days, at least not in the near future. They will, however, probably continue to be viable alternatives to conventional forms of religion.

These may be sobering thoughts for premies who still entertain world-saving fantasies. Yet, at this stage, such fantasies are a threat to the survival of the Mission as a spiritual alternative—a fact Guru Maharaj Ji seems to have grasped, for starting in 1977 he has encouraged premies to be realistic as they face the task of spreading the Knowledge. His current emphasis on the need to take stock of reality may check the unrealistic hopes of some premies and save them from disillusionment.

A Statement on the Method

Although this study is based largely upon the transcribed accounts of premies, questionnaire information was also gathered in the initial stages and I feel obliged to comment on it here. My original interest in using the questionnaire was to discover if the stories of the eighteen Boulder premies were similar to those of premies living elsewhere in the country. The questionnaire was constructed after the completion of about half of the interviews, so that it would reflect the issues premies regarded as influential in their development.

Besides the standard sociodemographic items, such as age, sex, race, education, employment, and parents' occupation and income, the questionnaire probed premies' attitudes about family, church, school, and friendship. For each of these areas, they were asked to characterize their experiences on a Likert-type continuum ranging from very good to very poor.

Family issues covered the incidence of broken homes due to divorce or the death of a parent, and the number and sex of siblings. Open-ended questions, which were not amenable to quantification, touched upon the quality of early family life and attitudes toward their parents.

227

A STATEMENT ON THE METHOD

Premies were asked to describe their religious background and to specify any denominations or sects in which they had been active. They were asked to identify religious practices in the family, to report whether they had left the church and, if so, to discuss their reasons for leaving and to specify at what point in life they had left.

The questionnaire also asked them to evaluate their school experiences through college and to discuss their friendship patterns. Friendship questions were primarily intended to discover if they had been socially isolated, which turned out not to be the case on the whole.

On the issue of drugs the questionnaire asked whether they had tried psychedelic drugs, what specific hallucinogens were used, the number of occasions on which they had been taken, the period of time over which they were used, whether they had discontinued their use before receiving the Knowledge, and, if so, what had influenced them to quit. There were also broader questions dealing with the impact of drugs on their general attitudes toward life and toward themselves, and the effect of hallucinogens on their spiritual awakening.

Curious to know what other experiences might have prepared them for commitment to Divine Light Mission, I also asked if they had been involved in any other eastern movement or religion before receiving the Knowledge and what influence such experiences had had on their spiritual interests.

Finally, they were asked to describe how they had come into contact with the Mission, and when and where they had received the Knowledge.

Besides the 18 local premies, 13 premies from Kansas City, Missouri, and 10 from Atlanta, Georgia, completed questionnaires, bringing the total premie sample to 41. In order to compare followers with nonfollowers, 40 nonfollower college students were drawn from two upper-division sociology classes at the University of Colorado. I intentionally selected upper-division students in the social sciences in order to roughly duplicate the age and college interests of the premies I had interviewed. To see how premies compared with followers of another eastern religion, the questionnaire was also given to 29 Krishna followers active in the Denver Hare Krishna movement. In

228

A STATEMENT ON THE METHOD

each group, every member was given the opportunity to fill out a questionnaire, on a volunteer basis.

On those items in which interval level data could be justified, as in the case of age, income, and Likert-type factors, a difference of means test was used. A difference of proportions test was employed for items in which arbitrary values were applied. Typically, these consisted of yes/no responses.

Comparisons between the Boulder, Kansas City, and Atlanta premies revealed a striking similarity. The 41 premies were young, with an average age of 23. Ages ranged from 19 to 29. All were white. They tended to come from middle-class families, with the average estimated income of the father being $21,000. On the average, they had attended one and one-half years of college.

On only two variables was there a statistically significant difference between the 18 local premies and the nonlocals. More local premies (66 percent) had been involved in other eastern movements before their initiation into the Mission than premies from Kansas City and Atlanta (34 percent). This difference might be explained by the fact that The Church of World Messianity (Johrei) was localized in the Boulder area and had attracted quite a number of premies living there. Also, while Boulder premies tended to rate their earlier church experiences as "poor," nonlocal premies were significantly more likely to rate their church experiences as "very poor."

Comparisons between the group of 41 premies and 29 Krishna followers indicated no statistically significant differences. Like premies, Krishna followers were young, white, and middle-class. However, there were a few apparent differences worth noting. Krishnas were considerably more critical of their college experience than premies. Premies, on the average, rated their college experience slightly below "average," but Krishnas tended to rate theirs as "very poor." Krishna followers were also more likely to have come from broken homes. Among Krishnas, 27 percent had come from broken homes as compared to 17 percent of the premies. Although the followers of Krishna had used psychedelics about as often as premies and over a similar time period, only 45 percent reported religious experiences while tripping, as against 65 percent of the premies. This would tend

229

A STATEMENT ON THE METHOD

to confirm the view that the Krishnas' turn toward spirituality was influenced as much by social factors as by drug experiences.

Most differences between the 41 premies and 40 nonfollower college students were slight. However, on four variables there were statistically significant differences. Premies were likely to rate their school experiences through high school on the "poor" side, while nonfollowers tended to rate theirs as "average." Premies also were less likely than nonfollowers to have been affiliated with a church in their youth: 21 percent of premies reported no church affiliation versus only 5 percent of the college students. This suggests that premies were somewhat less likely to have a strong religious orientation, a fact which might have made them more receptive to a new religious outlook. However, this view has to be tempered by the finding that only 11 percent of the Krishna followers had no earlier church affiliation, which diminishes the importance of that factor as an explanation for their conversion.

The most statistically significant differences between premies and college students were in the area of drugs. Among premies, 95 percent had used psychedelic drugs. Among Krishnas, 89 percent had, while only 67 percent of college students had. Equally important, premies and Krishna followers had tripped many more times and over a longer period. Premies also reported having many more spiritual experiences under the influence of hallucinogens.

Although not statistically significant, there were a few apparent differences between premies and college students which might warrant further investigation. Premies tended to be considerably more critical of their family experiences. They were more likely to rate their family experiences on the "poor" side than nonfollowers, who tended to rate theirs as "average." Premies also tended to come from homes where there was less equality between their parents: 25 percent of nonfollowers viewed the relative dominance of their parents as "equal," while only 9 percent of premies and 10 percent of Krishnas felt that way.

There were also a number of similarities between the two groups. On an average, neither premies nor college students were likely to have come from broken homes, the figures being 17 and 15

230

A STATEMENT ON THE METHOD

percent, respectively. Their early religious affiliations were compatible, with about the same percentages of Catholics, Protestants, and Jews in each group. Most striking was the fact that college students had dropped out of church at a rate comparable to both premies and Krishnas: 82 percent had left, as against 87 percent of the premies and 86 percent of the Krishna followers. Yet, college students judged their experiences at church somewhat above "average," while both premies and Krishnas rated them as "poor." Perhaps this is to be expected, since they were looking back after becoming enthusiastically involved in a new religion.

Premies and college students also shared a common evaluation of their success in making friends, both feeling they had above "average" success. Satisfaction with their college experiences showed only a small difference. College students were only a bit more pleased, judging their college experience to be just above "average," while premies evaluated theirs a little below "average."

Although drug use appears to be the major difference between premies/Krishnas and the nonfollower social science students, it is not wise to place too much emphasis on the influence of drugs as an isolated factor. The conversion process has to be viewed in its entirety to discover how people are led step by step into deeper involvement. For the premies in this study, drugs were just one of many factors.

Notes

Chapter 6. Growing Up

1. Edwin D. Starbuck, *The Psychology of Religion: An Empirical Study of the Growth of Religious Consciousness* (London: Walter Scoot, 1914).

2. William James, *The Varieties of Religious Experience* (New York: American Library, 1958).

3. Milton Mayeroff, *On Caring* (Evanston, New York: Harper and Row, 1971).

4. Armand M. Nicholi II, "A New Dimension of the Youth Culture," *American Journal of Psychiatry* 131 (April 1974), pp. 396–401.

5. Carl W. Christensen, "Religious Conversion in Adolescence," *Pastoral Psychology* 16 (September 1965), pp. 18–19.

6. Milton Rokeach, "Faith, Hope, Bigotry," *Psychology Today* 3 (April 1970), p. 58.

7. Victor D. Sanua, "Religion, Mental Health, and Personality: A Review of Empirical Studies," *American Journal of Psychiatry* 125 (1969), p. 1211.

8. Christensen, "Religious Conversion in Adolescence," p. 24.

9. Michael I. Harrison, "Preparation for Life in the Spirit: The Process of Initial Commitment to a Religious Movement," *Urban Life and Culture* 2 (January 1974), pp. 394–98.

10. George C. Anderson, "Maturing Religion," *Pastoral Psychology* 22 (April 1971), p. 20.

Chapter 7. Psychedelics: Blowing Open the Doors of Perception

1. *Guru Maharaj Ji : Reflections on an Indian Sunrise* (a short collection of Guru Maharaj Ji's satsang, 1973), p. 25. Dates noted in the text next to Guru Maharaj Ji's name are the years when his satsang was given.

2. *And It Is Divine* (the U.S. Mission's main publication) (January 1973), p. 45.

3. *Ibid.* (March 1975), p. 39.

4. *Guru Maharaj Ji: Reflections on an Indian Sunrise* (1973), p. 4.

5. Francine J. Daner, "Conversion to Krishna Consciousness: The Transformation from

233

NOTES

Hippie to Religious Ascetic," in Roy Wallis (ed.), *Sectarianism: Analysis of Religious and Non-Religious Sects* (New York: John Wiley and Sons, 1975), pp. 56–57. J. Stillson Judah, *Hare Krishna and the Counterculture* (New York: John Wiley and Sons, 1974), p. 135.

6. Armand M. Nicholi II, "A New Dimension of the Youth Culture," *American Journal of Psychiatry* 131 (April 1974), p. 397.

Chapter 8. Between the Sacred and Profane

1. Thomas Robbins, "Eastern Mysticism and the Resocialization of Drug Users: The Mehr Baba Cult," *Journal for the Scientific Study of Religion* 8 (Fall 1969), p. 309.

2. *And It Is Divine* (April 1973), p. 63.

3. Benjamin Weininger, "The Interpersonal Factor in Religious Experience," *Psychoanalysis* 3 (1955), p. 33.

4. *Guru Maharaj Ji: Reflections on an Indian Sunrise* (1973), p. 4.

5. *And It Is Divine* (December 1972), p. 4.

6. *Divine Light* (a British publication of the Mission) (April 1972), p. 23.

7. *Guru Maharaj Ji: Reflections on an Indian Sunrise* (1973), p. 25.

8. *Satguru Maharaj Ji* (a pamphlet; date unknown, but c. 1972), p. 7.

9. John Lofland, *Doomsday Cult: A Study of Conversion, Proselytization, and Maintenance of Faith* (Englewood Cliffs, New Jersey: Prentice-Hall, 1966), pp. 7, 44.

Chapter 9. Preparation

1. *Divine Light* (April 1972), p. 25.

2. *Ibid.*, p. 24.

3. *Divine Times* (the Mission's U.S. newspaper) (February 15, 1973), p. 6.

4. *Ibid.* (April 20, 1972), p. 3.

5. *Ibid.* (February 15, 1973), p. 7.

6. *Divine Light* (November 1972), p. 24.

7. *And It Is Divine* (December 1972), p. 7.

Chapter 10. Encounters with God

1. *Divine Light* (March 1972), p. 22.

2. *Ibid.* (April 1972), p. 23.

3. *Guru Maharaj Ji: Reflections on an Indian Sunrise* (1973), p. 5.

4. *Divine Light* (February 1972), p. 5.

5. *Ibid.* (November 1972), p. 18.

6. *Guru Maharaj Ji: Reflections on an Indian Sunrise* (1973), p. 15.

7. *And It Is Divine* (January 1973), p. 49.

8. William James, *The Varieties of Religious Experience* (New York: American Library, 1958), p. 157.

9. E. T. Clark, *The Psychology of Religious Awakening* (New York: Macmillan, 1929); Joel Allison, "Religious Conversion: Regression and Progression in an Adolescent Experience," *Journal for the Scientific Study of Religion* 8 (1969), pp. 23–38; Leon Salzman, "The Psychology of Religious and Ideological Conversion," *Psychiatry* 16 (1953), pp. 177–87; William Sargant, *Battle for the Mind: A Physiology of Conversion and Brain-Washing* (London: Heinemann, 1957); Theodore M. Levin and Leonard S. Zegans, "Adolescent Identity Crisis and Religious Conversion: Implications for Psychotherapy," *The British Journal of Medical Psychol-*

NOTES

ogy 47 (1974), pp. 73–82; and Carl W. Christensen, "Religious Conversion in Adolescence," *Pastoral Psychology* 16 (September 1965), pp. 17–28.
   10. Christensen, pp. 27–28.

Chapter 11. Metamorphosis
   1. *And It Is Divine* (March 1973), pp. 54–55.
   2. *Ibid.* (December 1972), p. 49.
   3. *Ibid.* (March 1973), p. 54.
   4. *Guru Puja* (a pamphlet) (1972), p. 12.
   5. *And It Is Divine* (October 1973), pp. 58–59.
   6. Rosabeth Moss Kanter, "Commitment and Social Organization: A Study of Commitment Mechanisms in Utopian Communities," *American Sociological Review* 33 (August 1968), pp. 504–5.
   7. Rosabeth Moss Kanter, "Commitment and the Internal Organization of Millennial Movements," *American Behavioral Scientist* 16 (December 1972), p. 238.
   8. Erik Erikson, *Childhood and Society* (New York: W. W. Norton, 1963).
   9. James V. Downton, Jr., *Rebel Leadership: Commitment and Charisma in the Revolutionary Process* (New York: The Free Press, 1973), pp. 241–70.
   10. J. Krishnamurti, *Think on These Things* (New York: Harper and Row, 1964), p. 98.
   11. Carlos Castaneda, *Tales of Power* (New York: Simon and Schuster, 1974), p. 231.
   12. *And It Is Divine* (July 1974), p. 34.
   13. Krishnamurti, *Think on These Things*, pp. 43–44.
   14. From a leaflet entitled "A Difficult Man."
   15. Shunryu Suzuki, *Zen Mind, Beginner's Mind* (New York: Weatherhill, 1970), p. 40.
   16. *And It Is Divine* (January 1973), p. 48.
   17. *Divine Light* (March 1972), p. 14.
   18. *Guru Maharaj Ji: Reflections on an Indian Sunrise* (1973), p. 28.
   19. Chögyam Trungpa, *Meditation in Action* (Berkeley, California: Shambala, 1970), p. 39.

Chapter 12. Changes
   1. Satsang given to a conference of premies in Denver, January 25, 1976.
   2. S. N. Eisenstadt (ed.), *Max Weber: On Charisma and Institution Building* (Chicago: University of Chicago Press, 1968).
   3. Sophia Collier, *Soul Rush: The Odyssey of a Young Woman of the '70s* (New York: William Morrow, 1978), p. 157, 162.
   4. Communication from a Mission official.
   5. *Ibid.*
   6. Satsang given to a conference of premies in late December 1975.
   7. Satsang given to a conference of premies in Denver, January 25, 1976.
   8. Satsang given to a conference of premies in Lima, Peru, November 18, 1976.
   9. *Ibid.*
   10. Satsang given to a conference of premies in Denver, January 25, 1976.

Chapter 13. Defection
   1. Armand L. Mauss, "Dimensions of Religious Defection," *Review of Religious Research* 10 (Spring 1969), pp. 128–35.

References

Abramson, E., et al. "Social Power and Commitment: A Theoretical Statement." *American Sociological Review* 23 (February 1958), pp. 15–22.

Allison, Joel. "Recent Empirical Studies of Religious Conversion Experiences." *Pastoral Psychology* 17 (September 1966), pp. 21–34.

—— "Adaptive Regression and Intense Religious Experiences." *Journal for the Scientific Study of Religion* 145 (1967), pp. 452–63.

—— "Religious Conversion: Regression and Progression in an Adolescent Experience." *Journal for the Scientific Study of Religion* 8 (1969), pp. 23–38.

Anderson, George C. "Maturing Religion." *Pastoral Psychology* 22 (April 1971), pp. 17–28.

Balswick, Jack. "The Jesus People Movement: A Generational Interpretation." *Journal of Social Issues* 30 (1974), pp. 23–42.

Beck, Robert N. "Hall's Genetic Psychology and Religious Conversion." *Pastoral Psychology* 16 (September 1965), pp. 45–51.

Becker, Howard S. "Notes on the Concept of Commitment." *American Journal of Sociology* 66 (July 1960), pp. 32–40.

—— "The Implications of Research on Occupational Careers for a Model of Household Decision-Making." In Nelson Foote (ed.), *Household Decision-Making: Consumer Behavior.* New York: New York University Press, 1961.

Berger, Peter L., and Thomas Luckman. *The Social Construction of Reality.* Garden City, New York: Doubleday and Co., 1966.

Bodemann, Y. Michal. "Mystical, Satanic, and Chiliastic Forces in Countercultural Movements." *Youth and Society* 5 (June 1974), pp. 433–47.

Cantril, Hadley. *The Psychology of Social Movements.* New York: John Wiley and Sons, 1963.

237

REFERENCES

Capps, Donald. "Contemporary Psychology of Religion: The Task of Theoretical Reconstruction." *Social Research* 41 (Summer 1974), pp. 362–83.

Castaneda, Carlos. *Tales of Power*. New York: Simon and Schuster, 1974.

Christensen, Carl W. "Religious Conversion in Adolescence." *Pastoral Psychology* 16 (September 1965), pp. 17–28.

Clark, E. T. *The Psychology of Religious Awakening*. New York: Macmillan and Co., 1929.

Coles, Robert. "Social Struggle and Weariness." *Psychiatry* 27 (November 1964), pp. 305–15.

Collier, Sophia. *Soul Rush: The Odyssey of a Young Woman of the '70s*. New York: William Morrow, 1978.

Daner, Francine J. "Conversion to Krishna Consciousness: The Transformation from Hippie to Religious Ascetic." In Roy Wallis (ed.), *Sectarianism: Analyses of Religious and Non-Religious Sects*. New York: John Wiley and Sons, 1975; pp. 53–69.

—— *The American Children of Krishna: A Study of the Hare Krishna Movement*. New York: Holt, Rinehart and Winston, 1976.

Downton, James V., Jr. *Rebel Leadership: Commitment and Charisma in the Revolutionary Process*. New York: The Free Press, 1973.

Durkheim, Emile. *Suicide*. New York: The Free Press, 1951.

—— *The Elementary Forms of the Religious Life*. New York: The Free Press, 1965.

Eisenstadt, S. N. *Max Weber: On Charisma and Institution Building*. Chicago: University of Chicago Press, 1968.

Eister, Allan W. "An Outline of a Structural Theory of Cults." *Journal for the Scientific Study of Religion* 11 (December 1972), pp. 319–33.

Erikson, Erik. "The Problem of Ego Identity." In Maurice Stein, Arthur Vadich, and David Manning White (eds.), *Identity and Anxiety*. New York: The Free Press, 1962.

—— *Childhood and Society*. New York: W. W. Norton, 1968.

Festinger, Leon; Henry Rieken; and Stanley Schachter. *When Prophecy Fails*. New York: Harper, 1956.

Frankl, Viktor E. *Man's Search for Meaning: An Introduction to Logotherapy*. New York: Washington Square Press, 1959.

Freud, Sigmund. *Group Psychology and the Analysis of the Ego*. New York: Bantam Books, 1960.

Furgeson, Earl H. "The Definition of Religious Conversion." *Pastoral Psychology* 16 (September 1965), pp. 7–16.

Gerlach, Luther P., and Virginia H. Hine. *People, Power, Change: Movements of Social Transformation*. Indianapolis: The Bobbs-Merrill Co., 1970.

Gerth, Hans, and C. Wright Mills (eds.). *From Max Weber: Essays in Sociology*. New York: Oxford University Press, 1946.

Goffman, Erving. *Asylums*. Garden City, New York: Doubleday and Co., 1961.

238

REFERENCES

Gordon, David F. "The Jesus People: An Identity Synthesis." *Urban Life and Culture* 3 (July 1974), pp. 159–78.

Harrison, Michael I. "Preparation for Life in the Spirit: The Process of Initial Commitment to a Religious Movement." *Urban Life and Culture* 2 (January 1974), pp. 387–414.

—— "Sources of Recruitment to Catholic Pentecostalism." *Journal for the Scientific Study of Religion* 13 (March 1974), pp. 49–64.

Hine, Virginia H. "Bridge Burners: Commitment and Participation in a Religious Movement." *Sociological Analysis* 31 (Summer 1970), pp. 61–66.

Hood, Ralph W., Jr. "Psychological Strength and the Report of Intense Religious Experience." *Journal for the Scientific Study of Religion* 13 (March 1974), pp. 65–71.

Horton, Paul C. "The Mystical Experience as a Suicide Preventive." *American Journal of Psychiatry* 130 (March 1973), pp. 294–96.

James, William. *The Varieties of Religious Experience*. New York: New American Library, 1958.

Judah, J. Stillson. *Hare Krishna and the Counterculture*. New York: John Wiley and Sons, 1974.

Jung, Carl G. *Memories, Dreams, Reflections*. New York: Random House, 1961.

—— *Man and His Symbols*. Garden City, New York: Doubleday, 1964.

Kanter, Rosabeth Moss. "Commitment and Social Organization: A Study of Commitment Mechanisms in Utopian Communities." *American Sociological Review* 33 (August 1968), pp. 499–517.

—— "Commitment and the Internal Organization of Millennial Movements." *American Behavioral Scientist* 16 (December 1972), pp. 219–43.

Kildahl, John P., "The Personalities of Sudden Religious Converts," *Pastoral Psychology* 16 (September 1965), pp. 37–44.

Krishnamurti, J. *Think on These Things*. New York: Harper and Row, 1964.

Lebra, Takie Sugiyama. "Millenarian Movements and Resocialization," *American Behavioral Scientist* 16 (November–December 1972), pp. 195–217.

Levin, Theodore M., and Leonard S. Zegans. "Adolescent Identity Crisis and Religious Conversion: Implications for Psychotherapy." *The British Journal of Medical Psychology* 47 (1974), pp. 73–82.

Levinson, Peritz. "Religious Delusions in Counter-Culture Patients," *American Journal of Psychiatry* 130 (1974), pp. 1265–69.

Lofland, John, and Rodney Stark. "Becoming a World-Saver: A Theory of Conversion to a Deviant Perspective." *American Sociological Review* 30 (December 1965), pp. 862–75.

Lofland, John. *Doomsday Cult: A Study of Conversion, Proselytization, and Maintenance of Faith*. Englewood Cliffs, New Jersey: Prentice-Hall, 1966.

Maharishi Mahesh Yogi. *The Science of Being and Art of Living*. New York: Signet Books, 1963.

239

REFERENCES

Marris, Peter, *Loss and Change*. Garden City, New York: Doubleday, 1975.

Maslow, Abraham H. *Toward a Psychology of Being*. New York: D. Van Nostrand, 1968.

Mauss, Armand L. "Dimensions of Religious Defection." *Review of Religious Research* 10 (Spring 1969), pp. 128–35.

Mayeroff, Milton. *On Caring*. Evanston, New York: Harper and Row, 1971.

McClelland, David C. "Toward a Theory of Motive Acquisition." *American Psychologist* 20 (1965), pp. 321–33.

Moran, Gerald F. "Conditions of Religious Conversion in the First Society of Norwich, Connecticut, 1718–1744." *Journal of Social History* 5 (Spring 1972), pp. 331–43.

Nicholi, Armand M., II. "A New Dimension of the Youth Culture." *American Journal of Psychiatry* 131 (April 1974), pp. 396–401.

Ritzer, George, and Harrison M. Trice. "An Empirical Study of Howard Becker's Side-Bet Theory." *Social Forces* 47 (June 1969), pp. 475–78.

—— "On the Problem of Clarifying Commitment Theory." *Social Forces* 48 (June 1970), pp. 530–33.

Robbins, Thomas. "Eastern Mysticism and the Resocialization of Drug Users: The Meher Baba Cult." *Journal for the Scientific Study of Religion* 8 (Fall 1969), pp. 308–17.

Roberts, F. J. "Some Psychological Factors in Religious Conversion." *British Journal of Social and Clinical Psychology* 4 (1965), pp. 185–87.

Rokeach, Milton. "Faith, Hope, Bigotry." *Psychology Today* 3 (April 1970), pp. 33–58.

Rosen, George. "Social Change and Psychopathology in the Emotional Climate of Millennial Movements." *American Behavioral Scientist* 16 (December 1972), pp. 153–67.

Salzman, Leon. "The Psychology of Religious and Ideological Conversion." *Psychiatry* 16 (1953), pp. 177–87.

—— "Types of Religious Conversion." *Pastoral Psychology* 17 (September 1966), pp. 8–20, 66.

Sanua, Victor D. "Religion, Mental Health, and Personality: A Review of Empirical Studies." *American Journal of Psychiatry* 125 (1969), pp. 1203–13.

Sargant, William. *Battle for the Mind: A Physiology of Conversion and Brain-Washing*. London: Heinemann, 1957.

Shupe, Anson D., Jr. "Toward a Structural Perspective of Modern Religious Movements." *Sociological Focus* 6 (Summer 1973), pp. 83–99.

Smelser, Neil. *Theory of Collective Behavior*. New York: The Free Press, 1963.

Starbuck, Edwin Diller. *The Psychology of Religion: An Empirical Study of the Growth of Religious Consciousness*. London: The Walter Scott Publishing Co., 1914.

Stark, Rodney. "A Taxonomy of Religious Experience." *Journal for the Scientific Study of Religion* 5 (1965), pp. 97–116.

REFERENCES

Stebbins, Robert A. "On Misunderstanding the Concept of Commitment: A Theoretical Clarification." *Social Forces* 48 (June 1970), pp. 526–29.

Suzuki, D. T. *The Training of the Zen Buddhist Monk.* New York: University Books, 1965.

Suzuki, Shunryu. *Zen Mind, Beginner's Mind.* New York: Weatherhill, 1970.

Trungpa, Chögyam. *Meditation in Action.* Berkeley: Shambala Publications, 1970.

Wallis, Roy. *The Road to Total Freedom: A Sociological Analysis of Scientology.* New York: Columbia University Press, 1977.

Weber, Max. *The Sociology of Religion.* Boston: Beacon Press, 1963.

Weininger, Benjamin. "The Interpersonal Factor in the Religious Experience." *Psychoanalysis* 3 (1955), pp. 27–44.

Wimberley, Ronald, et al. "Conversion in a Billy Graham Crusade: Spontaneous Event or Ritual Performance?" *The Sociological Quarterly* 16 (Spring 1975), pp. 162–70.

Yinger, J. Milton. "On Anomie." *Journal for the Scientific Study of Religion* 3 (Spring 1964), pp. 158–73.

241

Index

Alan, 15-29, 87, 95, 98-99, 106, 129, 142, 195-96, 199, 202, 206, 208, 210
Allison, Joel, 153
Anderson, George, 96
Andy, 136-39
Aquarian Gospel, 124-25, 168
Ashram: defined, 2; exodus from, 186; daily routine, 175; changes in function, 198; alternative living arrangements, 175
Attraction to movement: belief compatibility, 142; social influences, 129-30, 142-43; impact of satsang, 142
Availability, 99, 222-24

Baba Ram Dass, 41, 67, 119-20
Bal Bhagwan Ji, 3, 191
Benefits of involvement: coping, 28, 59; self-acceptance, 59, 207, 209; positive attitudes, 207-8, 210; unity, 209-10; meaning, 210
Bubba Free John, 179-80

Changes in movement: secular, 192-93; bureaucratic, 186, 196-97; charismatic, 187, 196, 201-4; balancing autonomy and dependence, 194-96, 204
Charisma: as catalyst of change, 187; charis-

matic revival, 187, 201-3; *see also* Surrender
Christensen, Carl, 89-90, 94, 153
Church: and discontent, 17-18, 31, 90; defection from, 47, 79, 84, 86, 91-92; hypocrisy of, 61-62, 82, 85, 92-93; comparing premies, Krishnas, college students, 91; attitudes about conversion, 93-94; Mauss on defection, 211; *see also* Discontent, Pentecostalism
Church of World Messianity (Johrei), 43, 172, 214-16
Clark, E. T., 153
Collier, Sophia, 191
Commitment: social enclosure, 138, 152, 165-66, 171-72, 214-15; investment and sacrifice, 141, 170-71; mortification, 172-75; surrender, 175-78; *see also* Conversion, Defection from movement, Surrender
Conversion: rebirth, 72; conservative nature of, 87, 185; sexual conflicts as cause, 89-90; Christensen's theory, 153; stages, 153-56; identity change, 155; human growth, 156; enthusiasm following, 157; normalization, 157-58; purification, 158; self-confidence, 168; *see also* Commitment, James, Starbuck, Surrender
Counterculture: Haight-Ashbury, 49, 103; so-

243

INDEX

Counterculture: (*Continued*)
 cial trends, 102-3; spiritual vanguard, 118; values changed, 127; *see also* Drugs

Darshan, 130
Defection from movement, 211-20; *see also* Church
Devotion, 2, 29, 73, 163; *see also* Surrender
Discontent: therapy, 19, 32-33, 80; idealism, 87; aimlessness, 96; need for meaning, 96-97; alienation, 97; social rescue, 97-99; need for love, 99; as poor predictor of commitment, 99; *see also* Church, Family, Friendship, School
Don Juan, 178
Drugs: psychedelics, 18, 21, 35-37, 49-50, 63-64, 106-11, 126; marijuana, 18, 32, 50, 63, 102; dealing, 19-20, 65-69; social influences, 32, 103-6; spiritual experiences, 36-37, 101-2, 111-12, 115; variety used, 101; extent of use, 101; morals about, 106; cosmic consciousness, 107; personal growth, 108-11; effect on religious concepts, 111; comparing premies, Krishnas, college students, 113-14, 126-27; durations of use, 114; loss of interest in, 126; *see also* Counterculture, Spirituality

Ego, 24-25, 73, 172-73, 181
Erikson, Erik, 177

Family, 15-16, 62, 79, 81, 84-85, 88-89
Family feud, 190-92
Friendship, 16-17, 19, 47-48, 61, 80, 82-83
Futility, 122-24, 128, 154, 164-65

Guru Maharaj Ji: satsang, 1-2, 102, 107-8, 110, 111, 119, 121, 123, 125-26, 130, 132-33, 134-35, 137, 140, 146, 147-48, 150, 152, 159, 161, 163-64, 179, 181, 192-95, 197, 204; childhood, 1-3; on Wall Street, 38-39, 67, 131-33; as link to God, 161, 164; compared to other gurus, 178-83; lifestyle, 183; changing attitudes toward, 198-205
Gurus, 178-83

Harrison, Michael, 94
Helen, 31-46, 87, 89, 102, 118, 126, 208
Hesse, Hermann, 51

I Ching, 39
Identity: change through conversion, 155; influence of mortification on, 172-73; identification with guru, 176; "psychosocial moratorium," 177; *see also* Commitment, Surrender
Investment and Sacrifice, 170-71

James, William, 77, 152-53
Joan, 213-16, 218-19
John, 83-84, 86, 92, 105-6, 109, 121, 139-41, 145, 149-50, 161-64, 170-71, 198-99, 203, 209
Jung, Carl, 51

Kanter, Rosabeth Moss, 170
Knowledge: defined, 3; session, 23, 40, 58, 71-72, 145-49, 151; as secret, 143; reactions to Knowledge session, 145, 148-52; impact on conversion, 155; *see also* Guru Maharaj Ji (satsang)
Krishnamurti, J., 178-79

Leary, Timothy, 36, 64, 119
Levin, Theodore, 153
Lofland, John, 127

Mahatmas, 2, 71, 134, 146, 192
Marc, 61-73, 87, 89, 96, 146-47, 208-9
Mary Anne, 81-83, 86, 95, 103-4, 107-8, 110, 112, 121-22, 211-13, 218
Maslow, Abraham, 86
Mata Ji, 2-3, 190-92
Matthew, 47-59, 87, 89, 96, 109, 120, 216-19
Mauss, Armand, 211
Mayeroff, Milton, 87-88
Meditation, 146-48, 179
Millennium 1973, 5-6, 188-91
Mission organization: worldwide membership, 5; staff size, 5, 196; community service, 4-5; beliefs, 6, 127, 140, 164, 199-201; India trip, 23-24, 41-42, 159-60, 216-17; pro-

244